THE LEGITIMACY OF ECONOM

An Empirical Approach to the Case of Chile

Juan Carlos Castillo

DISSERTATION.COM

Boca Raton

The Legitimacy of Economic Inequality:
An Empirical Approach to the Case of Chile

Dissertation.com
Boca Raton, Florida
USA • 2011

ISBN-10: 1-59942-376-6
ISBN-13: 978-1-59942-376-0

To my parents, Margarita Valenzuela and José Castillo

ABSTRACT

This research is an empirical study of the legitimacy of economic inequality with a focus on the case of Chile. Chile is an appealing case study in this regard because it has been one of the countries with the highest indexes of economic inequality over the past several decades. Theoretical perspectives based on the rational interest of the median voter have pointed out a negative association between high levels of inequality and legitimacy. Nevertheless, empirical evidence indicates that an unequal distribution of income is not necessarily challenged by the majority of a society, a phenomenon associated with the concept of *legitimacy of economic inequality*. Most empirical studies of this topic to date have considered social contexts that are not characterized by (comparatively) high levels of income inequality; thus, the impact of the level of inequality on its legitimacy remains largely unclear. The present study aimed at bridging this research gap, guided by the question: **How do high levels of income inequality in a society influence the legitimacy of economic inequality?**

Using data obtained by comparative public opinion projects including the International Social Survey Program (ISSP) and the International Social Justice Project (ISJP), this research considered individual preferences for occupational earnings inequality (the *just earnings gap*) as the main object of study. The central hypothesis was that individual preferences are strongly influenced by contextual standards such as the current income distribution, leading individuals of countries with high levels of inequality to have stronger average preferences for economic inequality (the so-called *existential* argument). Empirical evidence of legitimacy was related to two central dimensions based on David Beetham's *multidimensional concept of legitimacy:* (a) consensus regarding the inequality in the distribution of earnings in Chile and (b) the impact of the country level of income inequality on individual preferences for a larger *just earnings gap*. The empirical analysis provided partial evidence regarding the consensus about inequality in Chile, whereas in an international comparative framework, countries with higher levels of income inequality showed a stronger preference for a larger *just earnings gap*.

CONTENTS

TABLE INDEX

FIGURE INDEX

GRAPH INDEX

ACKNOWLEDGMENTS

The completion of this project was possible due to the support, encouragement, and patience of a number of significant people. My first acknowledgement is for my advisor, Prof. Bernd Wegener. He showed continuous confidence in this project, beginning with our first phone conversation when, while still in Chile, I proposed him some very vague initial research ideas. He offered me a place among his research team on social justice, considered me "one more" in the research methods department, made me part of weekly research meetings, invited me to present at international justice research conferences, and took many other considerations that have made me feel very privileged during the past three and a half years. His confidence and generosity encouraged me to move on, especially at the beginning of this project, when it was difficult to see the light at the end of the tunnel.

This research has profited in many respects from my advisor's invitation to work associated to the German research team of the International Social Justice Project at the Institute of Social Sciences. I was given the opportunity to learn from all its members what the implementation and analysis of an international public opinion research project entails, enjoying the constant support and good will of Kai Mühleck, Jean-Yves Gerlitz, Percy Scheller, Simone Schneider, Joscha Legewie, and Ingolf Böttcher. I also profited tremendously from weekly participation in the Methods Research Colloquium, where I was given the chance to present my project several times and receive insightful comments and critical remarks from Bodo Lippl, Martin Groß and Markus Schrenker, among others. I am particularly in debt to Markus for his generosity in sharing his statistical knowledge, his support in the design of the Factorial Survey, and his advice regarding multilevel models analysis. I want also to express my appreciation to Frau Timm, secretary of the methods department.

In addition to the research methods department, the Berlin Graduate School of Social Sciences (BGSS) served as an essential academic reference for my research. I learned many aspects of the dissertation research process from seminars and the BGSS colloquium, where I received advice from doctoral students of my generation as well as Prof. Glaessner, Prof. Müller, and Dr. Nagelschmidt. I want to particularly thank

Dr. Nagelschmidt for his dedication to making my stay at the BGSS a pleasant learning experience. I also owe a great debt to the BGSS for its generous funding of my presentations at several research conferences in places as Perú, Australia, the USA, México and Chile, as well as for providing me with the opportunity to attend a number of specialized empirical methods workshops conducted by leading scholars such as Bengt Muthén and Jeroen Vermunt.

My second advisor, Prof. Wolfgang Merkel, provided me with important guidelines upon which to focus my work as well as the opportunity to present at and participate in his Colloquium at the WZB in Berlin, from which I obtained relevant feedback. My friends Cristóbal Rovira and Matías Dewey conducted a careful review of my first draft of several theoretical chapters. Nir Levy and Simone Schneider from the BGSS also generously commented on my first draft, and Markus Schrenker offered me a detailed review of the empirical section. My final version was greatly improved due to your generous assistance, and the remaining mistakes and inaccurateness are undoubtedly due to my own shortcomings.

I am grateful to Dr. Thomas Krüggeler and Renate Flügel from the Latin-American department of KAAD, the institution from which I received the scholarship that made possible my stay in Germany during this research period.

My family and friends have also played an important role during this period. Among the friends that I have made during my stay in Berlin, I want to specially thank Matías Dewey and Carolina Dawabe, who were "there" at very special times. My father and mother-in-law have expressed a particular support and faith in me, for which I am very grateful. During the years that we have been separated, my family has continuously sent me intercontinental positive vibes from Chile, particularly my mother, sisters, as well as my father. I know that he never actually understood my option to travel to a far away country with a complicated language, leaving family, friends and my job to return to classrooms and books. Nevertheless, he always supported me, and the constant refrain that he has repeated to me from childhood — "Don't be afraid of going slow, just be afraid of not moving forward" — became a sort of *mantra* for me during this last period of completing my dissertation.

And last, but certainly not least, I extend my deepest gratitude to Andrea, my wife. I thank her not only for her direct contribution in reading parts of the draft and providing significant feedback but also for her constant encouragement and faith in me and in this project. Most of all, I am grateful for her patience and willingness to always listen to me, even during my often endless breakfast speeches about structural equations and random slopes. That definitely requires a tremendous heart.

INTRODUCTION

Social inequality is a topic of central interest for several disciplines, particularly economics, political science, and sociology. The growing concern with this topic in recent years has been associated with increasing levels of inequality within and between societies (Bergesen & Bata, 2002; Birchfield & Dion, 2007; Neckerman & Torche, 2007), bringing into consideration the issue of the legitimacy of distributive and political systems. According to Habermas, one of the central problems in the social sciences is "the distribution of the social product in an unequal but legitimate form" (Habermas, 1973, p. 132), a problem that certainly requires increased attention in societies with high and growing levels of inequality. The literature dealing with this phenomenon generally takes one of two main viewpoints. The first is a theoretical-normative approach that considers the existence of high levels of inequality a problem because it threatens the moral grounds of distribution in society (Sen, 1992) and has negative impacts in the forms of democratic instability, low economic growth, and/or the erosion of social cohesion (Lipset, 1959). The second approach is centered on explaining and describing the social structures of stratification in modern societies as well as accounting for the distributive rules that shape the structures of inequality. This approach assumes that inequality is a characteristic of all complex societies and does not rule out the possibility that economic inequality is supported by part of the population, a possibility related to the concept of legitimacy.

Providing support for economic inequality appears paradoxical. It contradicts a basic rational choice argument, which posits that a high level of economic inequality would be regarded as illegitimate. Such an argument is referred to in the literature as the *Meltzer-Richard hypothesis* (Meltzer & Richard, 1981; Borge & Rattsø, 2004), which predicts pressure for redistribution from the side of the median voter (Milanovic, 2000) in a context of high economic inequality. Therefore, to point out that economic inequality can be *legitimate* seems counter-intuitive vis-à-vis the rational interests of the actors. Such an idea finds its roots in the legitimacy concept of Max Weber. Weber was the first scholar who made reference to a belief in legitimacy or *Legitimitätsglaube* (Weber, 1947[1922]) for explaining submission to external structures of authority. Key to this conceptualization is the idea of *voluntary submission*, the suppression of the individual will on behalf of some external demand. This idea, initially applied to the concept of authority, has been expanded to encompass the distribution of goods and rewards in society (Della Fave, 1980, 1986a; Kreidl, 2000a; Stephenson, 2000; Wegener, 1992), thus linking beliefs regarding distribution and the legitimacy of economic inequality.

Several empirical studies have made use of the concept of legitimacy to explain support for an unequal distribution of rewards in society, particularly from 1990 onwards (Evans & Kelley, 2006; Gijsberts, 1999; Kelley & Evans, 1993; Kluegel, Mason, & Wegener, 1995; Mason & Kluegel, 2000). Research in the area of legitimacy has been closely related to research into distributive justice, since "the stability of a society, the absence of anomie, of normlessness, or even revolt, depends on a conception of justice that, if it is accepted by its members, provides legitimacy to the social institutions and the state" (Wegener, 2000, p. 75). The link between legitimacy and justice research has grown within the framework provided by comparative public opinion research into justice and inequality. In this framework, individuals preferences for inequality (*what ought to be*) are contrasted with the current

2

distribution of goods and rewards in society (*what is*). The level of income inequality that characterizes a society has become a central variable for the analysis of individual distributive preferences within different contexts. In this line of research, empirical evidence has shown that economic inequality is not necessarily evaluated as unjust (Hadler, 2005; Osberg & Smeeding, 2006). However, most empirical studies have not considered societies with high levels of income inequality among the countries that they have analyzed. The present dissertation aims at bridging this research gap, guided by the research question: **How do high levels of income inequality in a society influence the legitimacy of economic inequality?**

The difficulties encountered in addressing this research question to date have been related to two major concerns, which this study attempted to overcome:

i.   The first concern is related to the lack of participation of countries with high levels of economic inequality in comparative public opinion research on topics of inequality, distributive justice, and legitimacy. The implementation of specialized public opinion studies is a costly enterprise, not only in terms of the economic resources required, but also in terms of the academic capacities required for active participation. Since most countries with high levels of inequality are also characterized by high poverty indexes, the economic gap between countries often leads to an academic research gap. As a result, and somewhat paradoxically, to date the impact of economic inequality on the legitimacy of inequality has been primarily studied in countries with comparatively low levels of income inequality.

The focus of this research in a country with high inequality level as Chile opens the possibility to start facing this shortcoming. Currently, Chile is among the group of 15 countries throughout the world with the highest levels of income inequality (UNDP, 2007), a situation that has remained stable over the past decades. Chile has not had remarkable changes in income distribution since the recovery of democracy in 1990, despite the central place that this issue has acquired in the political agenda of the post-authoritarian governments over the past 19 years. My interest in this situation motivated me to propose the inclusion

3

of Chile in the *International Social Justice Project* (ISJP), the most comprehensive comparative public opinion research program addressing issues related to distributive justice. It is also because of this reason that this study was developed at the Humboldt University in Berlin, since the ISJP is coordinated from the Institute of Social Sciences of this university.

ii. The second limitation, which had been identified in previous research, relates to difficulties associated with the concept of legitimacy itself. Despite its widespread use in the social sciences, this concept lacks a clear definition, and as such is primarily used as a synonym for other terms, such as political support, evaluation of distribution, satisfaction, consensus, and/or stability (Easton, 1965; Fraser, 1974; Gibson, Caldeira, & Spence, 2005; Gilley, 2006b; Grimes, 2006; Ullrich, 2000). Due to the *diffuse* character of legitimacy (Zelditch, 2001), the areas of research pursued under this label have been quite different from one study to another. It is therefore difficult not only to identify a common research agenda in this area, but also to compare evidence obtained from previous research as well as to accumulate knowledge that orients further studies (Beetham, 1991a; Zelditch, 2001).

Conceptual problems with the concept of legitimacy can be traced back to Weber's inclusion of the term in sociology. Specifically, his definition of legitimacy as *der Legitimitätsglaube* has raised a series of questions in the literature, such as: Does a phenomenon stop being legitimate when a critical mass no longer believes in its legitimacy? Is simply asking individuals about their beliefs sufficient to determine the legitimacy of the phenomenon under study? The controversial character of the Weberian conception has been discussed by several scholars attempting to define the specific character of the belief in legitimacy and/or including elements to be considered in addition to individual beliefs. The diversity of approaches and the lack of exchange among them constitute major obstacles for the empirical study of legitimacy, which requires a definition of suitable for operationalization and analysis.

The problems of the diffuseness within the legitimacy literature and the difficulties that it creates for empirical study were addressed by David Beetham in *The Legitimation of Power* (1991a). Specifically, Beetham proposed a *multidimensional concept of legitimacy* that attempts to overcome previous confusion in the literature by specifying the basic elements or dimensions that must be taken into account when studying legitimacy. The majority of the theoretical section of this dissertation is based on this concept, since Beetham's multidimensional proposal presents two main advantages in addressing the research question. On the one hand, it is a comprehensive concept that allows for identification of previous theoretical and empirical contributions in particular dimensions of legitimacy, thus providing a common research agenda that orients future research. On the other hand, it offers criteria for evaluating the legitimacy of a particular situation in empirical terms.

The two mentioned contributions of this research—the inclusion of Chile (i) and the use of the multidimensional concept of legitimacy (ii)—have different emphasis in this study. Although this research started with a focus on the case of Chile, difficulties in identifying a clear concept of legitimacy suitable for empirical research led to a reorientation toward prioritizing the development of a conceptual explanatory model of legitimacy to be subsequently applied to the Chilean case. In other words, this research is not restricted to the description of a particular country's situation, but rather encompasses a general proposal for the empirical study of the legitimacy of economic inequality based on Beetham's multidimensional concept. Overall, this proposal considers the traditional aspect of legitimacy based on individual beliefs (the *subjective* dimension), but specifying that the beliefs must refer to the justification of economic inequality. Besides the subjective dimension, two additional dimensions are incorporated: the *consensual* and the *contextual* dimensions. The *consensual* dimension refers to the degree of agreement or consensus within a society regarding the justification of economic inequality, whereas the *contextual* dimension deals with the congruence between the level of economic inequality of a particular society and individual justifications of it or, in Homans' (1976) terms, the equivalence between *what is* and *what ought to be.*

5

A key aspect within this proposal is the definition and empirical assessment of individual justifications of inequality, from which emerges the link between legitimacy and social justice research. Empirical social justice research is an interdisciplinary field of studies mostly concerned with individual conceptions of how goods and rewards should be distributed within society (J. Berger, Zelditch, B. Anderson, & B. P. Cohen, 1972; R. Cohen, 1987; Frohlich, Oppenheimer, & Eavey, 1987; Kluegel et al., 1995; Jasso & Wegener, 1997; Wegener, 1999). An important aspect of social justice literature is the evaluation of rewards according to occupations, a research area known as the *justice of occupational earnings*. The literature on the justice of occupational earnings encompasses relative deprivation theory (Crosby, 1979; Runciman, 1966), equity theory (Adams, 1963), status value theory (J. Berger et al., 1972; Ridgeway, 1991), and justice evaluation theory (Jasso, 1980), all of which address the individual's experience of justice/injustice as well as the measurement of it. Building on this literature, I propose a means for the empirical assessment of the individual justification of inequality – the *just earnings gap* – which is the main dependent variable of this study. The *just earnings gap* assesses individuals' beliefs regarding occupational earnings based on their responses to questions about just salaries for low- and high-status occupations. With this conceptualization, it is possible to address the justification of inequality within large societies via public opinion studies such as the ISJP and the ISSP, both of which include items regarding just occupational earnings.

In addition to an empirical assessment of the justification of inequality, social justice theories provide the theoretical framework for the central hypothesis of this research. In this regard, two main determinants of justice standards are highlighted in the literature: the *utopian* and the *existential* (Kluegel, Csepeli, Kolosi, Orkeny, & Nemenyi, 1995; Shepelak & Alwin, 1986). The *utopian* determination of justice standards finds its roots in the normative literature of social justice, which argues for the existence of universal ideals of justice that orient social action, such as the principle of utility (Mill, 1863) and the principle of difference (Rawls, 1971). On the other hand, the *existential* perspective proposes that individual standards of justice are context dependent since the meanings of what is just changes over time and space (Walzer, 1983). Authors such as Berger et al. (1972) have suggested that what individuals consider just is generally oriented by the actual distribution of goods in a particular society instead of a general utopian principle of justice. In terms of the justice of earnings, this argument means that the evaluation of occupational earnings is based on the current distribution of earnings within a particular society. Extending this idea to the study of legitimacy, *societies with higher levels of inequality would show a stronger preference for earnings inequality than societies with lower levels of inequality.*

The central research hypothesis of this research builds on the existential determination of standards of justice regarding occupational earnings. In this sense, it is expected that countries with high levels of inequality, such as Chile, show evidence of legitimacy of economic inequality. In accordance with the multidimensional concept of legitimacy, the search for evidence is based on two main criteria: *consensual* legitimacy and *contextual* legitimacy. Consensual legitimacy refers to an overall agreement regarding the justification of inequality despite different positions in the stratification structure. If those at the top and at the bottom of the hierarchy share a similar preference for differences in earnings (just earnings gap), this will be interpreted as a sign of legitimacy of economic inequality. In other words, it is expected that status characteristics (independent variable) do not have a significant impact on the just earnings gap (the dependent variable). On the other hand, the analysis of the relationship between individual justifications of inequality and the level of income inequality (independent variable) delivers information regarding the *contextual* dimension of legitimacy. If the existential determination of standards of justice regarding occupational earnings holds, citizens of countries with higher levels of economic inequality, such as Chile, would be more likely to justify larger differences in earnings compared with countries with less inequality.

Organization of the Chapters

This dissertation is primarily organized into a theoretical section and an empirical section. The theoretical section is composed of three chapters that address the main concepts of this research—economic inequality, legitimacy, and social justice research — which can be conceived as partially encompassing aspects of the overall research question, as represented in the following scheme:

Figure 1: Structure of the theoretical section

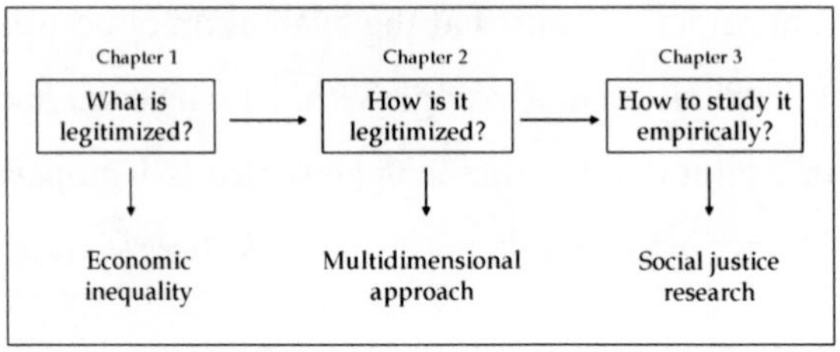

Chapter 1	Chapter 2	Chapter 3
What is legitimized?	How is it legitimized?	How to study it empirically?
Economic inequality	Multidimensional approach	Social justice research

Chapter 1 addresses the topic of economic inequality and describes the Chilean case. As economic inequality is the phenomenon to be studied under the optic of legitimacy, this chapter addresses the relevance of economic inequality, the main approaches to its study; and the role that the issue of legitimacy play in the general understanding of economic inequality. The chapter highlights the study of inequality both *within* and *between* societies, the latter consideration being particularly oriented towards understanding economic inequality in non- industrialized societies (Briceno-Leon, 2002; R. Cohen & Kennedy, 2000; Elizaga, 2006). The chapter concludes with the description of Chile's political and economic situation over the past 30 years, providing the background for the analysis of the high levels of income inequality that have characterized the country's recent history.

Chapter 2 examines the concept of legitimacy and its study from a social science perspective. Before applying the concept of legitimacy to the study of economic inequality, I discuss the general definition of the term based on Beetham's criticism of Weber's concept of *Legitimitätsglaube* (Beetham, 1991a, 1991b, 1993, 2004). From this debate, I propose an adaptation of Beetham's general multidimensional concept of legitimacy to the empirical study of the legitimacy of economic inequality. The second section of the chapter presents a review of the research in the area of legitimacy based on two main objects of study — authority and inequality — and two levels — the micro level and the macro level. In this framework, it is possible to locate the present study in the area of legitimacy of inequality at the macro level. Building on the previously reviewed perspectives regarding legitimacy, the final section of this chapter specifies the empirical assessment of each legitimacy dimension for the study of economic inequality, followed by an introduction to the basic explanatory model that orients the empirical analysis.

Chapter 3 introduces the topic of social justice and its link with legitimacy research. After discussing the origins of this perspective and its distinction from the normative study of justice, the chapter focuses on the justice of occupational earnings as a relevant aspect in the study of legitimacy, particularly in public opinion research (Gijsberts, 1999; Kelley & Evans, 1993; Kluegel, Mason, & Wegener, 1999; Lippl, 1999; Wegener, 1992). Building on the theories of status value (J. Berger et al., 1972) and justice evaluation (Jasso, 1978, 1980; Jasso & Rossi, 1977; Jasso & Wegener, 1997), I propose the use of the *justice earnings gap* as a measurement of the justification of economic inequality. In addition to discussing the research into the justice of occupational earnings, this chapter introduces two further elements from the justice research literature related to the utopian-existential determination of justice standards: *justice ideologies* and the *perception of inequality*. *Justice ideologies* represent general normative preferences regarding distribution, i.e. the utopian perspective, whereas the *perception of inequality* represents the influence of the immediate context, i.e. the existential perspective. If, as Homans proposes, "Justice depends on expectations, and expectations in the long run on actualities" (1976, p. 244), *perception of inequality* should have a positive impact on what is considered just earnings differences. In this case, *what is* would be influencing *what ought to be*, leading to a higher preference for inequality in contexts of high inequality. The chapter concludes by presenting an integration of social justice research into the multidimensional legitimacy model, a general explanatory framework which constitutes the basis of the research hypotheses.

Chapters 4, 5 and 6 represent the empirical section of this work. Chapter 4 describes the datasets, variables, and methods of analysis. This study analyzed three public opinion survey datasets: the Chilean data of the International Social Justice Project (ISJP 2006), the Factorial Survey of Occupational Earnings (FSOE, applied together with the ISJP in Chile), and the International Social Survey Program (ISSP 1999, social inequality module). Each dataset covered different aspects of the research hypotheses and placed emphasis on different dimensions of the explanatory model of legitimacy. The methods proposed for testing the hypotheses comprise structural equation models (Bollen, 1989; B. Muthén, 2002; B. Muthén & L. Muthén, 2007) and multilevel models (Heck & Thomas, 1999; Kreft & de Leeuw, 1998; Skrondal & Rabe-Hesketh, 2005).

Chapter 5 is centered on the analysis of the Chilean case based on two datasets: the FSOE and the ISJP. The FSOE, designed specifically for the case of Chile, is considered an exploratory study that covers a small sample of respondents from the capital city of Santiago. With this dataset, it was possible to achieve a comprehensive approach to individual beliefs regarding occupational earnings by assessing the impact of various determinants (besides occupation) in the evaluation of just earnings. The analysis of this dataset was centered on testing the assumption behind the *just earnings gap*, namely that occupational status is a relevant component in justice evaluations. This analysis introduces discussion regarding the impact of the perception of inequality on justice judgments, a crucial aspect in forthcoming analyses regarding the existential determination of distribution preferences. The second part of this chapter presents the analysis of the ISJP dataset with an emphasis on the analysis of the *consensual dimension* of legitimacy; that is, the extent to which there is evidence of consensus throughout the population regarding the just earnings gap.

Chapter 6 examines the explanatory model of legitimacy within a cross-national framework. The chapter focuses on the analysis of the ISSP survey of social inequality, which covers 28 countries and allows for estimation of the impact of the countries' income inequality level on individual perceptions and beliefs. The analysis of this dataset was based on a series of multilevel models in which individual level variables, including the just earnings gap, the perception of inequality, and justice ideologies, were predicted by context level variables such as the Gini Index of Income Inequality.

The main findings of the research are summarized in a final section, in which I discuss the principal theoretical and empirical contributions, the main shortcomings, and proposals of avenues for future research.

ECONOMIC INEQUALITY AND THE CHILEAN CASE

The aim of this chapter is to provide a theoretical framework for the understanding of economic inequality as a relevant object of study in terms of legitimacy, as well as to describe the situation of inequality in the particular case of Chile. The first section of the chapter refers to the study of economic inequality *within countries*, centered on the traditional sociological approaches to stratification and mobility research. This first section not only describes basic concepts in the study of social inequality from social sciences, but also shows how research in the area of social inequality connects with the study of legitimacy. The second section presents the study of economic inequality *between countries*. This perspective focuses on explaining the existence of higher inequality and poverty in some regions of the world (as Latin America) as based on historical power relationships among countries in a global stratification structure. Considering inequality between countries not only helps to understand the situation of economic inequality in Chile, but also introduces the discussion about the relationship between inequality and people's preferences for it, a central aspect to deal with in legitimacy research. The concepts and perspectives discussed in sections one and two are applied in the description of the Chilean case in section three. This last section also refers to the implementation of public opinion studies in Chile in the area of economic inequality, considered an important antecedent for the empirical study of legitimacy in this society.

1.1 ECONOMIC INEQUALITY WITHIN COUNTRIES

Throughout human history, a main characteristic of all societies has been the existence of unequal distribution of material and symbolic rewards among its members, in which a group of privileged individuals enjoy a disproportionate share of income, power, and other valued resources (Arts & Vermunt, 1989). *Social stratification* is a general term used to describe these systematic structures of inequality, or in the words of Lenski (1966) the study of the distributive process, which is aimed at answering the basic question *Who gets what and why?* The relationship between social stratification and inequality can be summarized as follows: "social stratification means that inequality has been institutionalized, and there is a system of social relationships that determines who gets what, and why [...] Such inequality may or may not be accepted equally by a majority in the society, but it is recognized as the way things are" (Kerbo, 1991, p. 12).

Social differentiation is a pre-condition of social stratification. People are differentiated in terms of biological characteristics, social roles and occupations. As a society becomes more complex, the division of labor increases leading to more differentiation (Durkheim, 1988[1893]). On the other hand, *social stratification* is the condition whereby people have unequal access to valued resources, services and positions in the society, related to different positions in the social structure (Grusky, 2006; K. Davis & Moore, 1945; Parsons, 1970). As a consequence, "inequality exists when socially distinct entities have differential access to strategic resources, and this differentiation gives those with access the ability to control the actions of others" (Paynter, 1989, pp. 369-370). Stratification emerges from social differentiation because social evaluation is often applied to differences in terms of superior or inferior value, and some roles place people in positions where they can obtain a greater share of goods and services. Therefore, the differentiated strata are not mere nominal categories, but hierarchically arranged sets with distinctions by ordinal rank in terms of status (Ridgeway, 2006; Ridgeway & H. Walker, 1995). In this sense, the *social* character of stratification not only makes reference to the classification of people in society into different kinds of strata, but also that the resulting ranks are based on societal definitions or attributions of differential value (Haug, 1977).

Based on this distinction between different economic positions and different values attributed to them, it is possible to identify two main concerns regarding the study of social inequality: the *stratification structure* and the *distributive norms*. The first one is centered on identifying the differential characteristics of social groups that are associated with a greater/lesser possession of valued resources, whereas the second one is related to the set of rules that guide the distribution of goods and rewards in society. Referring again to the main question to be answered in this area according to Lensky (*who gets what and why*), the stratification structure refers to *who gets what*, whereas the distributive norms are associated to the *why*. The empirical study of economic inequality from sociology has been traditionally associated with the area of *stratification structure*, classifying different occupational positions in society and analyzing processes of social mobility (Blau & Duncan, 1967; Erikson & Goldthorpe, 1992; Ganzeboom & Treiman, 1996). On the other hand, the study of the *distributive norms* has remained largely dominated by theoretical debate in sociology and normative orientations from political philosophy (Nozick, 1974; Rawls, 1971; Walzer, 1983). Nevertheless, from the 1970s onwards an empirical tradition regarding the study of distributive norms in society started developing, considering people's views regarding economic inequality by using public opinion studies (Huber & Form, 1973; Kelley & Evans, 1993; Kluegel & Smith, 1981, 1986; Mann, 1970; Wegener, 2000). This second perspective is the one that opens the possibility for the empirical study on the legitimacy of inequality, and that offers a complement to traditional studies in the area of social stratification.

This section is organized according to the two recently mentioned perspectives. It starts making a brief reference to the main concepts and strategies linked to the study of the *stratification structure and social mobility*. The second part describes the study of the *distributive norms*, which is complementary to the perspective of the stratification structure in the understanding of economic inequality, and that links the study of inequality to the concept of legitimacy.

1.1.1 Structural stratification and mobility research

Even though the focus of this research is more closely related to the study of the distributive rules than to structural stratification, I begin addressing this perspective based on three reasons. First, it is necessary to explore what the limits of structural stratification research are and how this area is complemented by the study of the distributive rules and later with the study of legitimacy. Secondly, some of the concepts presented here will be applied to the case of Chile when describing the stratification structure of the country in the last section of this chapter. Thirdly, as we will see in this section, the occupational status constitutes one of the central dimensions in stratification research, which will be the reason why I focus the study of legitimacy on differential earnings regarding occupations, as will be explained in the third chapter.

I begin by describing the concepts that make reference to the structural aspects of stratification and later I refer to the dynamics of the stratification structure based on the concept of social mobility.

Structural stratification. Stratification research emerges from sociology to account for the causes and consequences of social inequality (Crompton, 1998; Grusky, 2001; Neckerman & Torche, 2007), as expressed in areas such as income, gender and race (Grusky, 1994). The focus of this work will be on economic inequality, associated with the position that people hold in the occupational structure and in the differences in earnings among occupations. In this regard, the distinctive approach by sociology to the study of inequality is the idea that the occupational structure is relevant for the creation and maintenance of inequality. This basically means that properties or positions in the social structure are relevant for how much income and other rewards occupants of these positions obtain (A. Sorensen, 1996), and social inequality is fundamentally produced by divisive social relationships whereby the advantages of some groups could only be understood as related to the disadvantages of others (Savage, 2005). The Marxist theory of class is one of the main examples of such a structural theory, in which inequality is generated by differential positions in the social structure derived from the particular relationship to the means of production, generating different classes: capitalists own the means of productions, while the proletarians only owns its labor power (Marx & Engels, 1932[1848]). A large part of the discussion after Marx deals with the proper conception and indicators of social classes (Dahrendorf, 1959), and even about the relevance of class as an explanatory concept in itself (Blackburn & Prandy, 1997; C. Howe, 1992).

One of the main critics of the Marxist class conception concerns its reductionism to economic factors as determining the position in the social structure (Lipset, 1968). An alternative classical proposal to this perspective is usually associated with Max Weber, which will constitute a relevant influence on posterior empirical studies of stratification. The author points out that there are other dimensions of social stratification than just material or economic, expanding Marx's single class or economic dimension of social stratification into a multidimensional view, encompassing *class, status* and *party* (Weber, 1947). Unlike the *class* conception of Marx, Weber distinguishes between class situations and social classes. Whereas class situations refer to specific causal components in individual opportunities that are determined by property or lack of property, a social class comprises "the plurality of class situations between which an interchange of individuals on a personal basis or in the course of generations is readily possible and typically observable" (Weber, 1947, p. 747). Therefore, social classes are the actual strata that are formed on the basis of class situations[1] (J. Scott, 1996). The *status* concept refers to the life chances related to the social honor that is attributed to a style of life (Weber, 1947). The emergence of status conceptions are linked to religious world views and ideologies that serve as the basis for judgments of moral superiority and inferiority of status situations. At the same time, the "claims to honor that individuals make are made

---

[1] Based on this expanded definition of class, Weber constructs a typology of four classes: the working class, the petty bourgeoisie, the propertyless intelligentsia, and the propertied class (Weber, 1947).

effective whenever they are able to establish the degree of 'social closure' that allows them to monopolize access to specific occupations, forms of property and types of education" (J. Scott, 1996, p. 31). A consequence of social closure is the exclusion of those without the status attributes from access to particular resources, which occurs mainly through connubium (restrictions of intermarriage) and commensality (shared eating and leaving arrangements), giving rise to domination by virtue of prestige[2] (J. Scott, 1996).

The Weberian model of social stratification within advanced industrial societies became an inspiration to modern theories and research about stratification that proceeded to adopt this multidimensional perspective, particularly applied to the occupational structure and social mobility. The rationale behind this line is that "if we further argue that Weberian concepts of class, status and power are all manifested by occupational positions especially in industrial societies, occupation is perhaps the most useful indicator of differential position in a stratification system" (Nakao, 1992, p. 660). This position has been called the *synthesizing approach* (Grusky, 2001), since most of the social valuable goods or rewards are principally allocated through the occupations that individuals occupy in modern societies, an approach that is also fuelled by Durkheim's Social Division of Labor (Durkheim, 1988[1893]) as well as by posterior functionalist perspectives (K. Davis & Moore, 1945; Parsons, 1940). In this sense, the occupational structure is considered as the "backbone of the entire reward system of modern Western society" (Parkin, 1971, p. 18). Current class categories as those proposed in the Goldthorpe class schema (Erikson, Goldthorpe, & Portocarrero, 1979) are intended to reflect the differences in the distribution of desirable goods and attributes accruing to occupational roles (Marshall & Swift, 1993).

There are a series of challenges to the central role of occupation in social stratification. Alternative conceptions argue for the role of additional aspects besides occupation in the study of inequality, such as different combination of social

---

[2] I consider here only a description of class and status. The party dimension refers to bodies that are rationally oriented towards the acquisition of power, and as such constitutes a dimension of stratification less linked to the occupational structure than the other two.

categories (Tilly, 1998) as well as the pluralization of lifestyles, taste and consumer culture (Bourdieu, 1983; Featherstone, 1987). This has led to a cultural approach to the social structure analysis, where "milieus, not classes, lifestyles, not objective life opportunities, the lifestyle and not the distributive social system are in the center" (H. Müller & Wegener, 1995, p. 8). Nevertheless, in response to critics, Grusky and Sorensen (1998) have argued that occupations not only continue being the main channel through which rewards are distributed, but that they also constitute meaningful social communities and reference groups and provide stable bases of collective action. In this sense, the analysis of the occupational structure and mobility still constitutes one of the central areas for the study of stratification.

Social status and mobility research. The empirical study of stratification based on the occupational structure has as one of its main focuses in the mobility mechanisms that link the individual to occupations and generate unequal control over valued resources (Burton & Grusky, 1992; Kerckhoff, 1995). In this perspective, inequality is conceived as produced by two types of *matching processes*: "the social roles in society are first matched to 'reward packages' of unequal value, and individual members of society are then allocated to the positions so defined and rewarded" (Grusky, 2001, p. 3). These positions and associated reward packages are assumed to change only gradually over time, and the dynamics of this system are given by the flux of individuals that enter into the labor force, then exhibit different forms of stability or change along the positions, and finally retire from it. Given that the transmission of socio-economic advantage from generation to generation contradicts the meritocratic ideals at the foundation of the market economy in Western societies (D. Bell, 1972; Young, 1962), the analysis of social mobility has become one of the core interests in sociology (Ganzeboom, Treiman, & Ultee, 1991). In this sense, mobility analyses of the occupational structure approach us on the issue of the distributive norms that predominate in a society, in which such terms as *meritocracy* as well as *ascription* (the acquisition of status characteristics by factors other than personal achievement) often come into play (Breen, 1997). The interest in this core problem of sociology has led to a series of empirical studies that, based on different class categories, analyze the mobility pattern throughout generations and also compare it among different nations.

Ganzeboom et al. (1991) identify three generations in mobility research that deal differently with the problem of the transmission of socioeconomic advantage. The first (post war) generation is characterized by comparison among three highly aggregated occupational categories (farm, manual and non-manual occupations), in which the main findings were that the overall pattern of mobility was similar in industrial societies, and that these societies showed higher mobility rates than non-industrial societies (Fox & S. M. Miller, 1965; Lipset & Bendix, 1967). The second generation introduced the *status attainment model*, measuring status based on income and education as the major resources of individuals in the process of stratification (Blau & Duncan, 1967), and relying on continuous scales. The use of path analysis enabled decomposing the effects of ascription and achievement into the current position, measured respectively by the father's occupation and educational level, pointing to the hypothesis that industrialization promotes achievement and reduces ascription (Parsons, 1940). The third generation challenged some of the assumptions of the previous one, establishing that social classes are intrinsically discrete and unordered, and therefore mobility between social classes are not properly modeled using hierarchical continuous measures (Ganzeboom et al., 1991). This generation is characterized by the CASMIN[3] project and the EGP[4] class schema (Erikson et al., 1979; Erikson & Goldthorpe, 1992), which has become a standard in contemporary stratification research. In these schemas individuals are assigned to classes based on the categories of the International Standard Classification of Occupations (ISCO) (Ganzeboom & Treiman, 1996, 2003).

As we have seen, studies of structural stratification are usually analyzed in terms of distributive norms i.e. the criteria by which rewards are distributed, as represented by the terms *meritocracy* or *ascription* (Ganzeboom et al., 1991). Authors in the area of social stratification and mobility such as Goldthorpe point out conclusions like "no

---

[3] Comparative Analysis of Social Mobility in Industrial Nations.

[4] Erikson, Goldthorpe & Portocarrero.

society has yet become a true 'meritocracy' in the sense that an individuals' social origins and destinations are statistically independent once education – or IQ, motivation or other 'merit' variables – is controlled: a 'direct' effect of origins persists" (Goldthorpe, 2003, p. 17). Therefore, in the structural stratification approach it is possible to recognize some basic hypotheses regarding distributive norms such as the expected demise of ascriptive criteria as societies advance in the modernization processes. As Campbell points out, "we must realize that status attainment models provide a sophisticated numerical answer to questions about the balance between ascription and achievement at a particular point in time in a society with a particular structure and culture" (Campbell, 1983, p. 59). It is precisely this aspect which is derived somehow indirectly from stratification studies that become the focus of studies about distributive rules. Such studies adopt a different perspective: instead of deducing distributive rules from mobility patterns, they directly address people's views on distribution. It is in this framework that the concept of legitimacy starts appearing associated with economic inequality.

1.1.2. Distributive norms and the problem of economic inequality in modern societies

Historical changes in distributive norms. Although most people are aware of some evident consequences of economic inequality as the existence of poverty and wealth, they are usually less aware of the systematic social forces that structure such outcomes (Kerbo, 1991). Throughout human history, the characteristics of inequality and the meaning associated with it have been socially constructed, and therefore have changed over time. Social inequality has been seen at times as natural and as originating in a divine mandate, a common characteristic of pre-industrial societies (Lenski, 1966). In the case of tribal societies, the total size of distributable surplus was quite limited and properties were typically allocated evenly among tribal members, establishing limits on the overall level of inequality. With the emergence of agrarian forms of production, the economic surplus became large enough to support more complex systems of stratification (Grusky, 2006). The existence of surplus plays therefore a central role in the emergence of distributive norms, since with the surplus there are some accumulated goods that must be allocated according to some determined distributive principles (Cancian, 1976).

According to Lenski (1966), already in pre-Christian views it was possible to identify two ideal-typical contrasting viewpoints as far as distributive rules were concerned: the *conservative thesis* and the *radical antithesis*. The first perspective considered inequality as just, equitable and essential, while the second one saw it as unjust, unwarranted and unnecessary. It is commonly assumed that since the pre-Christian times, continuing through agrarian societies and concluding with the feudal system, the distributive norms were predominantly characterized by a conservative view, being reflected in justification and even promotion of inequality in philosophical and religious texts (Fleischacker, 2004; Kerbo, 1991). Despite the evidence that in pre-industrial societies there were attempts to question this allocation paradigm, the main manifestation of the radical antithesis ideas is principally identified with the emergence of the Enlightenment.

The arrival of modernity produced a critique of the traditional belief system that had served to explain and legitimate inequality. These ideas were not only restricted to the economic realm, but also referred to freedom and basic human rights. In this tradition, some philosophers such as Locke and Rousseau advanced the theory that sovereignty ultimately resides in the people as a whole, and not in traditional positions as of kings and aristocratic authorities (Lenski, 1966), proposing that all human beings were born equal rather than unequal. This discussion referred mostly to inequality in legal terms during the first stages of the Enlightenment. According to von Hayek (1976), it is only in the 19th century that the existence of economic inequality began to be evaluated by considering normative parameters related to justice in the distribution of goods and rewards in society. This is reflected in the emergence of egalitarian ideologies and the consequent delegitimation of the extreme forms of stratification found in caste, feudal and slave systems (Grusky & Kanbur, 2006; Kerbo, 1991). A classical example of the challenging perspective to the social order characteristic of capitalism is the writing of the Communist Manifesto by Marx and Engels in 1848, which offers an analysis of the causes and contradictions generated by social inequalities and exploitation of the working class (Giddens, 1979), while at the same time proposing a political program designed to achieve a more equitable social order.

Although the changes that were brought about by the French and English revolutions progressively eliminated the residues of feudal privilege, the continuing existence of different types of inequality (such as in income, gender and race) were made evident and became a central area of interest for the social sciences. One of the first key ideas of this analysis of economic inequality was that the feudal patrimony was replaced by economic groups, and distributive rules based on heredity were replaced by the belief in merit as the basis for a legitimate distribution (Foner, 1979; Young, 1962). This means, economic inequalities tended to persist but the distributive rule behind them was conceived differently: in the pre-modern era it was based primarily on ascription, in which roles are assigned on the basis of characteristics over which the person has no control, whereas in a modern conception the valid criteria usually emphasize achievement, individual effort and competition (Foner, 1979; Huber & Form, 1973; Lane, 1986).

The change in distributive rules is closely connected to institutional modifications in the political economic arena, especially due to the emergence of capitalist systems. Following Weber, modern capitalism is conceived as the provision of human needs by the method of enterprise, i.e. by private businesses seeking profit (Weber, 2003). Large scale and rationalized capitalism was accompanied by the development of a highly bureaucratized state that eliminated internal market barriers and "provided the basis for a reliable system of banking, investment, property and contracts, through a rationally calculable and universally applied system of law courts" (Collins, 1980, p. 932). At the same time, the state has acquired a predominant role in compensating market drawbacks such as unemployment and business fluctuations, particularly influenced by crisis periods (Greenwald & Stiglitz, 1987).

Role of the state in the distributive process and growing economic inequality. A great deal of the discussion regarding distributive norms and inequality in the last century is related to the role of the state in the economic process. Following the classical

22

analysis of Polanyi in economic distribution, it is possible to define two ideal-typical economies: *redistributive*, which collects and distributes goods through centralized decision making bodies, and *market*, in which the businesses and consumers decide what they will purchase and produce and decisions about the allocation of those resources are made with little government intervention (Nee, 1989; Polanyi, 1990; Waisman, 1992; Walder, 1996). Throughout the 20th century, the discussion in this area has mostly remained in the political-economic realm, highly influenced by the polarization of state regimes after the Second World War in the form of welfare states and central planned economies. The formation of *welfare states* oriented towards redistribution are based on principles of solidarity (such as progressive taxation), which broadly speaking are aimed at compensating the inequality produced by market economies[5] (Amiel & Bishop, 2003; Arts & Gelissen, 2001; Esping-Andersen, 1990). Still, after some decades of income compression, advanced European welfare societies are experiencing a rise of income inequality (Esping-Andersen, 2007; Merkel, 2007). Such a trend, which contradicts the prevailing consensus of the inverted U shaped Kuznets curve of inequalities and economic growth[6] (Aghion, Caroli, & Garcia-Peñalosa, 1999), has brought up the issue of the legitimacy of the welfare states and their capacity to offset market inequalities through redistribution (Birchfield & Dion, 2007; Korpi & Palme, 1998; Merkel, 2001). On the other hand, despite the lower economic inequality of the central planned economies, their capacity to reach an egalitarian distribution has been questioned[7], particularly in the former socialist eastern European bloc (Szelenyi, 1978). Besides, the fall of the Berlin wall produced an overall rise in income inequality levels similar to those of West-European and middle income countries (Forster, Jesuit, & Smeeding, 2005).

---

[5] Types of welfare regimes (Esping-Andersen, 1990) vary in inequality levels, being the Anglo-Saxon (or liberal) type of welfare regime traditionally associated to higher economic inequality (Gottschalk & Joyce, 1998; Kenworthy, 2007; Morris & Western, 1999; Devroye & Freeman, 2001).

[6] According to Kuznets' (1955) influential hypothesis, income inequality should follow an inverse-U shaped pattern along the development process, first rising with industrialization and then declining as more workers join the high-productivity sectors of the economy.

[7] Along with the new class approach (Djilas, 1957), the bureaucracy of socialist regimes constituted de facto a new class since control over the means of production could be interpreted as an ownership form of productive private property. This new class of socialist regimes has been associated with the fact that, contrary to the expectations, the redistributive mechanisms in socialist economies actually originated increasing social inequality (Szelenyi, 1978).

The confidence in the equalizing effects of redistributive politics on both sides during the cold war period led to consider income inequality mainly as a problem of the third world, where nations actually presented the highest indexes of inequality worldwide (Deininger & Squire, 1996). Nevertheless, the increasing economic inequality within and between countries during the last decades has caught the attention first of economists and then social scientists towards the consideration of inequality as a global phenomenon (Birchfield & Dion, 2007). Still, despite the relevance of the situation of growing income inequality, it has been criticized that "sociologists have been strangely and remarkably silent on this issue. While stratification and inequality are among the few undisputed core areas in the field of sociology, sociological research in this area has continued to focus on trends in the earning 'gaps' – gender and race- or on poverty alone, leaving the broader trends – stagnation in earning levels and growing polarization in earning distributions – to the economist"(Morris & Western, 1999, p. 624).

The empirical study of the legitimacy of inequality from the side of sociology constitutes an approach to the understanding of the growing economic polarization. This perspective takes into account the existing distributive rules in society and its institutional context, but it also considers the extent to which people support the system of distribution, a research area that has been possible due to the implementation of specialized public opinion in topics of inequality and social justice.

<u>Distributive norms, public opinion and legitimacy</u>. The brief consideration of welfare and socialist regimes in the previous part serves to illustrate the growing relevance of the distributive norms regarding the allocation of goods and rewards. Besides that, it represents a final stage in the historical review of the changing distributive norms and economic inequality, which as we can see does not seem to have solved the issue of increasing inequality despite an assumed general consensus for greater equality, especially from the Enlightenment onwards (Adloff, 2005). It is at this stage where it is possible to point out a different perspective to the one presented so far in the study of stratification, in which distributive norms are not deduced from mobility patterns

or economic indicators of countries with different political orientations towards distribution. Instead, it considers people's preferences regarding distribution as expressed by themselves, a research area that is characterized by the development of public opinion studies regarding inequality (Haller, 1989; Kelley & Evans, 1993; Kluegel et al., 1995; Kluegel & E. Smith, 1981, 1986; Mason & Kluegel, 2000).

Considering people's views on distribution opens a series of possibilities regarding the understanding of income inequality, from which I emphasize three. Firstly, it enables one to find out to what extent people support different distributive principles, as for instance the ones referred to before as ascription and achievement. Secondly, it makes it possible to evaluate the degree of consensus in a society regarding these different distributive norms. Finally, with the information on people's preferences regarding distribution in a society, it is possible to analyze its congruence with some external standards of the society. An example of this last possibility could be to analyze the extent to which people of social democratic types of welfare regimes (external standard) support an active role by the state in the redistribution, or to what extent people living in a society with high income inequality (external standard) exhibit support for greater inequality.

Some of these possibilities have already been addressed by comparative public opinion projects such as the International Social Survey Program (social inequality module), and particularly the International Social Justice Project. With analysis of these datasets it is common to make reference to the concept of the legitimacy of economic inequality, specially to denote those situations where people's preferences for distribution are mostly characterized by principles that emphasize individual factors such as achievement and merit (Gijsberts, 1999; Kelley & Evans, 1993; Kelley & Zagorski, 2004). Nevertheless, although the analysis of the degree of legitimacy is certainly related to people's preferences, from the literature it is still not clear whether legitimacy concerns only support for some distributive norm. Further, there is not consensus about, what information we need to know from the respondents of public opinion surveys to analyze legitimacy, and whether legitimacy is restricted to some type of belief (as the *Legitimitätsglaube* in Weber) or are there additional aspects to take into account besides people's beliefs. These inquiries actually correspond to the second chapter of this work, which deals with the concept of legitimacy and its empirical measurement. For the time being these questions will remain open until we complete the presentation of a relevant aspect in the understanding of economic inequality and its legitimacy: the economic inequality between societies.

Summarizing the main ideas of this first section, the analysis of the stratification structure represents a traditional approach from sociology to the study of inequality within societies. This perspective considers occupation as one of the central dimensions of the stratification structure associated with differential criteria for reward distributions. Different generations of mobility research have been concerned with the description of the mobility patterns between generations, pointing to the status attainment processes in different societies and how these processes allow characterization of the distributive criteria in a society as more meritocratic or more ascriptive. The predominant distributive rules are deduced in an *indirect* way through the analysis of mobility patterns. On the other hand, a second perspective in inequality research tackles the study of distributive rules as a central object of study in a *direct* way. Such an approach has its origins in the analysis of the changing distributive norms across history, particularly in the contradictions presented in modern societies between egalitarian ideals and the economic inequality generated by market mechanisms. Along this line we find analysis regarding the role of the state as a redistributive body particularly throughout the 20th century, which in the last decades has been accompanied by an interest in people's views regarding inequality. Such development has led to the implementation of public opinion studies on topics of inequality and distribution, which have raised the issue of the legitimacy of inequality as an area of empirical concern.

1.2 ECONOMIC INEQUALITY BETWEEN COUNTRIES

The previous section dealt with the traditional sociological approach to the study of economic inequality based on the concept of social stratification. This perspective has remained largely focused on particular societies and most of the time with the nation state as the unit of analysis and the boundary of the term *society*. Nevertheless, the existence of economic inequality not only within but mostly between nations, as well as the growing relevance of phenomena such as globalization, have progressively led to expanding the analysis of inequality to consider inequalities both within and between countries under concepts such as *global stratification* or *global inequalities* (Bergesen & Bata, 2002; Elizaga, 2006; Held & Kaya, 2007; Melchior, Telle, & Wiig, 2000; Milanovic, 2007; Morris & Western, 1999; Wade, 2004). Considering such a perspective in this research has two main reasons. The first one is that the amount of inequality within countries has been related to the position that a country occupies in a global structure. In other words, the inequality within a country is affected not only by the system of stratification and the occupational structure, but also by external forces concerning the relationship to other countries. Such consideration acquires relevance particularly when analyzing the situation of inequality in a country as Chile. The second reason for considering the topic of inequality between countries is of theoretical-methodological order. When studying people's views regarding inequality and when adding the concept of legitimacy, we run the risk of confounding the direction of causation, i.e. to state that people's beliefs are the cause of the actual level of inequality in a society. Establishing that economic inequality has structural causes other than people's preferences helps support the argument that people's beliefs are influenced by the context in which they live (Bowles, 1998; Greif, 1994; P. Hall & Taylor, 1996; March & Olsen, 1984), and that this situation can be tackled under the concept of legitimacy.

This section begins by presenting the main points related to the relevance of incorporating inequality between countries' perspective as a complement to the study of inequality within countries. The second part describes three main theoretical approaches that have dealt with the explanation of inequality between countries, providing a framework for addressing the topic of economic inequality in Chile in the last section of this chapter.

1.2.1 Inequality as a global phenomenon

With a few exceptions, analysis of between and within dimensions of economic inequality belong to two conceptually different literatures (Goesling, 2001). Traditionally, the analysis of economic inequality beyond national boundaries has been left to economists and political scientists, and only recently the study of economic inequality as a global phenomenon has started to be tackled more systematically by sociologists. According to Neckermann and Torche (2007), the importance of considering economic inequality in a global context is based on three main grounds:

- *Quantitative:* most of the world's inequality is rather between than within countries (Korzeniewicz & Moran, 1997). The balance of inter-country and intra-country inequality has shifted dramatically over time (Bornschier & Trezzini, 1996; Gottschalk & Smeeding, 1997). Whereas in the late eighteenth century most of the world's inequality was found within nations, with the industrial revolution and economic development in Europe, the between-nation inequality rose significantly (Goesling, 2001). Even though since the 1950's the between country inequality has declined mostly due the influence of economic growth in China and India, between two-thirds and three-quarters of global income inequality remains between nations (Bourguignon & Morrisson, 2002; Neckerman & Torche, 2007). In fact, recent statistics show that about 15% of the world's population that live in industrialized countries control about 80% of the global product (Pogge, 2007).

- *Generalization:* a global perspective can show whether stratification patterns observed in industrialized countries are specific to them or have more general applicability. This issue brings about the problem of ethnocentrism of social sciences (R. Cohen & Kennedy, 2000), where most of the concepts explaining social phenomena have their origin in explanations about European nation states and the USA. Considering different contexts, especially in empirical research, allows one to test the degree of generalizability or particularity of the cumulative knowledge, which is certainly an ongoing challenge for sociology.

28

- *Recursivity*: some consequences of inequality such as relative deprivation and concentration of power may have an analogue when taking into account the relationships among countries instead of among individuals. This point appears especially relevant in the study of inequality, since the concentration of income between countries seems to replicate the distribution found within most developing countries. Besides, empirical evidence supports the hypothesis that the two levels of inequality show covariation (Alderson & Nielsen, 1999; Bergesen & Bata, 2002), i.e. countries that have a low position in the global stratification structure have higher inequality indexes.

Given the relevance of economic inequality between societies as expressed in these three points, some authors have called into attention the lack of research and theorization coming from sociology in this area (Morris & Western, 1999). But apart from a lack of research, what is possible to find are a series of theoretical proposals and research lines that have developed somehow in a parallel way and that only recently appear under the umbrella of so-called *global inequality* (Noel & Therien, 2002). The interest in addressing economic inequality between countries can actually be traced back to the 1950s and the debate on the modernization theory, in which poverty and inequality seemed to be only a problem of underdeveloped nations. With increasing inequalities in European welfare states from the 1990s onwards, the topic acquired its global accent and the attempts to develop a sociology of economic inequality that encompasses inequality within and between nations began.

The origins of the studies about inequality between countries is closely related to the development of the *dependency* and *world systems* theories, in which the position of a country within the world system and the patterns of interactions among countries are emphasized as potential causes of internal inequality (Alderson & Nielsen, 1999). Given that Chile traditionally belongs to the so-called developing world – countries with higher poverty rates than industrialized countries – its socio economic situation needs to be situated and understood in a broader context where the existence of poverty and inequality has causes that go beyond the limits of the nation state.

1.2.2 Inequality beyond the nation state: modernization, dependence and world systems theory

One of the most frequent questions in the literature of between-nation inequality is whether the average national incomes are converging over time (Firebaugh, 1999; Goesling, 2001), where convergence means a decline in between-nations income inequality, and divergence the opposite. Divergence in average incomes exploded between the early 1800s and the mid 1900s, a period in which the average income in the richest nations grew from 4 to 30 times than that of the poorest nations (Firebaugh, 1999). The growing economic gap between countries and the socio-economic consequences associated with absolute poverty in a large number of nations led to a series of theoretical debates. The discussion was accompanied by political and economic proposals aimed at overcoming the situation of under-development of poor countries, an approach known as *modernization theory*. This perspective is considered a starting point in explaining poverty and inequality in developing nations, which will later be criticized by alternative approaches to modernization such as *dependence* and world *systems theory*.

- *Modernization theory* is an attempt to explain the processes of industrialization and development. In the traditional version of this theory[8], all societies, once they begin the modernization process, must move from one development stage to the next in a predetermined order (A to B, B to C, and so on) (Chirot & T. Hall, 1982). A classical proposal in modernization literature about the stages of development was proposed by Rostow as going through five consecutive stages: traditional economies, the adoption of scientific methods of technology, capital accumulation and early industrialization, high industrialization and the age of high consumption (Rostow, 1959). The sociological perspective under this vision of evolutionary development was based on functional theories (K. Davis & Moore, 1945; Parsons, 1951) that pointed out increasing differentiation as a key to modernization. This differentiation in an evolutionary perspective could be promoted by interventions such as foreign

---

[8] Subsequent generations of modernization theory depart from this traditional perspective and focus on the link with democracy (Boix & Stokes, 2003; Inglehart & Welzel, 2005; Przeworski & Limongi Neto, 1997).

aid, motivation of individuals[9], and/or economic reforms, as has been the logic behind a series of political reforms motivated by Bretton Woods[10] institutions under the *Washington Consensus* premises (Griffith, 2006). In addition, modernization theory "tended to refuse the idea that deep structural factors might prevent economic progress" (Chirot & T. Hall, 1982, p. 83). Rather, obstacles to modernization were assumed to be in the cultural sphere, where modernization was viewed as a primarily Western process that "non-Western societies could follow only in so far as they abandon their traditional cultures and assimilated technologically and morally superior 'western' ways" (Inglehart & Baker, 2000, p. 19). Therefore, underdevelopment was seen as a consequence of the internal characteristics of a society, such as traditional psychological traits, institutions and cultural values. As Lipset pointed out: "the comparative evidence from the various nations of the Americas sustains the generalization that cultural values are among the major factors which affect the potentiality for economic development" (Lipset & Solari, 1967, p. 30).

Arguments of modernization theory bring about the problem of the causation regarding the relationship between the economic situation and people's preferences for it. In line with this theory, the structural situation of a country is dependent on cultural determinants, such as normative preferences regarding distribution. If we considered this perspective as a framework for the study of legitimacy, we would be assuming that economic inequality is actually caused by people's preferences. In other words, it would lead to a correspondence between support for an actual situation of inequality and the origins of inequality. This certainly constitutes an oversimplification that ignores influences other than cultural preferences (and even psychological characteristics) in the origin of inequality. Alternative approaches have emerged partially as a reaction to the proposal of modernization theory, attempting

---

[9] The motivational aspect corresponds to a socio-psychological approach to modernization theories from authors such as Mclelland (1961) who pointed out the idea that people from western nations were characterized by a high need for achievement and rationality.

[10] Bretton woods is a small town in New Hampshire where representatives of 44 countries (USA allied) met in July 1944 to formulate policies and design institutions for global economic cooperation, the World Bank and the International Monetary Fund.(IMF) being the most well known (R. Cohen & Kennedy, 2000).

to give a more complete account of the generation of economic inequality. Such approaches provide a most adequate framework for studying the role of people's preferences regarding distribution in the legitimacy of inequality.

- *Dependence theory* appears as one of the first critical perspectives that reacted against modernization theory. This approach emerged in Latin America and is commonly associated with Raúl Prebisch (1950; 1972) as his first representative and also with the Economic Commission for Latin America and the Caribbean (ECLAC) as the institution in which this school of thought mainly developed (Cardoso & Faletto, 1979). Its origins in the mid 1950s were related to the crisis of colonialism initiated in World War I and accentuated after World War II, where such theses as racial superiority were rejected and modernity was assumed to be a universal phenomena that all nations could achieve (Santos, 1998; J. Valenzuela & A. Valenzuela, 1978). In this scenario, the modernization approach was criticized for its emphasis in Europe and the United States as an ideal of modernity and where the backwardness of developing countries was explained by obstacles of the same countries to their development or modernization, leading Latin American intellectuals "to re-evaluate both historical and contemporary characteristics of the so-called 'southern' societies" (Elizaga, 2006, p. 413). Some of the basic ideas of dependence theory are that underdevelopment is closely connected with the expansion of industrialized countries, that development and underdevelopment are different aspects of the same process (Frank, 1979; Nohlen, 1999), and that underdevelopment cannot be considered the first condition of an evolutionary process (Blomström & Hettne, 1987; Santos, 1998). Therefore, the dependency perspective rejects the assumption made by modernization writers that the unit of analysis in studying underdevelopment is the national society, and further they state that "the interdependent nature of the world capitalist system and the qualitative transformations in that system over time make it inconceivable to think that individual nations on the periphery could somehow replicate the evolutionary experience of the now developed nations" (J. Valenzuela & A. Valenzuela, 1978, p. 545).

An already traditional distinction that lies beneath these ideas is the one between *core*, *pheripheral* and *semi-pheripheral* societies: core societies are economically diversified, rich, and relatively independent of outside controls; peripheral societies are economically overspecialized, relatively poor and weak, which are subject to manipulation or direct control by core powers; finally, semi-peripheral are midway between core and periphery, trying to industrialize and diversify their economies (Bollen, 1983). This distinction first made reference to the economic dependence of peripheral and semi-peripheral countries and to the unequal terms of trade between exporters of raw materials and exporters of manufactured goods, but then was connected with historical and sociological analysis of the relationships of inequality between societies (Santos, 1998).

- *World systems theory* expanded the core-periphery vision pointed out by dependence theorists attributing the existence of poverty and inequality mainly to global capitalism and not to the internal performance of the countries (Robertson & F. Lechner, 1985; Rossem, 1996; Wallerstein, 2004). This perspective states that the development paths followed for peripheral societies have been imposed by Western powers, since the core needs the peripheries to extract the surplus that fuelled capitalist expansion (Chirot & T. Hall, 1982; Frank, 2000; Wallerstein, 1974). Such an approach has been characterized by some authors as a feudalization or re-feudalization of peripheral areas (D. Johnson, 1981), and its origins are actually attributed to the beginnings of capitalism in the sixteenth century, when some countries were able to specialize in industrial production of manufactured goods, obtaining the raw material from the peripheral areas of the world which they had colonized. The gap between core and periphery widened as labor became coerced in order to lower production costs. As a consequence, the labor force remained less skilled and capital was withdrawn to the core instead of accumulating. In this sense, under this conception uneven development "is not a recent development or a mere artifact of the capitalist world-economy; it is one of capitalism's basic components" (Chirot & T. Hall, 1982, p. 85).

Despite the critics of economicism and overdeterminism made to dependence theory (D. Johnson, 1981), and the lack of empirical support in world systems theory (Alderson & Nielsen, 1999; Firebaugh, 1999), their contribution to the understanding of the economic situation of peripheral countries has certainly been decisive. The consideration of these perspectives in this work is related to underpin the argument that economic inequality is to an important extent determined by the relative position of a country with regard to other countries in economic and historical terms. Again, this line of argumentation provides us with a framework for clarifying the direction of the causation between people's preferences for distribution and the actual distribution in a society, a point of central relevance for guiding the interpretation of empirical findings in this research. This means, evidence for a high degree of inequality support in a country with high inequality will not be regarded as that people's preferences are the cause of high inequality (as in line with modernization theory). Rather, this evidence will be considered in terms of the *legitimacy* of this situation, independent of people's participation or agreement with the origin of it. Actually, a key in the concept of legitimacy, as we will see in the next chapter, is that people support a situation even though it does not necessarily directly benefit them (J. Berger & Zelditch, 1998; Dornbusch & W. Scott, 1975; Hegtvedt & C. Johnson, 2000; Zelditch, 2001).

Summing up the main aspects of this section, there is a growing tendency to consider a *global* perspective in the study of economic inequality, meaning the inclusion of inequality between societies as a central aspect in the understanding of the phenomenon. Such an approach is specially pertinent when developing countries are part of the analysis, since it is in this context where one can appreciate that poverty and inequality, as country characteristics, are related phenomena. Even though the phenomenon of underdevelopment was initially attributed to internal characteristics of the affected nations from modernization theory, alternative approaches such as dependence and world systems theories have raised the issue of the historical inequality between countries to understand the existence of poverty and inequality. Such theories have been considered to support the argument related to the direction of the causation between income inequality and people's preferences for it, a relationship that will be analyzed under the concept of legitimacy in the next chapter. Before that, the last section of this chapter deals with economic inequality in the case of Chile.

1.3 THE CASE OF CHILE: ECONOMIC GROWTH WITH INEQUALITY

As with most Latin American countries, Chile has experienced significant political and economic transformations during the last decades. These series of transformations have impacted the income distribution of the country, locating Chile among the nations with the highest income inequality worldwide. On the other hand, the high inequality has been accompanied by steady economic growth and a decrease in the rate of people living under the poverty line, making Chile the most successful economy in Latin America for most international observers (Hojman, 1996). Both factors – high inequality and decreasing poverty associated with economic growth – are to be considered since they shape social stratification structure in the country, which is a key aspect to take into account when studying preferences regarding inequality and the legitimacy of inequality in Chile.

To understand the economic situation in Chile, this section begins by describing the historical context of economic reforms in Latin America that affected the income distribution in most countries of the region. The second point to deal with refers to the particular situation of Chile and the political economic reforms during the last 30 years that have had an impact on current income inequality level, which are the context of socio-economic indicators presented in a third moment. In the fourth point I discuss some studies that show evidence of how the income inequality indicators are reflected in the stratification structure of the country. Finally in the last part I review empirical research that have tackled the issue of inequality from the point of view of public opinion, which is considered an antecedent to empirical studies of legitimacy of inequality in this country.

1.3.1 The regional context: Economic reforms in Latin America

Theoretical approaches such as dependence and world systems theories have associated the existence and stability of poverty and income inequality in parts of the world – usually referred to as *the south* – to the relationships among nation states in a global stratification order (R. Cohen & Kennedy, 2000; Elizaga, 2006; Neckerman & Torche, 2007). But besides their emphasis on theoretical analysis, such approaches have influenced concrete political decisions, as for instance the generation of local industries capable of exporting manufactured goods in order to overcome economic dependence from core economies. Such emphasis is particularly clear in Latin American governments under the influence of the CEPAL[11] in the 1950s and 1960s. In the proposal from the CEPAL, the state occupied a central role in the development process, in which widening and reinforcing the state apparatus was the basic instrument of economic policy (Iglesias, 2006). This led to implementing political economic reforms such as *Import Substitution Industrialization* (ISI), which was expected to lead the way toward "greater economic autonomy, less reliance on raw export commodities, progressive weakening of the power of the landowning aristocracy, and the diffusion of economic benefits to the impoverished masses" (Portes, 1976, p. 75). Import substitution industrialization fostered local industry with protected economic barriers, which was conceived as a *second industrialization* that would give dynamism to the manufacturing industry (Filgueira, 2001).

From 1959 to 1970 the processes of incipient industrialization and urbanization created some upward mobility, particularly for the middle classes of Latin America. Nevertheless since the 1970s, the debt crises and the ensuing economic stagnation were the primary factors responsible for increasing poverty and inequality in the 1980s. After a series of economic crises it became clear that the wealthy were better prepared to protect themselves from the impact of recession than the poor (Korzeniewicz & W. Smith, 2000), leading to the situation that almost every country

---

[11] CEPAL is the Spanish acronym for ECLAC (Economic Commission for Latin America and the Caribbean), an organization of the United Nations which is headquartered in Santiago, Chile. It is one of the five regional commissions of the United Nations and it was founded with the purpose of contributing to the economic development of Latin America.

in the region experienced: an increase in the concentration of income and wealth. The effects of misdistribution in the 1970s were exacerbated by further economic declines such as the economic crisis in the 1980s that strongly affected Latin America (K. Hoffman & Centeno, 2003). The 1980s has been called *the lost decade* by the CEPAL, characterized by increased foreign debt, high inflation rates, loss of competitiveness in the international economy and widening social gaps. Negative capital flows during most of the 1980s certainly weakened governments' abilities to improve distribution or attenuate poverty (K. Hoffman & Centeno, 2003; Kaminsky & Pereira, 1996). Part of the failure of the state-centered development model has been attributed to the imperfect democracies and the domination of particular interests groups such as political parties, economic groups, military, caudillos and dictators, who strengthened their economic and political power throughout the state (Iglesias, 2006). In this scenario, public policies were not able to attend to the demands of the majority, leading to exclude them from the benefits of economic growth.

The gravity of the crisis led to abandoning this model and adopting the orthodox economic policies as a condition for borrowing money from international financial institutions (Iglesias, 2006), producing a radical change in the role of the state in the development process, and also in the levels of economic inequality (Korzeniewicz & W. Smith, 2000). Lending institutions such as the World Bank and the International Monetary Fund (IMF) fostered a minimalist state, justified by the crisis of state-centric reforms of the previous period that was attributed inefficiency, excessive bureaucracy and corruption (Kenworthy, 1999). In this view, state redistribution interferes with the functioning of the market and the operation of its *invisible hand*, which most efficiently aligns production, consumption and distribution (Coburn, 2000). Consequently, characteristic of this period is the implementation of structural adjustment programs (SAPs) that drastically influenced the role of the state in the development process (Kay, 1993). Structural adjustments typically comprise on the one hand a phase of *stabilization*, consisting of fiscal adjustment, inflation control and a new competitive exchange rate through devaluation, and on the other a phase of *structural* change, that includes liberalization of trade and capital flows, privatization, regressive tax reform, deregulation of labor relations, a new model of social protection, and administrative reforms to introduce market forces in the public sector (Laurell, 2000).

As a consequence of the economic crises and structural adjustment programs, the past two decades have been characterized by a *regressive bias* in policy making (K. Hoffman & Centeno, 2003). The combined effect of fiscal adjustment, wage cuts and unemployment necessarily led to the deterioration of public social institutions, which were put under financial strain. The reforms were applied in key areas such as health, pensions and education, as proposed in the World Bank 1990 report on poverty, in which social services and benefits are consequently defined as private goods that should obey market forces, believed to distribute resources efficiently (Laurell, 2000). As a result of these reforms that dismantled the redistributive role of the state in Latin American countries (Rudra, 2002) – starting actually in Chile in the early 1980s – inequality indicators like the Gini index have increased steadily in those countries that have adopted neoliberal policies (Coburn, 2000; Laurell, 2000; Kenworthy, 1999), keeping Latin America as the region with the highest economic inequality worldwide, as illustrated in the following table:

Table 1: Average Gini Coefficients by regions and decades

Region	Gini Coefficients				
	1960s	1970s	1980s	1990s	Average
Latin America and the Caribbean	53.24	49.06	49.75	49.31	49.78
Sub-Saharan Africa	49.90	48.19	43.46	46.95	46.05
Middle East and North Africa	41.39	41.93	40.45	38.03	40.49
East Asia and the Pacific	37.43	39.88	38.70	38.09	38.75
South Asia	36.23	33.95	35.01	31.88	35.08
Industrial countries	35.03	34.76	33.23	33.75	34.31
Eastern Europe	25.09	24.63	25.01	28.94	26.57

Source: Deininger & Squire (1996) .

As depicted in the table, not only is the Latin American income distribution the most unequal in the world, but it has been that way at least since the 1960s (A. Berry, 1997; De Ferranti et al., 2003; Portes & Canak, 1981). What appears remarkable is that the high inequality has not reversed significantly during the economic recovery in Latin America since 1990, which was also accompanied by democratic regimes in the region. The high concentration of income in Latin America has been associated with

38

a disintegration of public life, producing high crime rates in most Latin American cities and the erosion of the middle class (E. Hoffman, 2003).

1.3.2 Economic reforms and inequality in Chile

Income inequality has characterized the history of Chile and most of Latin America since the time of the Spanish conquerors and the implementation of the *encomienda*[12] system, which gave members of an upper class (Spaniards) control over the supply of Indians' labor (Góngora, 1975; Keith, 1971). The structure of land ownership made inequality perpetuate over the colonial period, and even though some of the middle sectors began to acquire a degree of political and economic importance with the independence from Spain in 1810, this was restricted mostly to urban areas (Hojman, 1996). Nevertheless, it was not until the great depression of 1929 and its effects on the local economy that the topic of redistribution associated with a development strategy clearly appeared in the Chilean political agenda, strongly influenced by the CEPAL (Chase-Dunn, 1975; G. Palma, 1978; Santos, 1998).

The growing social demands associated with the high levels of economic inequality evidenced in the 1960s (Altimir, 1996), along with a massive urban migration, helped progressive governments reach power in the decades of the 1960s and 1970s: a Christian Democratic government in the year 1964 and a Socialist government in the year 1970. These governments conducted significant redistributive reforms, including the nationalization of industries as well as agrarian and educational reforms (Torche & Wormald, 2004), leaving a great part of the economy under state control (Beyer, Rojas, & Vergara, 2000). Specially Allendes' socialist regime (1970-1973) was conceived as the *Chilean road to socialism*, a unique case of a Marxist-oriented government democratically elected (Kay, 1979). The state-centered reformist path was abruptly cut by the military coup of 1973, which marked the beginning of the dictatorship of Augusto Pinochet that lasted 17 years.

---

[12] The *encomienda* system gave individual Spaniard conquerors the right to demand labor and tribute to the Indians assigned to them.

During the dictatorship, the military regime carried out a deep economic transformation, including macroeconomic adjustment, privatization of industries and states services, liberalization of prices, and deregulation of the labor market (Marcel & Solimano, 1993; Riedemann, 1984). The key principle behind these reforms was to give the market a preeminent role in economic activity. As a consequence, Chile was transformed from a closed economy with a large state influence to one of the most open and free market economies of the world, even being considered a sort of laboratory for political and free market economic experimentation (Martínez & Díaz, 1996). Economic reforms were implemented through the alliance between the military and economists from the Chicago school – known in Chile as the *Chicago boys* –, who were formed in the neoliberal tradition following theorists like Friedman and von Hayek (Trottier, 1997). For them, the state intervention and Keynesianist policies were responsible for the economic crises of the socialist government in Chile, and therefore the first task during the military regime was a radical reduction of the size of the state. Paradoxically, this restructuration was only possible due to a strong and decisive state intervention (Borzutzky, 2005), which was accompanied by a repressive policy towards the opponents of the regime.

After ending a dictatorship of 17 years, the country has been in a process of democratic consolidation since the early 1990s, as are many of its Latin American neighbors (Colodro, 2002; Merkel, 1998). The transition from authoritarian to a democratic regime has implied a re-settlement of the democratic procedures and institutions (O'Donnell, 1996), as well as facing up to the subject of the human rights violations carried out by members of the previous military regime. Despite the increase in social expenditures and the drastic diminishing of the poverty rate, the free-market model inherited from the military regime has been associated with the maintenance of income inequality (Waissbluth, 2006), even though the democratic governments have been explicitly committed to reducing inequalities in income as one of the top priorities in the political agenda (Hojman, 1996). The maintenance of neoliberal policies as well as the stable level of inequality in the democratic period actually constituted one of the main motivations for considering the question of to what extent people support income inequality in this country, and whether it is possible to talk about a legitimacy of inequality in a context with high inequality, as characterized in the following section.

1.3.3 Income distribution in Chile

A number of different measures are available for gaining an overview of income inequality (Morley, 2001), the most direct and straightforward being a comparison of household income per capita across the population, ordered by income level. One classical standard index of inequality based on household income is the Gini coefficient, which measures the difference between the actual distribution and a perfectly equal distribution in which each person receives exactly the same income[13]. Based on this index, in the World Development Report (UNDP, 2007) Chile occupies 14th place in the ranking of countries ordered according to unequal distribution of income, a situation that has not significantly varied in the last 20 years (Kremermann, 2004). On the other hand, in this same report Chile is considered among the 40 countries with high human development, according to the Human Development Index (HDI). These two indicators (high Gini and high HDI) illustrate again the situation of the country in a simple and summarized way: successful macro-economic and development indicators, and at the same time high inequality indexes (Ruiz-Tagle, 1999; Valda, 2007).

The analysis of income deciles delivers a closer picture of the stability of income distribution in Chile in the last years. The following table shows the evolution of the income distribution from 1990 to 2006, based on the Survey of Socio-Economic Characterization CASEN, conducted by the Ministry of Planning and Cooperation (MIDEPLAN, 2006):

---

[13] The Gini coefficient varies between zero and one, with zero representing perfect equality and one a hypothetical situation in which one individual receives all the income. Alternative measures of inequality are the Atkinson index and the Theil index, but Gini is preferred in this case because of its widespread use in different inequality datasets.

Table 2: Evolution of income distribution according to income deciles

Decile	1990	1992	1994	1996	1998	2000	2003	2006
1	1.4	1.5	1.4	1.3	1.2	1.3	1.2	1.2
2	2.7	2.8	2.7	2.6	2.5	2.7	2.7	2.9
3	3.6	3.7	3.5	3.5	3.5	3.6	3.6	3.9
4	4.5	4.7	4.5	4.5	4.5	4.5	4.7	4.9
5	5.4	5.6	5.6	5.4	5.3	5.7	5.4	5.6
6	6.9	6.6	6.4	6.3	6.4	6.2	6.6	7.0
7	7.7	8.1	8.1	8.2	8.3	7.9	8.2	8.7
8	10.4	10.5	10.6	11.1	11.0	10.4	10.7	11.1
9	15.2	14.8	15.4	15.4	16.0	15.1	15.3	16.0
10	42.2	41.8	41.8	41.8	41.4	42.7	41.5	38.6
Total	100.0	100.0	100.0	100.0	100.0	100.0	100.0	100.0

Source: Mideplan 2006, CASEN survey

Throughout the last 16 years, on average more than 40% of the total income has been concentrated in the richest (10th) decile, whereas less than 1,5% of the total household income corresponds to the poorest decile. Even though in the last year of the survey (2006) there was a decrease in the income share of the richest decile (38,6%), the poorest decile also experienced a diminishing of their participation in the total income, from 1,4% in 1990 to 1,2% in 2006. As a consequence, the income inequality remains stable overall as it is presented in the following indicators:

Table 3: Inequality indexes

	1990	1992	1994	1996	1998	2000	2003	2006
Index 10/10	30.1	27.9	29.9	32.2	34.5	32.8	34.6	31.3
Index 20/20	14.0	13.2	14.0	14.7	15.5	14.5	14.6	13.1
Index 10/40	3.5	3.3	3.5	3.5	3.5	3.5	3.4	3.0
Gini coefficient (*)	0.57	0.56	0.57	0.57	0.58	0.58	0.57	0.54

Source: Mideplan 2006, CASEN survey - (*) Calculated based on individuals.

The indexes refer to decile ratios, in which the numerator is the highest decile and the denominator the lowest. This means, the index 10/10 is the highest decile (10th) divided by the lowest decile (1st). The value of 30.1 in 1990 establishes that households in the highest decile obtained 30,1 times more income when compared to households in the lowest decile. The index 10/10 tells us that there have been variations in income distribution, but not remarkable differences between the year 1990 and the year 2006. However, the indexes 20/20 and 10/40 show negative variation in the year 2006, which can be interpreted as a reduction of inequality between the richest deciles and the lowest deciles, specially the poorer 40% of the population, but still the gap between the richest and the poorest remains relatively stable. The differences between the indexes 10/10 and 20/20 are related to the extreme concentration of income in the richest decile. Actually, Chile becomes the most egalitarian country of Latin America when taking this decile out of the comparison among income groups (Torche, 2005a).

Regarding economic growth and poverty alleviation, since the end of the 1980s Chile experienced a significant economic expansion, with an average GDP per capita growth of more than 4,1% yearly during 1990-2005 (Schmidt-Hebbel, 2006). At the same time, the economic development – and the consequent destination of greater resources to reforms in the social area – led the country to a remarkable decrease in the rate of population living in poverty: from 38,6 % of people living under the poverty line[14] in 1990 to 13,7% in 2006 (Mideplan, 2006), as depicted in the following chart:

Graph 1: Evolution of Poverty Rate - Chile 1990-2006

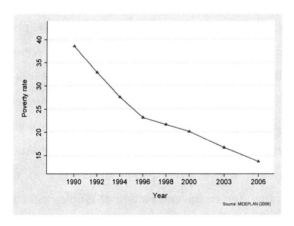

The proportion of people in absolute poverty has steadily decreased in the last two decades (Borzutzky, 2009), locating Chile as the country with the lowest poverty rate in Latin America (CEPAL, 2006). The particular combination of high income inequality and steady economic growth has produced a remarkable impact on the current stratification structure of the country, characterized by an increase in average

---

[14] The poverty line is estimated as total per capita income basis on the household. If that income does not reach the value of two *basic baskets of goods* per capita, that household is considered poor. Among the poor, it is possible to distinguish the indigents, which are people whose income is not enough to reach the value of one basic basket of goods. The basic basket of goods is defined by CEPAL, and it has a minimum caloric requirement in order to assure individual subsistence, estimated at 2,176 calories per day per person (Escobar, 2003).

salaries accompanied by widening gaps in earnings associated with the occupations (Contreras & Gallegos, 2007). The impact of income inequality on occupational earning gaps will be later used as an argument for the consideration of survey questions regarding just earnings, when we discuss the operationalization of a legitimacy measure in public opinion surveys.

1.3.4 Social stratification, earning gaps and mobility in Chile

This section center the analysis on the occupational stratification structure as a way of approaching the issue of income inequalities from a sociological perspective in Chile. Among the analyses of the Chilean stratification structure, a study by Manzano (2006) deals with the impact of the economic transformation on the occupational structure during the military dictatorship. Based on a Weberian class categorization, the author analyzes the changes in group composition and income participation of entrepreneurs, employees, freelancers and unskilled workers. The results indicate an increase in the number of entrepreneurs in the period considered, as well as a growing distance between their income and other occupational groups. As a consequence, in the year 1990 the income of the employer was on average 11,6 times the income of the unskilled worker. In the employee's category, privatization of state sectors generated a high level of unemployment, leading a large part of them to experience downward mobility to the worker's strata. Workers and marginal employees are the groups whose participation diminished in the occupational structure the most, mainly due to the contraction of employment in the fiscal and public sectors, which along with the economic crises led to high unemployment rates that even reached 63% in 1980. Working conditions of this group were the most affected by the deregulation of the labor market, resulting in a significant reduction of their average salary and also of their social protection.

Based on the analysis of data from the Superintendence of Administrators of Pension Funds (SAFP), Escobar (2003) observes that 57.4% of individuals in labor force in Chile have monthly incomes of US$ 430 and lower which, after deducting the contributions to the pension system actually reduces it to US$ 344. On the other hand, a 6.9% obtains income higher than US$ 1,720. The wide occupational earnings gap existent in the country has been topic of national and international reports (Beyer & Le Foulon, 2002; Borghi, 2005; ILO, 2008b; INE, 2007; Núñez & Tartakowsky, 2007; A. Palma, 2008; Ruiz-Tagle V, 2007). Occupational income differences are not only characteristic of the private but also of the public sector (Claps, 2007), and at an international comparative level Chile has been classified as one of the countries with highest wage inequality (ILO, 2008b). The low participation in the total income on the side of workers and employees has been seen as a challenge to the premise of equality of opportunity that underpins free market reforms. A closer look to the stability of this situation is given from sociological research about social mobility mechanisms in Chile.

- *Social mobility and the stability of earnings inequality.* Torche (2005a, 2006; 2004) analyzes some of the scarce comparative research data on social mobility that includes Chile and which is based on the Goldthorpe class schema (Erikson et al., 1979; Goldthorpe, 2003). In comparison with other countries of the dataset (Israel, USA, Sweden, England, France, Ireland and Scotland), Chile appears to show a more fluent mobility, which appeared to the authors as surprising for a country with a high income concentration at the top of the occupational hierarchy. This seems initially to support the *incentives perspectives*, which is one of the alternatives to relate social mobility and inequality, by pointing out that the higher the inequality, the more the incentive for upward mobility and therefore, more social mobility. The incentives perspective is the opposite of the *resources perspectives*, which indicates that the increase in inequality would reduce the mobility, given that it benefits those who have more resources in the competition for upward mobility. As a way of clarifying these results, Torche proposes that there is a high social mobility in lower classes that do not differ much in terms of socioeconomic status. On the other hand, there are significant hierarchical barriers between the superior strata and the rest of the structure, characterized by low social mobility (Contreras, Cooper, Herman, & Neilson, 2004). Therefore, an important distinction to include here is that of *decisive* and *non-decisive* barriers, whereby if a barrier is situated between two classes that have a similar position in the hierarchy of socioeconomic status, this is less decisive for equality of opportunity since those who cross them will not improve their welfare opportunities significantly, as occurs in the Chilean case.

Stability of inequality and the lack of influence of the mobility patterns on the distribution of income have led to focus the attention on the educational system, conceived as one of the main sources of social mobility in modern societies (Gaviria, 2007). Given that educational opportunities are closely associated with the income level of the family, the maintenance of inequality in Chile has been characterized by Atria (2006) as the *Matthew effect*, following Merton's conceptualization on the accumulation of advantages (and disadvantages) in the scientific community[15] (Merton, 1988). Actually, in the Chilean case, educational levels are highly correlated to the family income level, which is expressed in the fact that only 3.1% of the poorest quintile reaches tertiary education, in contrast to the 48.2% of the richest quintile (Torche, 2005b).

Disparities in education have been related to the effects of the drastic privatization of the public education system during the dictatorship period, which was characterized by establishing parental choice through a *voucher system* in primary and secondary levels[16] (Bellei, 2005; Torche, 2005b; Carnoy, 1998). After the reform and up to now, schools are classified into public, private-voucher, and private schools, where the private-vouchers are administrated by private agents allowed to profit from state resources. After privatization, public schools concentrated mostly low income groups, private-vouchers were used by middle income sectors, and private schools were paid for by the highest income groups[17]. Such reform in the educational system has had as a consequence a rise in the effect of the father's education on the probability of entering secondary schooling, signaling an increase of inequality over

---

[15] This differential accumulation characterized by Merton makes reference to the Gospel of Matthew in the New Testament, where states that: "for unto everyone that hath shall be given, and he shall have abundance; but from him that hath not shall be taken away even that which he hath" (Matthew 13:12 and 25:29).

[16] Vouchers were first conceptualized by the economist Milton Friedman as a way to increase school quality, control public spending on education, and privatize the delivery of schooling. In Friedman's proposal, each child would receive an entitlement (voucher) from the government that could be used at any school, public or private, willing to accept it (Carnoy, 1998, p. 309).

[17] 9%, 33% and 55% of the students are enrolled in private, private voucher and public (municipal) schools, respectively (Mizala, Romaguera, & Ostoic, 2004).

time (Torche, 2005b). An extreme example of the influence of the educational system in the perpetuation of the stratification structure is the concentration of high income students in a small number of schools, increasing social closure. As one of the effects of the concentration of opportunities, networks and economic power, in Chile 50% of the corporate managers have graduated from one of the five elite schools of the country (Simonsen, Padilla, & Vargas, 2008).

Besides inequality in the occupational structure and the educational system, other social factors such as discrimination by social origin in the labor market have also been related to the stability in income disparities. A study of Núñez & Gutiérrez (2004a) considers discrimination in the labor market in the sense of *employer status discrimination*, meaning the consideration of variables different from meritocratic criteria in the determination of salaries. They associate the concept of status with socio-economic origin, operationalized according to the family name of the subjects in study. The reason for choosing last names is related to the historical origins of the Chilean elite or *Aristocracia*, formed largely from descendants of Basque and European immigrants, who towards the turn of the 20th century concentrated political and economic power (Collier & Sater, 1996; Pike, 1963)[18]. Taking a representative sample of students who graduated from Business and Economics from a Chilean university, they found that socio-economic origins measured by last name seemed relatively more important than academic performance in determining occupational earnings in the labor market. According to the analysis: "an average student from an upper-class background is likely to earn 50% more than an average student from the poorest socio-economic background" (Núñez & Gutiérrez, 2004b, p. 127), as represented in the following graph:

---

[18] It is estimated that around 25%of the Chilean population are descendants from Europeans, while 70% are mestizos and 5% are predominantly of Amerindian ethnic background, most of them Mapuches (Núñez & Gutiérrez, 2004b).

Figure 2: Academic performance and salaries according to social origin

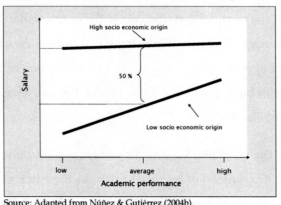

Source: Adapted from Núñez & Gutiérrez (2004b).

The figure shows that, besides the income gap according to socio-economic origin, there are differential rewards for academic performance: an increase in academic performance raises the income of a low status student, but the salaries still remain lower than those of high status students.

The studies presented in this section regarding the labor market, mobility and discrimination help illustrate how the situation of income inequality in Chile is expressed in earning differences according to status characteristics. Besides, it shows how earning differences are anchored in processes of social closure that generate a concentration of wealth especially in the richest 10% of the population. Studies such as the ones of Torche and Núñez & Gutiérrez reflect the contradictions of an economy characterized by free market reforms but in which the allocation processes seem far from reaching the meritocratic ideal that serve as a basis of this type of economic policy. Such a situation has raised interest in the impact that economic inequality generates on public opinion, assuming that inequality is something that should be challenged by the population. But the results of these studies generate a rather more complex picture, as we will see in the next section, raising some doubts on theories that predict that higher inequality represents a threat to its legitimacy.

1.3.5 Social inequality and public opinion in Chile

In this final section I will discuss some results of public opinion studies regarding inequality and income distribution in Chile. Since this research will tackle the issue of the legitimacy of inequality based on public opinion studies, it is relevant to know what has been done so far in this domain, and also to note how this research represents a distinctive approach when compared with other studies in this area. All in all, few studies have been conducted in Chile that cover public opinion regarding such issues. Among them the most relevant and representative nationwide are the *Paradoxes of Modernization* (UNDP, 1998), the *Latinobarómetro* survey (Lagos, 2005), and the *Cultural Perceptions of Inequality* (Cumsille & Garretón, 2000).

Paradoxes of Modernization is the title of the UNDP report for Chile in the year 1998. This report is a general analysis of the economic situation of the country at that time, including as a source of analysis a public opinion study regarding attitudes towards the economic system and state services. The title of this report attempts to reflect that, despite macroeconomic advances in economic growth and poverty reduction, there was evidence of a perceived lack of security regarding the health, education, work and social security systems. This perception is based on the fact that the social policies are deficient, because neither do they cover the whole population nor do they assure fair access to the services, originating strong feelings of inequity and invalidity. The results were interpreted as a product of the tension between the process of modernization and the individual's subjective experience of it. According to Lechner (1999) the *wounded subjectivity* generated by exclusion processes associated with the socio-economic situation puts in danger the sustainability of the development process as a whole, since among the ways to react against this tension are progressive individualization, the decrease of civic participation, and the consequent crisis of legitimacy of the political system. Such consideration of legitimacy in the UNDP report appears based on arguments that oppose the existence of high inequality to the legitimacy of the distribution (Meltzer & Richard, 1981). Based on the interest in the impact of high inequality on the legitimacy of the distributive system, some public opinion studies started to focus more specifically on the issue of perceptions and preferences for inequality in Chile.

Latinobarómetro is an annual public opinion survey applied in 18 countries of Latin America that started in the year 1995 (Lagos, 2005). Some of the areas covered are democracy, economy, civic culture and participation, discrimination, and other special topics. This survey is not specialized in the area of economic inequality, but still some of the descriptive results reported deliver interesting comparative information in some of the areas related to this research. The descriptive analysis of the data indicates that Chile has the highest perception of progress within the country in Latin America (62%), and consistently three quarters of the population believe that their children will live better than themselves. With regard to the market economy, 41% are satisfied with this system (3rd place in Latin America), and 62% think that the market economy is the only way to achieve economic development. Further, 72% believe that private enterprise is indispensable for the country's development, and there is high confidence in the country's elite (65%). Other figures show that only 43% are satisfied with the democratic system, and 59% of the population supports democracy over other types of government. Nevertheless, 52% of the Chileans would not care about having a non-democratic government if this could solve the economic problems. In this area, a majority of the Chileans is worried about being left unemployed (54%), and only 18% feel that people are protected by labor laws. In general, the descriptive results of Latinobarómetro are consistent with the successful image of the country in economic terms and show support of the majority for the market economy system, despite feelings of insecurity in the labor market. Such evidence opens the question regarding the relationship that people establish between a distributive system based on market rules and economic inequality, particularly in the labor market. Unfortunately, Latinobarómetro does not include specific questions regarding inequality in occupational earnings, and this research area remains largely unclear at the Latin American level.

Overcoming some of the limitations of Latinobarómetro, the *Cultural Perceptions of Inequality Study* (Cumsille & Garretón, 2000; Garretón & Cumsille, 2002) was implemented in Chile in the year 2000 with the objective of knowing people's conceptions about inequality, its causal factors, as well as the role attributed to the state in its reduction. Among the descriptive results reported by the authors, it is stated that 76% of the surveyed affirm that economic development has only benefited a minority. Besides, it draws attention to the fact that 63% consider the inequality as inherent to social relations in the country, and that this is something that will always exist. 60% of the interviewed believe that the distance between the poor and the rich will increase with time, and only 13% of the population thinks that economic growth will eliminate poverty in 20 years. 22% see inequality as something positive, in the sense that it motivates people to improve. The state is considered mainly responsible for existent inequalities, and improvement in income distribution is the first preference of the measures to overcome inequality. The authors of the study conclude that there is not a predominance of an individualistic market ideology in the country and that people question the situation of inequality.

Since conclusions of the *cultural perceptions of inequality* study are based on descriptive results without specific research hypotheses, it is difficult to establish a meaningful relationship between the percentages reported and the extent to which people support economic inequality. Actually, based on the same dataset, other authors conclude quite the opposite. In two consecutive publications under the title "The poor cannot wait, the inequality can wait" (Lehmann & Hinzpeter, 2000, 2001), researchers of the Public Studies Center (CEP – Centro de Estudios Publicos) point out that equality and redistribution are not a priority for the poor people, but rather the economic development of the country. Forcing the decision between these two variables, 43% of the poor prefer economic development and 36,3% greater equality. They also maintain that for the poor it is more important to overcome their economic situation (68%) instead of achieving more equality in economic matters (30,6%). The poor would also trust in *responsible work* and *individual initiative* as the main mechanisms of economic mobility, and consequently they are willing to accept higher income differences.

As can be appreciated, the public opinion studies conducted so far in topics of inequality in Chile show a number of contradictions in the descriptive results as well as in the interpretations. On the one hand, the *Latinobarómetro* points out general support for the market economy and at the same time a feeling of insecurity and scarce support for democratic institutions, along the line advanced before of the UNDP report *paradoxes of modernization*. On the other side, the *cultural perceptions of inequality* study argues for a distributive role of the state and negative evaluation of inequalities, whereas further analysis of this data performed by CEP points out that people prefer economic growth rather than the diminishing of inequality gaps. Even though these somehow contradictory interpretations of the results could be attributed to political bias of the organizations behind the studies[19], they are also afflicted with additional shortcomings. Actually, the studies conducted so far are not of a scientific-academic character, in the sense that there is neither a clear research question nor a theory that orients explanatory relations in the data. Therefore, the interpretations are mainly based on descriptive analysis about how much or how little a percentage means, which certainly offers a lot of room for maneuver in the interpretation, and makes it difficult to identify a research agenda in the area.

The present research is aimed at overcoming some of the limitations identified in previous studies. On the one hand, it proposes a conceptual framework for interpreting the results of public opinion studies regarding inequality and distributive issues, based on the concept of legitimacy. On the other hand, the proposed conceptual framework is characterized by a series of explanatory relationships, offering criteria for establishing research hypotheses to determine when a situation of inequality can be described as legitimate. The conceptual framework for the analysis of the legitimacy of economic inequality is the topic of the next chapter.

1.4 SUMMARY

This chapter focused on the topic of economic inequality, developing first a framework for the analysis of inequalities within and between societies, and then presenting the case of income inequality in Chile based on this framework. Starting with *inequality within countries*, one of the basic motives of stratification research is to evaluate the extent to which societies accomplish the requisite of open positions according to meritocratic criteria, based on the industrialization thesis that proposes

---

[19] The *cultural perceptions of inequality* study was financed by the government of the Concertación (middle-left coalition) through the Ministry of Planning and Cooperation (MIDEPLAN). On the other side, CEP is a think tank funded by economic groups commonly associated with the promotion of liberal ideas regarding economic reforms.

increasing equality of opportunity through the process of modernization. Notions of class and status as well as social mobility have been used to study the degree to which ascriptive criteria such as the father's status is determinant of class membership. Consideration of the criteria that underlies the distribution of goods and rewards is the focus of the study of distributive rules, constituting a complementary approach to stratification research in understanding income inequality from social sciences. The predominance of distributive rules has changed throughout history and from one society to another, and people's support for the way in which rewards are distributed brings the concept of legitimacy to the fore. Public opinion studies regarding distribution commonly interpret their results in terms of legitimacy, but from these studies it is not clear what the specific meaning of this concept is and to what extent it differs from mere support or endorsement of distributive rules, a problem that will be addressed in the chapter referred to legitimacy.

The analysis of economic inequality within societies has been complemented in the second part of the chapter considering the relative position of a society regarding other societies, i.e. inequality *between societies*. The between-societies approach to the study of inequality has acquired relevance in the last years due to the increase in inequality in industrialized welfare states as well as between countries, and it is essential to consider when explaining the comparatively higher rates of inequality that exist in developing countries. Theoretical approaches such as dependence and world systems theories point out that the causes of poverty and inequality in some regions of the world are related to the historical economic relationship between countries. Such approaches provide a particular framework for the empirical analysis of legitimacy based on public opinion studies, since inequality is not considered as originated on people's preferences for it. The specific meaning of *preferences* will be the topic of the third chapter, when introducing the link between legitimacy and people's conceptions of distributive justice.

The last part of the chapter was dedicated to present the case of economic inequality in Chile. It started considering economic reforms in Latin America as an overall context for the Chilean case, since it is the region with the highest income inequality worldwide. Historical reasons related to processes of colonialism, economic reforms and a series of economic and political crises are related to the implementation of radical free-market reforms, which have had a strong impact on economic inequality and the stratification structure. Such an impact is well reflected by the Chilean case, which leads the rankings in terms of poverty reduction and economic growth in Latin America, but on the other hand shows consistently high rates of economic inequality even after 19 years of democratic regimes. Current levels of inequality appear influenced by the neoliberal transformation of the welfare system, which was based on the idea that the market should replace the state as the main allocation mechanism. The economic reforms have affected the stratification structure of the country, as reflected in wages according to occupations of different status, inequalities in the educational system, and the influence of factors such as discrimination by social origin in the labor market. The few public opinion studies implemented in this regard offer different and even contradictory results, mostly due to the lack of theoretical frameworks and scarce theoretically-driven analysis, aspects that this work attempts to overcome by proposing an explanatory model for the empirical study of the legitimacy of economic inequality.

Chapter 2

THE LEGITIMACY OF ECONOMIC INEQUALITY

Most authors in social sciences agree that legitimacy is a relevant concept, but most of them also disagree on what legitimacy actually means. Already classical authors in sociology such as Max Weber gave legitimacy a central place, with a definition of legitimacy that has fuelled numerous debates in social sciences. The topic has also been raised in more recent conceptualizations such as the one of Habermas (1973) in *Legitimation Problems in Late Capitalism* as well as in *Legitimation through Procedures* by Luhmann (1969), generating a series of debates and a growing body of literature around the concept of legitimacy (J. Berger & Zelditch, 1998; Kopp & H. P. Müller, 1980; Thome, 1981). But the growing interest in the concept does not seem to have contributed to clarifying the meaning of the term itself. Commonly, legitimacy is mentioned to highlight the relevance of some social research area, since the topic studied has an *influence on the legitimacy* of a particular situation, but legitimacy as such remains largely undefined. On the other hand, the large list of objects associated with the concept in the literature (power, authority, political regimes, democracy, stratification, distribution) as well as the different levels of analysis (persons, groups, organizations, societies) makes it difficult to identify the commonalities among different perspectives. In this regard, Morris Zelditch points out that legitimacy has become a "diffuse phenomenon, a kind of auxiliary process that explains the stability of any sort of structure, at any level, that emerges and is maintained by any other basic social process" (Zelditch, 2001, p. 40).

[handwritten: Zelditch's point]

The diffuse character of the concept of legitimacy as pointed out by Zelditch generates difficulties for its empirical research. An empirical study of legitimacy applied to economic inequality requires clear criteria in terms of legitimacy indicators and possibilities for their operationalization, something difficult to find particularly in the current literature referred to large society scale studies. The tension between the theoretical diffuseness of legitimacy and the need of precise orientations for empirical research is at the core of this chapter. In this regard, the first section discusses the meaning of the concept of legitimacy from its historical origins to its entrance in social sciences. This first section ends by introducing a concept based on the works of Beetham (1991a) that attempts to overcome limitations of previous approaches, called the *multidimensional concept of legitimacy*. The second section is a review of the different research perspectives associated with the concept of legitimacy, divided into two main areas: the legitimacy of authority and the legitimacy of economic inequality. The description of the main research lines in both areas will allow us to identify common aspects in the empirical approach to legitimacy, as well as to place the contribution of this particular work in a broader research agenda. Based on the definition of legitimacy of the first section and on the different areas of legitimacy research of the second, the third section proposes a concept of legitimacy that attempts to integrate the central aspects of previous definitions for the study of economic inequality. At the same time, the proposed definition offers the possibility of empirical operationalization and will guide the empirical study of the legitimacy applied to economic inequality in the Chilean case.

[handwritten: tension theoretical diffuseness & empirical precision]

[handwritten: Beetham's concept multi-dim.]

2.1 THE CONCEPT OF LEGITIMACY

2.1.1 Origins of the concept: between coercive power and voluntary submission

The latin word *legis* means *according to a rule*. Most definitions of legitimacy entail a reference to a rule or a norm as well as compliance or agreement from a group of individuals (Zelditch, 2001), which is one of the oldest problems in the history of social thought. The use of the term legitimacy to denote this problem can be even traced back to the *Melian Dialogs* of Thucydides, from the *History of the Peloponnesian wars* (Thucydides, 1954[431 b.C.]). In this text, the expanding Athenian empire offers the inhabitants of the island of Melos the choice between submission or being destroyed, and the dialog is actually a discussion about the legitimacy of both alternatives. Athenians try not to conquer, but to convince, since they want their subjects not only to accept their rule but also their philosophy (Wassermann, 1947). The historical reference to the *Melian Dialogs* serves to illustrate the two aspects at the origin of the discussion about legitimacy: (i) the *impotence of pure power* and (ii) the *paradox of voluntary submission.*

i.   According to Zelditch (2001), the origin of the concept of legitimacy is related to the problem of *impotence of pure power*. As the Athenians seem to assume in the Melian Dialogs, seeking to gain influence over others based solely on the possession of coercive power is regarded as costly and inefficient (Grimes, 2006; Tyler, 2005) particularly when the size of a society increases and the capacity of administrative control decreases. Such a problem was already referred to in The Prince by Machiavelli as "although one may be very strong in armed forces, yet in entering a province one has always need of the goodwill of the natives" (Machiavelli, 1908 [1515], p. 4). Even though instrumental incentives can help to gain compliance, they rely on the variable preferences of individuals, and therefore the problem for people in positions of authority consists in finding a basis of loyalty that is voluntary and at the same time not purely instrumental (Linz, 1988). In this framework, legitimacy appears as a concept associated with the requisites of political stability and compliance with the law, which according

57

to Cipriani (1987) acquires relevance based on two historical facts. The first one is related to the absence of warfare that allows the circulation of ideas and freedom of thought and expression, making relevant the consideration of people's views regarding the political order. A second historical factor derives from the French revolution, after which the usual taken-for-granted formulas such as succession to power began to waver. It was particularly at times of the discussion about the Bourbon restoration during the Bonapartist dictatorship that the words legitimacy and legitimation began to appear frequently as an argument in the political arena (Holmes, 1982; Richter, 1982), linked to the importance of considering public opinion in supporting political decisions.

ii. The *paradox of voluntary submission* presents a different approach to the concept of legitimacy. Whereas the analysis based on the *impotence of pure power* conceives legitimacy in instrumental terms (i.e. as necessary for political stability), the *paradox of voluntary submission* reflects the interest in explaining why people consider legitimate a given situation. It draws attention to the fact that the existence of legitimacy relies on a paradoxical fact by which people voluntarily submit to an external will. Linz (1978) characterizes this situation as *loyal opposition*, in which people comply with external demands despite personal criticism of the rules or system involved (Gibson et al., 2005; Martin, Kleindorfer, & Brashers, 1987). This approach started at the beginning of the 20th century and is based on the idea that legitimacy is associated with some kind of belief held by individuals. In this view, "legitimacy does not refer to whether authorities or structures follow some concrete set of objective legal rules but to which extent members of a political system believe that the authorities and structures are adequate to meet members' own expectation" (Fraser, 1974, p. 118). Such a position is strongly linked to the conceptualization of Max Weber. He shared with contemporary intellectuals such as Freud and Durkheim the idea that "social norms and values become part of people's internal motivational systems and guide their behavior separately from the impact of incentives and sanctions" (Tyler, 2006, p. 378).

Whereas the *impotence of pure power* perspective has an interest in the process of legitimation (i.e. achieving legitimacy), *voluntary submission* emphasizes the phenomenon of *legitimacy*. Such an apparently subtle distinction between a process (legitimation) and a state (legitimacy) (Barker, 2001; Bourricaud, 1987; Dewey, 2008) permits to clarify that the main interest in this research is not to analyze the process of *legitimation* of economic inequality but rather the *legitimacy* of it. In this sense, this study is not aimed at identifying the different actors playing a role in the generation and maintenance of economic inequality, but rather to consider to what extent people in a society with high inequality consider that such a degree of inequality is legitimate.

2.1.2 Legitimacy as *Legitimitätsglaube*: problems and extensions

Most of the theoretical controversies and confusion regarding the definition of legitimacy rests in its link with subjective elements such as personal beliefs. A central figure in the origin of this debate is Max Weber with his definition of legitimacy as a belief, or *Legitimitätsglaube*. This conception has been criticized by a series of scholars, but most of the critics are summarized in the perspective of David Beetham, particularly in the book *The Legitimation of Power* (1991a). Both positions are described next, and from this conceptual controversy I intend to identify the central elements present in a concept of legitimacy that is suitable for empirical research.

To understand the position of Weber regarding legitimacy it is necessary to start with the notions of power and domination. Weber defines power as "the probability that one actor within a social relationship will be in a position to carry out his own will despite resistance, regardless of the basis on which this probability rests" (Weber, 1947, p. 152). He was particularly interested in the forms of power that involved stable social relationships and that were beyond the use of coercive power, called *domination*, from which it is possible to identify two forms. The first form is related to a process of instrumental rationalization and calculations of expediency, generating a type of domination in which subordinates perceive that it is in their own interest to allow the dominant actors to realize their interests. Nevertheless, "purely material interests and calculations of advantage as the basis of solidarity between the chief and his administrative staff result [...] in a relatively unstable situation" (Weber, 1947, p. 325), and therefore the domination associated with instrumental rationalization does not form "a sufficiently reliable basis for a system of imperative coordination. In addition there is normally a further element, the belief in legitimacy" (Weber, 1947, p. 325). This belief in legitimacy is associated by Weber with a second form of domination, which is the domination by virtue of *authority*. In this form of domination, the dominant groups are able to issue commands that subordinates accept as the basis for their own behavior (J. Scott, 1996; Schluchter, 1985), making it possible for a legitimate authority not to depend primarily on surveillance or immediate rewards (Blau, 1963; J. Cohen, Hazelrigg, & Pope, 1975; Grafstein, 1981; Matheson, 1987; Pope, J. Cohen, & Hazelrigg, 1975). For this conceptualization, a fundamental criterion of authority is a "certain minimum of voluntary submission" (Weber, 1947, p. 324), which is different from persuasion since people suspend their own judgment and accept authority without having to be convinced that this is correct (Blau, 1963).

With the concept of *Legitimitätsglaube* Weber attempts to solve the paradox of voluntary submission, for which the notion of *validity* is of central character. According to the author, "what is important is the fact that in a given case the particular claim to legitimacy is to a significant degree and according to its type treated as 'valid'; that this fact confirms the position of the persons claiming authority and that it helps to determine the choice of means of its exercise" (Weber, 1947, p. 327). The validation of the claims to legitimacy can be based on different sources, of which Weber identifies three: rational, traditional and charismatic[20], giving origin to his well known typology. In short, for Weber, people believe that the authority is legitimate when his or her claim to obedience is based on some of these

---

[20] For Weber, authority is based upon a claim to legitimacy based on three different types of grounds:
"1. Rational grounds – resting on a belief in the 'legality' of patterns of normative rules and the right of those elevated to authority under such rules to issue commands (legal authority)
2. Traditional grounds – resting on an established belief in the sanctity of immemorial traditions and the legitimacy of the status of those exercising authority under them (traditional authority); or finally
3. Charismatic grounds – resting on devotion to the specific and exceptional sanctity, heroism or exemplary character of an individual person, and of the normative patterns or order revealed or ordained by him (charismatic authority)" (Weber, 1947, p. 328).

three valid grounds, leading to a convergence between legitimacy beliefs and legitimacy claims (H.P. Müller, 2007).

The Weberian identification of legitimacy with the *Legitimitätsglaube* is considered by several authors as vague and misleading. From the numerous critical remarks and reformulations to Weber's definition of legitimacy (Blau, 1963; Gronow, 1988; Luhmann, 1989; Spencer, 1970), the approach of David Beetham (Beetham, 1991a, 1993, 2004) attempts to summarize previous contesting points in three main objections to Weber:

i. The disregard of elements of legitimacy besides the belief itself: Beetham argues that the acquisition and exercise of power within a legal framework is something that does not only depend on people's beliefs, but that must be evaluated taking into account the established rules. In this context something can be considered legitimate when it conforms to the rules, which makes the identification of a particular rule a first aspect of concern in legitimacy research.

ii. The misrepresentation of the relationship between legitimacy and people's beliefs: an authority is not legitimate because people believe in its legitimacy, but "because it can be justified in terms of their beliefs" (Beetham, 1991a, p. 11). Therefore, in assessing legitimacy we should not focus on a direct report about beliefs in legitimacy, but on the extent to which the object of legitimacy is justified according to people's shared values and normative expectations.

iii. The lack of consideration for the role of consent: people confer legitimacy through actions that demonstrate consent within the rules and conventions of a given society, not only through beliefs.

Based on these three critical remarks, Beetham proposes a *multidimensional concept* of legitimacy that attempts to overcome the critical aspects mentioned before. According to this proposal, power is legitimate when "i) it conforms to established rules; ii) the rules can be justified by reference to beliefs shared by both dominant and subordinate, and iii) there is evidence of consent by the subordinate to the particular power relation" (Beetham, 1991a, p. 16). Even though Beetham points out his definition in opposition to Weber, in my view it represents a clarification in some aspects and an extension in others. It offers greater precision associating the belief with a *justification*, something that appears close to the Weberian notion of valid grounds for a legitimate authority. Secondly, it introduces two clear criteria for determining legitimacy: *conformity with rules* and *consent*. And thirdly, the definition is not centered only on authority but is expanded to the more general object of *power*, which can be associated not only with the phenomenon of authority, but also with the notion of economic power and economic inequality (Beetham, 1991a).

Even though the definition of Beetham presents a series of criteria for evaluating the legitimacy of a situation, it still remains in the theoretical arena and besides it is not directly associated with the issue of economic inequality. In order to make this definition suitable for empirical research, in the next section I describe a series of approaches to the study of legitimacy that will help shed light on the empirical assessment of legitimacy. In the last section of the chapter, I come back to the multidimensional definition and propose a way for its empirical implementation in the study of the legitimacy of economic inequality.

2.2 OBJECTS AND LEVELS IN THE STUDY OF LEGITIMACY

As mentioned at the beginning of this chapter, the multiplicity of concepts associated with the term legitimacy in social sciences literature is one of the main sources of confusion about its meaning (J. Berger, Ridgeway, Fisek, & Norman, 1998). According to Beetham, "social scientists have in fact been thoroughly confused about legitimacy, and their confusion has its starting point in their failure to conceptualize adequately" (Beetham, 1991a, p. 7). The problem is not only caused by the diversity of objects and situations associated with legitimacy, but mostly the different meanings of the term and the lack of interaction between research lines that actually deal with the same concept. My argument in this regard is that this confusion is partially caused by the focus on different dimensions of one single concept, as those proposed by Beetham. In this sense, the consideration of different theories of legitimacy can provide input to the empirical assessment of each of the dimensions, being also an attempt to identify a common research agenda behind the different approaches.

Authors as Della Fave (1980), Hegtvedt (2000), Tyler (2006) and Johnson et al. (2006) have advanced the work of reviewing and classifying different areas of legitimacy research. Some of these reviews are ordered according to disciplinary perspectives, such as the one of Tyler regarding the psychology of legitimacy, whereas Johnson refers to sociological conceptualizations. A more encompassing view is the one offered by Morris Zelditch (2001). The author proposes that it is possible to identify two broad research areas: the *legitimacy of authority* and the *legitimacy of economic inequality*[21]. *Legitimacy of authority* is the traditional approach from sociology and political sciences, and refers to the conditions under which actors accept a moral obligation to obey a system of power and also to comply with the law (Tyler, 1990). On the other hand, *legitimacy of economic inequality* is a more recent research area concerned with the allocation of goods and rewards in society, associated with studies in the areas of sociology and social psychology. Nevertheless, Zelditch only enunciates the possible classification of legitimacy theories in the areas of authority and inequality, without detailing the specific theories that correspond to each area.

Besides the distinction between two main objects of legitimacy – authority and inequality – there is a general agreement on different conceptualizations that legitimacy occurs at different *levels*. Zelditch (2001) recognizes the existence of theories that analyze legitimacy as a macro phenomenon (societal / institutional level), also theories at a meso level (large formal groups), at the micro level (small informal groups) and finally a psychological level. Based on the distinction between objects and levels of legitimacy, in the following I propose a classification of perspectives in the study of legitimacy, by considering two objects – *authority* and *economic inequality* – and two levels – *macro* and *micro*. The consideration of only two levels (instead of the four suggested by Zelditch) is a more simplified and

---

[21] Zelditch actually refers to legitimacy of distribution. I have replaced this term with legitimacy of inequality because as discussed later in this chapter, legitimacy of distribution is conceived as one of the aspects studied under the general umbrella of legitimacy of inequality.

parsimonious classification based on the character and size of the collective body to which the theory makes reference. *Macro level* theories of legitimacy are characterized by considering legitimacy as an attribute of large societies, whereas *micro level* theories deal with organizations and groups. Accordingly, the classification is summarized in the following table:

Table 4: Objects and levels in the study of legitimacy

Levels	Objects	
	Legitimacy of authority	Legitimacy of economic inequality
Macro	Political order	Stratification system / distributive rules
Micro	Authority in organizations and informal groups	Allocation of rewards in organizations and informal groups

The different fields that appear in the table by crossing levels and objects emerge as an attempt to classify the diverse research lines in the area of legitimacy. It mainly represents an analytical exercise and does not exclude possible interactions between the fields. This means, the legitimacy of distribution can certainly affect the legitimacy of authority at different levels (or the other way around), but this is an empirical question that can be answered only when the two fields are analytically differentiated. The objective of this proposal is to go beyond a historical review, but to identify the research emphasis in the different areas according to the legitimacy dimensions mentioned in the last section. Besides, the classification reflects a broad research agenda which specifies the place of the present research, namely in the legitimacy of economic inequality at the macro level.

2.2.1 Legitimacy of Authority

Even though the legitimacy of authority lies outside the scope of this research, it is the traditional area in the study of legitimacy that has shaped the conceptual basis that will be later applied to the issue of economic inequality. More than a review of all authors that have named the concept of legitimacy, the description of theories is based on key references that represent a particular emphasis in the study of legitimacy. Even though Weber introduces the term legitimacy to social sciences associated with authority, this perspective is not mentioned again here since it was already described in the previous section given its central character.

a) Legitimacy of authority at the macro level

Macro level theories about the legitimacy of authority are based on the idea that societies are characterized by an asymmetrical distribution of political power. A main concern in this area is to explain a process that entails exercise of power on the part of a few members of society, as well as to ascertain the possible causes of revolution against this asymmetrical order. In this area, legitimacy is conceived as "a generalized sense of identification with and feelings of obligation toward the regime that motivate citizens to comply" (Gurr, 1971, p. 185), which has as a consequence the reduction of political violence and government instability. This idea was earlier advanced in classical elite theory by Mosca in *The ruling class* (2001[1939]), distinguishing between two classes of people: a class that rules and a class that is ruled. This *ruling class* is always a minority of the population and maintains its power by a high degree of organization, by draining off the talented members of inferior classes and by the use of *political formulas* to justify their position (Zuckerman, 1977), aiming at counting with a moral basis recognized and believed to be right. Even though Mosca, Pareto, C.W. Mills and other elite theories do not directly deal with the concept of legitimacy, they are considered some of the first sociological analyses introducing people's beliefs as a key element in supporting the political order.

Lipset (1959) is one of the first scholars of the post-war era in directly addressing the role of legitimacy in the political field. He was particularly interested in the requisites of the democratic system and in this context he conceived legitimacy as "the capacity of the system to engender and maintain the belief that the existing political institutions are the most appropriate ones for the society" (Lipset, 1981, p. 84). He made the distinction between legitimacy and another dimension called *effectiveness*, related to "the actual performance of the government, the extent to which it satisfies the basic functions of governments as defined by the expectations of most members of a society" (Lipset, 1959, p. 86). By linking people's expectations to their instrumental interests, Lipset's approach appears close to the original conception of Weber that separates legitimacy from short-run evaluations based on mere instrumental interests (i.e. effectiveness).

The distinction between legitimacy and effectiveness appears further elaborated by David Easton in the concepts of specific and diffuse support, one of the central references in political sciences as far as the empirically-oriented study of legitimacy is concerned. Easton pointed out that "given its long and venerable history as a central concept in political science, legitimacy has yet to receive the attention it merits in empirical research" (Easton, 1965, p. 451). Accordingly, his theoretical propositions are based on a classification of different objects and types of *political support*, attempting to specify research fields in the study of legitimacy. He conceives political support as "the way in which a person evaluatively orients himself to some object through either his attitudes or his behavior" (Easton, 1975, p. 436). To explain situations in which despite discontent with the political regime there seems to be no pressure for political change, Easton proposed the existence of two kinds of support: *specific* and *diffuse*. *Specific* support is directed towards political authorities and institutions, and it varies with perceived benefits or satisfactions. This kind of support, analogous to the notion of effectiveness in Lipset, is limited to the instrumental output evaluation of the authorities and regimes. On the other hand, *diffuse* support consists of "a reservoir of favorable attitudes or good will that helps members accept or tolerate output to which they are opposed or the effects of which they see as damaging to their wants" (Easton, 1965, p. 273). Therefore, diffuse support is defined as output-independent and related to the stability of the political system (Easton, 1975, 1976; Muller, Jukam, & Seligson, 1982; Westle, 1989). It is this second aspect of support that is closely associated with the notion of legitimacy as already specified by Weber since it occurs "independently of the specific rewards which the member may feel he obtains from belonging to the system" (Easton, 1965, p. 125).

Nevertheless, there is divergence in the literature regarding the relationship between the two types of political support – specific & diffuse – and the notion of legitimacy.

Easton sometimes conceives legitimacy itself as a type of diffuse support, although the usages are somewhat inconsistent (Fraser, 1974). However, concepts such as diffuse support have strongly stimulated the debate and empirical research in legitimacy (Gilley, 2006a, 2006b; Weatherford, 1987, 1992; Westle, 1989). Research on direct support certainly presents fewer problems in terms of operationalization when compared to diffuse support, since the first refers to concrete objects of evaluation about government effectiveness and performance of authorities[22]. In the case of diffuse support, there have been different attempts to bring this concept into the empirical arena, and as the adjective attached to the concept anticipates (diffuse), the issue of the operationalization has been a rather difficult enterprise (Fletcher & P. Howe, 2002). Initial proposals such as the *Trust in Government Index* (A. Miller, 1974) were criticized by Easton himself as a measure of diffuse support since it might be "simply picking up evaluations of the general performance of various incumbents" (Easton, 1975, p. 450). Further attempts such as Citrin's *Political Alienation* (1977) emphasized the distinction between support for the *incumbent's officeholders* and for the *system*, where the first one refers to the performance of concrete authorities and the second one to the political system itself. The incumbent-system distinction (Muller et al., 1982; Seligson, 1983) appears as a way of differentiating direct support of authorities from diffuse support, since "the hypothesis behind the distinction between incumbent affect and system affect is that the latter is more consequential for the stability of a political regime than the former"(Muller & Jukam, 1977, p. 1563). Despite this distinction, there is still no standard measure of diffuse support, and the debate on the specificity of the concept and its measurement still continues (Grimes, 2006, 2008; Kaina, 2008).

Even though there is not a consensual proposal for the measurement of legitimacy based on Easton, the major contribution from this line of research is the discussion on the difference between direct support and legitimacy. From here on, direct evaluations of performance or effectiveness of authorities and regimes are not regarded as a measure of legitimacy. Therefore, many studies that use the term

---

[22] A review of the research on topics such as government support or evaluations of welfare state regimes fall out of the scope of this research, and besides some reviews have already been presented (Dalton, 1999; Grimes, 2006).

legitimacy to characterize attitudes towards the government and welfare state would not be considered under this perspective as studies of legitimacy, rather only of direct support. But besides Easton's contribution, there is one important shortcoming that generates ongoing conceptual debates about terms such as diffuse support, political alienation and trust[23] , namely the restriction of legitimacy to a type of belief. Such an approach bears the same critical aspects discussed in the previous section regarding the limitation of legitimacy to one specific dimension. In this sense, the debate has circulated around the best way of operationalizing and measuring a certain kind of belief, disregarding relevant elements such as the level of consent associated with diffuse support and/or the extent of conformity with rules of the context. This belief-centered emphasis in macro level research on the legitimacy of authority is contrasted by studies at the micro level that incorporate additional dimensions in the study of legitimacy.

b) <u>Legitimacy of authority at the micro level</u>

It is possible to identify two main research areas in the legitimacy of authority at the micro level: legitimacy in organizations and legitimacy of procedures.

- *Legitimacy in organizations*. Research in this area has been strongly influenced by the Weberian conceptualization of authority and its links with the study of leadership. In this literature it is possible to find two different perspectives: the *managerial* and the *cultural* (M. Suchman, 1995)[24]. The *managerial* approach to legitimacy is aimed at increasing compliance with norms and to improve the organizational performance on the side of subordinates, especially in situations of crisis (Raven & French, 1958; Massey, 2001). Besides, this perspective also attempts to identify and promote sources for enhancing the legitimacy of organizations in their social context (Elsbach, 2001; Elsbach & Sutton, 1992), since legitimate organizations are most likely to receive support and resources from constituents (Tyler, 1990). In this managerial approach, legitimacy is auxiliary of performance and organizational effectiveness,

---

[23] See the recent Kaina-Grimes debate (Kaina, 2008).

[24] Suchman uses the terms managerial and institutional. Here I replace institutional by cultural since it is a broader term in which the study of legitimacy within organizations is also embraced.

and usually the term is interchangeable with trust or support (Kaina, 2008). On the other hand, the *cultural* approach conceives legitimacy as a set of constitutive beliefs that are shaped by cultural definitions (DiMaggio & Powell, 1991; M. Suchman, 1995). In the case of legitimacy of authority studies within the organization, the emphasis is on the validity of authority claims, whereby validity is characterized by being a collective process in which the support for norms and authorities goes beyond instrumental interests (Dornbusch & W. Scott, 1975; Hegtvedt & C. Johnson, 2000; Zelditch & H. Walker, 1998). Within the cultural approach there is also a line of research that tackles the relationships of the organization with its context, strongly influenced by the neo-institutional perspective. This framework rejects traditional adaptation theories such as those of the managerial approach and instead emphasizes institutional organizational conformity with social rules and rituals (Kraatz & Zajuac, 1996; Meyer & Rowan, 1977). Organizational legitimacy emerges as a consequence of *institutional isomorphism* (Deephouse, 1996; DiMaggio & Powell, 1991) or the resemblance of an organization to other organizations in its environment, and in this sense the principal dimension of legitimacy emphasized by this perspective is the one of conformity with the rules of the context. Scholars in this area have called attention to concepts such as cultural conformity and the idea that legitimacy implies "congruence between the social values associated with or implied by (organizational) activities and the norms of acceptable behavior in the larger social system" (Dowling & Pfeffer, 1975, p. 122).

The cultural approach to the legitimacy of organizations expands the traditional consideration of legitimacy as a belief by considering two additional dimensions proposed in Beetham's multidimensional concept of legitimacy: consent and conformity. In this sense, it is possible to appreciate that the multidimensional concept is not proposing something completely new, but rather that it integrates aspects that appeared separately in the previous literature about legitimacy. Still from the legitimacy of organizations it is not clear to what extent consent and conformity are related to a particular belief. The integration of the three dimensions in the legitimacy of authority is better accomplished in the area of procedural justice, particularly with the works of Tom Tyler.

- *Legitimacy of procedures*. Scholars of the procedural justice approach to legitimacy point out that perceptions of fairness of the processes through which the authorities make decisions and exercise their power reinforces the legitimacy of authorities, organizations and the government (Epp, 1998; Sunshine & Tyler, 2003). The main idea behind this perspective is that "perceived fairness in decision processes can affect citizens' overall assessments of political institutions and even their willingness to defer decisions to those institutions" (Grimes, 2006, p. 286). This conception was initially introduced by Thibaut & Walker (1975), who emphasized that those procedures that provide individuals with control over outcomes and promote equitable distribution are considered fair. Accordingly, people's willingness to accept and cooperate with legal authorities is linked to evaluations of performance (Sunshine & Tyler, 2003) and also to deterrence – the threat of sanctions that would accompany non-compliance. This perspective has received the name of *self-interest model*, characterized by the evaluation of fairness based on the outcome of the process.

The self-interest model has been contrasted by the *group-value model* of Lind and Tyler (1988), who proposed a different approach to the notion of legitimacy in this area. Lind & Tyler's theory of procedural justice attempts to explain why people willingly comply with legal authorities, even though this compliance does not necessarily match people's instrumental interests. They propose that internalized norms are responsible for the judgments about procedures, and as a consequence what is considered moral and just is not directly dependent on the instrumental interests as stated by the self-interest model (Tyler, 1988). Rather, in the *group-value model* the willingness to comply depends upon a belief that legal authorities are legitimate, and this belief at the same time relies on the perception of fair procedures on the part of authorities (Herbert, 2003). More than the outcomes of the legal processes, people consider two aspects as critical: the assessment of the fairness of the procedures, and the assessment of the authority's motives when employing the procedures. When both elements are positively evaluated, people consider the procedures legitimate regardless of the outcome (Tyler & Huo, 2002).

The group value model of Lind and Tyler presents a link between two dimensions of legitimacy: the belief (in this case, the belief in fairness) and the consent of the group independent of the personal benefit associated with the outcome. As Hegtvedt & Johnson point out, "the group value model in particular implies what is largely missing from distributive justice approaches: the collective context, which is the key to legitimacy processes" (Hegtvedt & C. Johnson, 2000, p. 303). In empirical terms, the incorporation of the collective context suggests not only considering a particular belief, but also the *level of consensus* in the group regarding the belief as a criteria for legitimacy. The level of consensus will play an important role in the final section of this chapter, when proposing an empirical implementation of the multidimensional concept of legitimacy for the study of economic inequality.

2.2.2 Legitimacy of economic inequality

The legitimacy of economic inequality constitutes the particular research area in which this research is situated. Economic inequality is conceived as a broad category that encompasses different aspects that have been separately associated to legitimacy. These aspects are related to the two areas in the study of economic inequality referred to in the previous chapter: the *stratification system* and the *distributive rules*. Most of the theories and research about legitimacy of inequality has been related to distributive rules behind structures of inequality, generally addressed under the concept of ideology. On the other hand, the stratification system has only later become an object of study from the perspective of legitimacy, by research that focuses on people's evaluations of occupational earnings and justification of economic inequality. The present research includes both perspectives in the empirical study of legitimacy at the macro level.

a) Legitimacy of inequality at the macro level

Macro level theories of the legitimacy of economic inequality are mostly concerned with explaining social stability under conditions of inequality in the distribution of resources in society. The problem tackled at this level can be summarized by contrasting two positions in the explanations of legitimacy of inequality. On the one

71

hand it is possible to find a perspective that opposes inequality to legitimacy based on the rationality assumptions of the median voter (Milanovic, 2000), usually called the *Meltzer-Richard hypothesis* (Meltzer & Richard, 1981). This hypothesis points out that when the median voter has less income than the mean, they will support income taxation and pressure for redistribution (Borge & Rattsø, 2004). As a consequence, the higher the economic inequality, the less the legitimacy and the higher the pressures for redistribution. The assumption behind this is that "the government's share is set by the rational choices of utility-maximizing individuals who are fully informed of the state of the economy and the consequences of taxation and income redistribution" (Meltzer & Richard, 1981, p. 915). On the other hand we find a research tradition in sociology that has its origins in concepts such as ideologies (Marx & Engels, 1953), moral ideas (Durkheim, 1982) or belief in legitimacy (Weber, 1947) that aim at explaining why people do not necessarily oppose rules that they might not agree on (Lichbach, 1989). In this view, people are considered moral agents that make decisions following values and personal beliefs and not primarily on the basis of utility maximizing criteria. Such a perspective has acquired growing interest for empirical research on the legitimacy of inequality in the last decades, particularly on the side of sociology and social psychology (Castillo, 2009; Jost, Pelham, Sheldon, & Ni Sullivan, 2003; Kelley & Evans, 1993; Kreidl, 2000a; Mau & Veghte, 2007; Scharpf, 2007; Sidanius, Levin, Federico, & F. Pratto, 2001; Sutphin & Simpson, 2009; Tyler, 2006; Wegener, 1992). Before addressing the empirical aspect of the legitimacy of inequality, I will start with a general sociological background that has fuelled the empirical research and which represents two contesting approaches to the study of legitimacy: the consensus and conflict approaches (Horton, 1966; Mann, 1970).

- *Consensus and conflict approaches to economic inequality*. The consensus approach to the sociological study of legitimacy can be traced back to Durkheim and the concept of *moral ideas* (Durkheim, 1982[1895]), which has been later extended to a general functionalist view of society. The author considered shared values necessary to put constraints on the behavior of the members of society in a scenario of scarce material resources and infinite desires. Human beings would not have the faculty to hold back their own desires, which must be restrained by the transmission of moral ideas that lead to consider social constraints as appropriate and just (Arts & van der Veen, 1992). The author presupposes that each society cherishes moral ideals that determine the value assigned to different occupations and the consequent living standard, and also the minimum requirements for those at the bottom of the social hierarchy and maximum requirements for those at the top.

Following Durkheim's approach, functionalists such as Parsons (1940) and Davis and Moore (1945) assumed that differences in social rewards which are legitimized by the value system are grounded in the differences in importance of occupations for the performance of the society. In the functionalist view, inequality is not only inevitable, but also necessary for the survival and balanced functioning of a society (Arts & Vermunt, 1989). The market, the political processes and institutional mechanisms based on law and tradition are the coordinating mechanisms that allocate roles to its members and motivate them by means of differentiated distributions of rewards (Horton, 1966; Savage, 2005). This perspective emphasizes integration and consensus in society on inequality of social rewards in order that the best-qualified people be encouraged to occupy those positions that are regarded as more important to society than others (Van der Sar & Van Praag, 1989). Rewards are institutionally transformed into right and legitimate claims according to different occupational positions in society, generating stability in the system of social stratification (Arts & van der Veen, 1992). The legitimacy of claims to social rewards is currently judged by impersonal standards, especially standards of individual achievement and less on the basis of ascription. According to functionalism, in industrial societies characterized by a complex division of labor, a new consensus based on rationality and meritocracy has replaced an old consensus grounded on religion and tradition (Crompton, 1998).

In contrast to functionalist-order theories that emphasis the consensus, Marxism has usually been labeled as a *conflict* perspective. The Marxist view emphasizes the irreconcilable conflict of interests between the bourgeoisie (or capitalists) and the proletariat, a conflict originating in their differential access to the means of production and the relations of exploitation derived from it (Marx & Engels, 1932). In explaining why conflicts of interest between proletarians and capitalists do not necessarily translate into class conflict, Marxism points to concepts such as *ideology* and *false consciousness*. Dominant classes develop a set of beliefs that are more dense and coherent than those of the subordinate classes, becoming hegemonic (Gramsci, 1971). This set of beliefs or ideologies penetrates the consciousness of the working class, leading them to see reality through the categories of the dominant class, termed the *false consciousness* of the proletariat. As a consequence of the false consciousness, the proletariat is incorporated into a system that operates against their material interests, which explains the coherence and integration of the capitalist society (Abercrombie, S. Hill, & Turner, 1980). In this view, ideology appears as a mechanism of intellectual legitimation of social domination, as a solution in the mind that hides contradictions that cannot be solved in practice (Chiapello, 2003; Izzo, 1987; Larraín, 1983; McClosky, 1964).

The issue of legitimacy acquires a central role for both conflict and consensus approaches, even though with quite a different meaning. Consensus scholars point out that a widespread commitment to values, norms and beliefs confers legitimacy and stability to the social structure. On the other hand, conflict scholars also agree on this widespread commitment, but deny that such a consensus confers legitimacy to economic inequality (Mann, 1970). For both perspectives, a key aspect to solve is to find out the actual degree of consensus in a society, which is actually a matter of empirical research. Under this premise, a series of empirical studies began to be implemented in the 1960s under the framework of the consensus-conflict discussion and the concept of dominant ideology (Abercrombie, 1990; Abercrombie et al., 1980), which later have derived into the empirical study of the legitimacy of inequality.

- *Empirical research on the legitimacy of inequality at the macro level.* It is possible to distinguish among three different periods related to the empirical research of the legitimacy of income inequality.

i.   The first period started in the US in the 1960s and relied on the assessment of attitudes and beliefs[25] towards inequality and redistributive politics. The

---

[25] Attitudes are generally defined as a "learned predisposition to respond in a consistently favorable or unfavorable manner with respect to a given object" (Ajzen & Fishbein, 1975, p. 6), and consist of three different

fundamental inquiry in this period was the apparent support of the distributive system in a country with high economic inequality when compared to industrial European societies. This debate was fuelled by early empirical evidence of a lack of support for egalitarian values in lower classes (Huber & Form, 1973; Lane, 1959), as well as by empirical studies about beliefs and ideologies in the general public (Converse, 2004[1964]) in the era of the "end of ideology" debate (D. Bell, 1960; Waxman, 1968). The empirical research of this first period has been summarized by Mann (1970), who searched for evidence of consensus and dissensus in different social classes. Based on the concepts of dominant and deviant values of Parkin (1967), Mann established that working class individuals exhibit less internal consistency in their values than middle class people, and "there is little truth in the claims of some Marxists that the working class is systematically and successfully indoctrinated with the values of the ruling class" (Mann, 1970, p. 435). Rather, for the author the lack of consensus in the working class is the empirical demonstration of the existence of false consciousness, a conflict between dominant and deviant values within the individual. Further evidence (Feagin, 1972) revealed that an overwhelming majority even among the poor does not support the idea of more equality in the distribution of income and wealth. Much of the research that followed in the 1970's was aimed at testing the existence of an *American stratification ideology*[26] (Huber & Form, 1973; Huber, Form, & Pease, 1970), defined as a set of emotionally held beliefs and myths throughout status groups that explain and vindicate the unequal distribution of rewards in society.

ii. A <u>second period</u> of research is characterized by the appearance of a series of conceptualizations regarding beliefs about inequality and with a strong empirical emphasis (Feagin, 1972; Huber & Form, 1973; Kluegel & E. Smith, 1986; R.

---

components: cognitive, affective and conative (Kiecolt, 1988). Beliefs are considered part of the cognitive component of an attitude, characterized by linking an object with an attribute (Ajzen & Fishbein, 1975).

[26] According to Huber & Form (1973), the American stratification ideology was characterized by the following syllogism: i) opportunity to get ahead is available for all, ii) if opportunity is available, the position of an individual in the stratification order is a function of personal efforts and abilities, instead of economic or structural factors, and iii) since people are personally responsible for the rewards they receive, the current distribution of rewards is fair, and therefore inequality is positively evaluated.

Robinson & W. Bell, 1978). Kluegel & Smith (1981) systematized most of the work of previous research in the area, and proposed a theoretical and empirical framework for further studies based on the concept of *split consciousness* (Kluegel, 1989). The split consciousness theory is an attempt to subsume previous proposals such as the notions of divided selves (Sennett & Cobb, 1972), compartmentalization of beliefs (Lane, 1962) or contradictory consciousness (Cheal, 1979). In this attempt, Kluegel is mostly interested in the empirical test of the two-dimensional nature of the beliefs about inequality, in opposition to the one-dimensional solution from the previous period of research. In this view, beliefs about inequality are formed by two broad influences: firstly they are the product of the inculcation of dominant-ideology beliefs, but they are also influenced by beliefs originating from one's own stratification-related experience, or *challenging beliefs*. The challenging beliefs are related to conditions of working class life, socialization, or specific personal experiences. In this conceptualization, it is possible that low status people support the dominant ideology and challenging beliefs at the same time, since both influences are separated or 'compartmentalized' (Lane, 1962) in people's minds, giving origin to the label of *split consciousness*. In this framework it is possible to account for the lack of consistency in the beliefs of the working class found in the previous research period. Further, one of the major contributions of Kluegel lies on the empirical realm, firstly by using national representative samples for the analysis, and secondly by introducing multivariate methods such as confirmatory factor analysis and structural equation models (Bollen, 1989; Jöreskog & Sorbom, 1986) in testing the dimensionality of the beliefs and their determinants.

A second element in this research period is the beginning of the association between studies of legitimacy and research into distributive justice. Such an approach is advanced by Lane (1986), who proposed a theoretical link between legitimacy, ideology and justice with his influential distinction between *market justice* and *political justice*. He points out that "our aim is not to clarify philosophical justice; we do attempt to illuminate concepts of the legitimacy of markets and politics, to contribute to an understanding of the forces of social change, and above all, to help explain the tenacious hold of market capitalism on the public mind" (Lane, 1986, p. 384). Lane proposes that *market justice* beliefs involve preferences for non-egalitarian criteria of earned deserts over criteria of equality or need, as well as preferences for limited government involvement in the economy (Kluegel et al., 1999; Lane, 1986). The key element of this approach is the inclusion of an active sense of justice that "seems to influence people's judgments more than does perceived self-interest" (Lane, 1986, p. 397). Influenced by the works of Tyler in procedural justice as well as by the idea of the *justice motive* of Lerner (1980)[27], Lane brings up the idea that the legitimation of market mechanisms is mostly related to beliefs about distributive justice, or about what people think regarding how goods and rewards are and should be distributed in society.

Besides the contributions of Lane and Kluegel & Smith on the topics of ideology and justice in relation to legitimacy, there is an additional theory in this second period of research which strongly influenced the research about legitimacy of stratification, namely the *self evaluation theory* from Richard Della Fave (1974, 1980, 1986a, 1986b). Della Fave was particularly concerned with why people consider stratified social orders legitimate, "despite the fact that this seems to contradict their own self-interest" (Della Fave, 1986b, p. 478), a situation that he related to the concept of self-evaluation. Self evaluation theory argues that people in the upper reaches of the stratification system are seen as contributing more to society and deserving control over greater resources. Based on an assumption of cognitive consistency and the use of the distributive principle of equity (Adams, 1963), people of high status think they deserve their position and the poor see their disadvantages as justified, leading to legitimation of inequalities in a process "through which perceptions of what is are transformed into notions of what ought to be" (Della Fave, 1986b, p. 485). The works of Della Fave represent one of the first comprehensive approaches to the study of the legitimacy of the stratification system that offered an alternative explanation to the idea of external

---

[27] See next section on legitimacy of inequality at the micro level.

ideological domination, by also incorporating other explanatory elements such as self evaluation and perception. In this sense, self identity theory is considered an important precedent for this research that will also look for alternatives to the idea of ideological domination in explaining legitimacy processes.

iii. A third period of research is characterized by the link between the concepts justice and legitimacy in the context of comparative public opinion studies (Kluegel et al., 1995; Wegener, 2000, 1992). Besides including the concepts developed in the second period (such as split consciousness, market justice and self evaluation), this stage incorporates into the discussion an important theoretical and research tradition in sociology in the area of social justice, such as equity, status value and justice evaluation theory (J. Berger et al., 1972; Berkowitz & E. Walster, 1976; Jasso, 1978; Jasso & Wegener, 1997; E. Walster & G. Walster, 1975; Wegener, 1999). By making this theoretical link with justice literature, and with the availability of country representative data sets since the 1990's onwards, this period of research allows a more comprehensive approach to the study of the legitimacy of economic inequality. In this context, comprehensive means that with public opinion studies about distributive justice it is possible to cover the different elements included in the multidimensional concept of legitimacy, which constitutes the reason for basing the analysis of legitimacy on these kind of studies in the present research.

The explanation of the link between social justice and legitimacy requires additional elaboration and will constitute the central aspect of the following chapter. Before tackling this issue, the last point of this section completes the review of the classifications of legitimacy theories considering micro level approaches in the area of economic inequality.

b) Micro level legitimacy of inequality

The study of the legitimacy of economic inequality has occupied an important part in socio-psychological literature, even defining a whole area of studies known as the *psychology of legitimacy* (Jost & Major, 2001a). This area groups a series of approaches

78

that converge toward the idea that "people use ideas and beliefs to reinforce the legitimacy of the stats quo" (Jost & Major, 2001b, p. 33). They are particularly interested in psychological processes linked to the legitimation of inequalities within and between groups, such as stereotypes, prejudice and rationalizations. The accent on these psychological processes is related to critics of the equity approach, which in its basic formulation states that people accept outcomes as just when they are proportional to inputs. Authors such as Folger (1984) argue that a legitimate distribution goes beyond calculations of proportionality such as the ones equity theory proposes, and that people are able to accept disproportional outcomes as long as this is evaluated as appropriate based on principles other than equity, as for instance based on normative orientations for equality or for need (Deutsch, 1975).

Research at the micro level in legitimacy of distribution has been related to concepts such as relative deprivation (Crosby, 1979; Runciman, 1966) attributions of poverty and wealth (Ben-Ari, Schwarzwald, & Horiner-Levi, 1994; Bullock, 1999; Calder, 1977; Donald & Montiel, 1999; Kreidl, 2000b; Solomon, 1978; Yzerbyt & Rogier, 2001) and social identity (Hornsey, Spears, Cremers, & Hogg, 2003; Mummendey, Kessler, Klink, & Mielke, 1999; Tajfel, 1982), particularly in the case of small groups and organizations, as well as in the relation between groups. Most of these approaches at the micro level use the term legitimacy as auxiliary to justify the relevance of the research, but two recent research lines where legitimacy occupies a central place deserve special attention: the *system justification theory* (Jost & Major, 2001a) and the *social dominance approach* (Sidanius, Levin, & Pratto, 1996; Sidanius, Liu, Shaw, & Pratto, 1994).

- *System justification theory* is concerned with the paradoxical phenomenon of people who are materially disadvantaged and who at the same time fail to express discontent with their situation. Characteristic of this approach is the focus on people who, despite being socially disadvantaged, are reluctant to challenge the system and report levels of self-esteem equal or greater than members of socially advantaged groups (Major & Schmader, 2001). The theory starts with the assumption that economic inequality does not necessarily represent a threat to the legitimacy of the current economic order (Jost & O. Hunyady, 2003). In fact, this theory maintains that (a) there is a motive to justify the existing social order, and (b) paradoxically, this motive is sometimes strongest among those who are most disadvantaged by the social order (Jost & Major, 2001a). The first argument (a) builds on the belief in a just world theory (Lerner, 1980), that postulates the existence of a basic motive that leads to the belief that people get what they deserve, and deserve what they get. A consequence of this motive is to attribute responsibility to low status people for their situation. The second argument (b) is related to the theory of cognitive dissonance (Festinger, 1962), in which empirical research has demonstrated that people who are more socially and physically disadvantaged develop the strongest needs to justify their own suffering in order to reduce the dissonance associated with a situation of deprivation. According to system justification theory, the reduction of dissonance has been empirically tested in the case of a negative relation between income level and ideological support for authority and for law and order (Jost & Major, 2001a).

- As far as the *social dominance approach* is concerned, it departs from a different point than system justification theory by assuming that all social systems are characterized by the establishment of stable, group based social hierarchies. Social hierarchies consist of at least two social categories: the dominant group, at the top of social categories, and on the other hand the subordinate group, whose members get allocated a disproportionate quantity of negative social value (Sidanius & Pratto, 1999). These hierarchical structures are related to the influence of ideology in the form of legitimizing myths: "ideologies that provide support for group-based social inequality are referred to as hierarchy-enhancing (HE) legitimizing myths (LMs), while ideologies which provide support for group-based equality are referred to as hierarchy-attenuating (HA) legitimizing myths (LMs)" (Sidanius et al., 2001, p. 31). The theory asserts that the greater the degree to which both dominant and subordinates agree on the veracity of hierarchy-enhancing legitimizing myths, the less physical violence will be necessary to keep the stratification system intact.

The social dominance theory shares with system justification an ideological consensus across groups as a result of the spread of dominant ideology and cultural hegemony. Nevertheless, they differ in that social dominance tends to view the social order as something imposed by one group on another, whereas system justification theory conceptualizes the social order in terms of a collaborative process. Both perspectives emphasize different dimensions of legitimacy: whereas with system justification the role of consent by those not benefiting from the distribution is central, for social dominance it is the conformity with context rules in the form of legitimizing myths.

The description of the micro level theories of the legitimacy of inequality closes the presentation of empirical and theoretical based on objects (authority and economic inequality) and levels (micro and macro). The next section considers the contributions of the approaches reviewed for the empirical assessment of the multidimensional concept of legitimacy.

2.3 MULTIDIMENSIONAL APPROACH TO THE EMPIRICAL STUDY OF THE LEGITIMACY OF ECONOMIC INEQUALITY

The objective of this last section is to define a concept of legitimacy of economic inequality suitable for empirical research. The definition of such a concept builds on two main sources: the first one is the multidimensional concept of legitimacy (Beetham, 1991a) presented in the first section, and the second are the diverse approaches for the empirical study of legitimacy described in the second section of this chapter.

As discussed in the first section, Beetham's concept of legitimacy attempts to overcome the limitations of the Weberian conceptualization by expanding the limits of the concept beyond the *Legitimitätsglaube*. In doing so, the concept is constituted by three elements: one is related to a belief in the form of justification, a second to consent as expressed in some concrete action, and the third to conformity with the established rules. Despite critics regarding the possibilities of an empirical implementation of this concept (O'Kane, 1993), in the following I propose a way for the empirical assessment of each dimension. In order to simplify the description of the dimensions and to facilitate their association with previous empirical research, I will name the first one *subjective dimension*, the second *consensual dimension*, and the third *contextual dimension*.

i. Subjective dimension. This dimension is broadly related to "what people think", and it constitutes the basic element that has been considered in previous legitimacy research in the form of ideology, beliefs or support. Nevertheless, the distinctive character of legitimacy in this dimension is that it embraces the *justification* of rules and authorities according to normative criteria in the form of values or beliefs (P. Berger & Luckmann, 1967). Something is not legitimate because people support it, but because *it can be justified in terms of people's beliefs* (Beetham, 1991a; Luckmann, 1987). In empirical terms, this means that what we need to know from people in a society in order to evaluate legitimacy is not what they consider good or appropriate, but first and foremost what they consider just. Recent developments in the empirical study of legitimacy advance precisely along this line, such as the commented works of Tyler in the area of procedural justice, public opinion research by Kluegel, Mason & Wegener in the area of distributive justice, and psychosocial research by Jost in the system justification theory. Consequently, for the assessment of the legitimacy of inequality in the subjective dimensions, I will consider people's *justifications of economic inequality*, as it is further elaborated in the next chapter.

ii. Consensual dimension. The fact that the content of the subjective dimension of legitimacy is related to justice does not automatically mean that something considered just is then legitimate. Rather, "legitimacy involves the demonstrable expression of consent on the part of the subordinate for the particular power relation in which they are involved" (Beetham, 1991a, p. 18). To elucidate the way in which consent can be empirically evaluated we need some additional considerations. One central aspect in most of the theories presented is that something is considered legitimate when individuals believe that they must obey the norms regardless of whether they obtain immediate benefits (Hegtvedt & C. Johnson, 2000), i.e. beyond instrumental interests or calculation of expediency in Weberian terms. In this context, a criterion of consent is that people should exhibit a similar level of justification, disregarding their personal benefits from the situation. This idea is at the basis of the conceptualization of legitimacy as a *collective process* rather than a matter of private consent (Hegtvedt & C. Johnson, 2000) which is characteristic of research in the area of authority. To translate this notion into the area of economic inequality, the justification of inequality should be similar across groups with different instrumental interests, as for instance status groups. In other words, in a situation of no-legitimacy it would be expected that individuals of low status justify less inequality than those of high status, since they appear the less benefited in the stratification structure. But if, despite differences in individual status, there is evidence of *consensus in the justification of inequality*, this would be interpreted as an indicator of legitimacy.

iii. <u>Contextual dimension</u>. "Power can be said to be legitimate in the first instance if it is acquired and exercised in accordance with established rules" (Beetham, 1991a, p. 16). Consequently, an empirical assessment of any legitimacy object requires to evaluate the degree of conformity with a given rule, which is close to the idea of isomorphism described in the approach to legitimacy by neo-institutional analysis. Applied to the legitimacy of income inequality, it implies a definition of the distribution rules that characterize a particular society. The problem for empirical research is actually the identification of the distribution norms, since they are not as clear as written laws or procedures in the area of the legitimacy of authority. In this regard, it is possible to find two alternatives in previous empirical approaches. A <u>first possibility</u> is to consider a theoretical classification regarding the distributive rules that predominate in a given society as part of their political culture. This approach is exemplified by a series of studies that compare western societies (assumed to be mostly guided by market rules) and post-communist societies (assumed to bear the influence of egalitarian rules) and that evaluate the extent to which people of these societies support the corresponding distributive rules (Kluegel et al., 1995; Verwiebe & Wegener, 2000; Wegener, 1992; Wegener, Lippl, & Christoph, 2000). The <u>second possibility</u> is to consider a concrete indicator of societies regarding economic inequality, such as the level of income inequality (expressed in measures as the Gini index). The income inequality level reflects the way the distribution of economic resources in a particular period of time, and this indicator of *what is* can be contrasted with people's justification for inequality, i.e. *what ought to be* (Evans & Kelley, 2006; Hadler, 2005; Lübker, 2007; Osberg & Smeeding, 2006). The advantage of this perspective is that the context indicator is a continuous quantitative measure, which permits greater precision and flexibility at the moment of testing explanatory models in international comparison. Legitimacy of economic inequality in this contextual dimension occurs when individuals in a society with high inequality (as Chile) exhibit a corresponding large justification of economic inequality.

The following figure summarizes in a schematic way the multidimensional concept of legitimacy applied to empirical research about economic inequality:

Figure 3: Multidimensional model of legitimacy of economic inequality

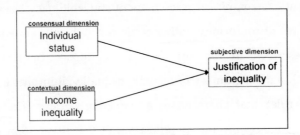

Figure 3 illustrates the three dimensions as well as the relationships among them. For the empirical test of the model, I will first consider the influence of individual status on the justification of inequality, represented by the arrow between both elements in the figure. According to the consensual hypothesis, justification of economic inequality should be similar across status groups, and therefore an indicator of legitimacy is when individual status does not have significant influence on the justification of inequality. I call this general hypothesis the *consensual legitimacy*. The second criterion of legitimacy is represented by the lower arrow. For evaluating conformity with context rules, the model considers the influence of the level of economic inequality on the justifications of inequality. In this case, a positive association between high economic inequality and greater justification of inequality is considered a criterion of legitimacy, called *contextual legitimacy*. From the conceptual model, this relationship could be expressed as a correlation and not a causal path, since in empirical terms conformity implies that income inequality and justifications of inequality covariate, not that one is the cause of the other. Nevertheless, the causal sense of the relationship is based on further arguments to be developed in the next chapter regarding the influence of context factors on people's beliefs (C. Anderson, 2008; Vijver, Hemert, & Poortinga, 2008; J. Berger et al., 1972; Homans, 1976; Blomberg & Kroll, 1999).

A final aspect to highlight at the end of this chapter is that legitimacy is evaluated in the relationship between dimensions. Therefore, even though the *justification of inequality* appears as the dependent dimension (variable) in the model, this does not mean that the justification of inequality corresponds to legitimacy. If this were so, we would again be confounding legitimacy with a particular belief, which was the starting point of the theoretical discussion at the beginning of this chapter. Rather, legitimacy is expressed by relationships among the elements of the model: consensus in the justifications (consensual legitimacy), and the extent to which the justification of inequality conforms to the level of inequality (contextual legitimacy).

Still there is a central aspect of the model that requires further elaboration, namely how to measure *justifications about inequality* in empirical terms and how to explain individual differences in these justifications. The assessment of the justification of inequality is the topic of the next chapter, in which I complete the missing elements of the explanatory model and propose the specific research hypotheses that will guide the empirical analysis.

2.4 SUMMARY

This chapter focused on the proposal of a concept of legitimacy that was suitable for empirical research in the area of economic inequality. I started by introducing the discussion on legitimacy in social sciences and highlighting the diversity of perspectives and the ambiguity of the concept itself. Much of the diffuse character of the concept of legitimacy is attributed to the conceptualization of Weber and the identification of legitimacy with *Legitimitätsglaube*, a debate that was illustrated presenting first the Weberian position and then the critical perspective exemplified by David Beetham. Based on the critics towards Weber, Beetham proposes a multidimensional concept of legitimacy that goes beyond the belief aspect and is based on three aspects: justifications of a rule, consent with the rule, and conformity with the rule.

In the second part of the chapter I proposed a framework for the classification of the different research lines in the area of legitimacy based on two main objects (authority and distribution) and two levels (micro and macro). The objective of this overview was to identify previous empirical evidence, to establish that the legitimacy of economic inequality constitutes an independent research area, and to critically analyze some concepts of legitimacy according to the multidimensional definition proposed before. Most of the attention was paid to the legitimacy of distribution at the macro level, the research area in which this study is located. In this area, three research periods were identified: the first one centered on the consensus-conflict debate and the dominant ideology, the second introduced concepts such as split consciousness and self evaluation, and the third characterized comparative public opinion research on topics of distributive justice. It is possible to observe an evolution through the research periods by progressively incorporating dimensions in the study of legitimacy other than the subjective one, and the last period of research opens the possibility for the study of legitimacy of economic inequality in a multidimensional perspective and in large scale societies.

Finally, the third section of the chapter was oriented to the development of a multidimensional model of legitimacy of economic inequality based on the concept of Beetham and previous empirical research. The model is constituted by a *subjective dimension* that entails justification of inequality, a *consensual dimension* referred to an overall justification of inequality beyond instrumental interests, and finally a *contextual dimension* that considers the conformity or congruence between people's justifications of inequality and the actual level of inequality in the particular society in study. A last element to develop in order to complete the multidimensional model corresponds to the empirical measurement of the *justification of inequality*, which is the topic of the following chapter.

Chapter 3

LEGITIMACY AND SOCIAL JUSTICE RESEARCH

Social or distributive justice is a broad area of theoretical and empirical studies basically concerned with how goods and rewards should be distributed in society. A traditional approach to this field is of *normative* orientation and characterizes the philosophical-political debate about the most adequate principles of distribution since the Nichomaquean Ethics of Aristotle (1999[350 b.C.]) onwards. A second and most recent approach to social justice is characterized by *empirical* studies which do not aim at defining normative principles, but at addressing lay people's conceptions about justice, i.e. what people think about how goods and rewards should be distributed in society. By considering peoples views, the empirical study of social justice opens the possibility of addressing a relevant question for the study of legitimacy, namely to what extent inequality in the distribution is considered just, or in more general terms, the justification of economic inequality.

The justification of economic inequality constitutes the central aspect of the multidimensional concept of legitimacy discussed in the last chapter, which corresponds to the subjective dimension of legitimacy. Since the objective is to characterize a society regarding justification of inequality in empirical terms, it is necessary to define what information is going to be considered as an indicator in this sense, facing the restriction that this information is obtained through public opinion studies. In this regard, people's views about justice are far from a simple matter, and a yes-no question such as "Do you think that inequality is just?" is certainly not enough to account for the complexity that an issue such as social justice implies. Therefore, in this last theoretical chapter I am going to concentrate on defining the elements that constitute the subjective dimension of legitimacy as well as on how to address them empirically on a large societal scale (i.e. through public opinion studies), for which I built on theoretical and empirical approaches to social justice research of the last 50 years. The definition of the concepts that constitute the justifications of economic inequality (i.e. subjective dimension) represents the last step in completing the multidimensional model of legitimacy for its empirical implementation.

The chapter is organized in four sections. The first one is a general background to the study of social justice, attending to the links between normative and empirical approaches and defining particular areas of research in the empirical realm. The second section focuses on the elements that allow the empirical analysis of people's justification of inequality. Based on the theoretical traditions of status value and justice evaluation theory, I propose alternatives to the empirical assessment of the justification of inequality based on the justice evaluation of occupational earnings differences. The third section introduces two contesting perspectives regarding the explanation of justice judgments about occupational earnings, namely the utopian and the existential. This distinction allows advancement toward explaining why larger differences in occupational earnings can be endorsed in contexts of high inequality, a discussion that is at the base of the main hypothesis of this research. In the last section, I proceed to the completion of the multidimensional model of legitimacy by adding the elements related to the justification of economic inequality. Based on the complete model I specify the explanatory relationships in the form of research hypotheses that will guide empirical analysis regarding the Chilean case and also in international comparison.

3.1 SOCIAL JUSTICE: NORMATIVE AND EMPIRICAL APPROACHES

A basic distinction in social justice studies is the one between normative and empirical traditions (Wegener, 1999, 2001). Both cover different aspects in the study of social justice that complement each other and that provide the general background of the concepts that relate social justice and legitimacy of inequality. Even though the main interest in this chapter is the empirical approach in social justice and its link to the study of legitimacy, it is relevant to consider previously that some of the developments in the empirical arena are connected to and have been stimulated by the normative philosophical contributions (Hasse, 2002; Kluegel et al., 1995; Liebig & Lengfeld, 2002; Sabbagh, 2001). As Sabbagh states, there is as growing call for considering possible exchanges between both traditions, and for "examining how philosophical-normative and empirically oriented research can contribute to one another" (Sabbagh, 2001, p. 237). To understand this contribution among the perspectives, I start with a brief description of the normative area in distributive justice, to then highlight how the link with empirical approaches is related to the study of legitimacy.

3.1.1 About the normative perspective in social justice

Social justice is a *normatively charged* concept (Merkel & Kruck, 2004) characterized by the definition of the principles according to which implement and evaluate a just distribution. Such a perspective was initiated by Aristotle in the Nichomaquean Ethics, in which he pointed out that the general sense of justice states that everyone should have their own in proportion to their relevant differences, treating equals equally and unequals unequally (Aristotle, 1999[350 b.C.]). Based on this general principle, he further differentiates between two types of justice: rectificatory, related to the preservation of order and the payment of damages in accordance with caused injuries, and *distributive justice*, stating that goods and honor should be allocated proportional to individual contribution, also called the principle of proportional equality (or equity). From here onwards the relationship between justice and equality will constitute one of the main axes in the normative debate about distributive principles, attempting to define what is (or are) the appropriate distributive principles that allow an unequal distribution of goods possible to be considered just. As characterized by Barry, the normative discussion in social justice can be conceived as "the defensibility of unequal relations between people" (Barry, 1989, p. 3). In another way, it is about establishing which particular kind of inequality could be considered a principle of distributive justice, known as the *equality of what* debate (Krebs, 2000): equal to contributions in the case of Aristotle, equality of resources (Dworkin, 1981, 2000), basic goods (Rawls, 1971), opportunity for welfare (Roemer, 1982) or equality of capabilities (Sen, 1992).

To understand the framework of the justice-equality debate we must consider the relationship of distributive justice and economic resources in modern societies. Authors such as Fleischacker (2004) and Jackson (2005) point out that the meaning of the term distributive justice has radically changed throughout history and has only in a recent phase been linked to the distribution of material goods. Actually, the original Aristotelian conception of distributive justice was not mainly concerned with material goods, but mostly with political participation (Fleischacker, 2004). Justice in association with the distribution of economic resources started with the discussion of property rights in the 18th century by Adam Smith (von Hayek, 1976; Jackson, 2005), and according to Fleischacker "not a singular jurisprudential thinker before Smith – not Aristotle, not Aquinas, not Grotius, not Putendorf, not Hutcheson, not William Blackstore or David Hume – put the justification of property rights under the heading of justice. Claims to property, like violations of property, were matters for commutative justice; no one was given a right to claim property by distributive justice" (Fleischacker, 2004, p. 27). The discussion about the right to property and material goods assumes that an individual's fair share can be defined in relation to the shares held by others, in the context of a bounded community. In such a community, a central agency such as the state and its governmental institutions are attributed a central role as far as distribution is concerned (D. Miller, 2003).

Both the right to material goods and the role of a central agency in the distribution characterize the modern debate on distributive justice (Jackson, 2005). In this framework, most of the 19th and 20th century were dominated by political theories of Marxism and utilitarianism that were actually inhospitable to the concept of distributive justice: Marx and Engels considered the notion of justice as a mere ideology (McBride, 1975; Wood, 1972), whereas the utilitarians subordinated individual rights to the general goal of utility maximization (Jackson, 2005; Gargarella, 1999; Cullen, 1992). Even though social justice can be regarded as one of the central political ideas in the twentieth century, it was not until the publication of *A theory of Justice* from Rawls in 1971 that the topic newly obtained a philosophical political dimension (Maffettone, 2001). Rawls emerges as an alternative to the utilitarian conceptions that tolerated the misery suffered by part of the society under the principle of utility maximization, proposing that "each person possesses an inviolability founded on justice that even the welfare of society as a whole cannot override" (Rawls, 1971, p. 3). The definition of the justice principles is achieved by creating a hypothetical situation called *the original position*, which is a type of virtual agreement between two parts that are deprived of the knowledge of their interests behind the *veil of ignorance*. Justice principles derived in the original position lead to a conception of *justice as fairness* based on two principles of universal applicability: each individual should have the same right to basic freedoms, and all social valuable goods should be distributed equally unless an unequal distribution benefits the most disadvantaged (Rawls, 1971). The emphasis on individual rights can be conceived as opposed to the Aristotelian view based on distribution according to personal characteristics, since for Rawls such characteristics are dependent on fortunate social or familiar circumstances and do not constitute criteria for a just distribution (Merkel, 2001).

Rawls has not only become a central figure in contemporary theoretical debates about justice, but he has opened the door to the consideration of people's conceptions about distributive justice and its role in the legitimacy of distribution. Actually, the formulation of the original position already relies on people's conceptions about justice since "justice as fairness is the hypothesis that the principles that would be chosen in the original position are identical with those that match our considered judgments" (Rawls, 1971, p. 48). Further, the link between people's conceptions and justice principles is emphasized by Rawls in the *liberal principle of legitimacy*, in which "our exercise of political power is fully proper only when it is exercised in accordance with a constitution, the essentials of which all citizens as free and equal may reasonably be expected to endorse in the light of principles and ideals acceptable to their common human reason" (Rawls, 1971, p. 137). The endorsement of justice principles from the side of individuals is associated with the Rawlsian notion of *reflective equilibrium*. Following the analysis of Wegener (1995), in further publications of Rawls (and partly as a response to communitarian critics[28] of the universalistic appeal of the justice principles), he restricts the applicability of the distributive principles to modern democracies where the justice conceptions are "implicitly present in the political culture of constitutional democracies" (Rawls & Hinsch, 1992, p. 365). Such statements refer us not only to the relevance of the empirical study of justice, but also to consider people's justice conceptions in relation to the particular context, which corresponds to one of the key dimensions in the study of legitimacy presented in the last chapter (contextual dimension).

3.1.2 Empirical justice research and the study of legitimacy

Empirical social research is an area concerned with the study of what people consider as a just distribution and with what are the determinants (i.e. causes of individual variability) of justice conceptions or beliefs (R. Cohen, 1987). Empirical justice can be traced back to concepts such as relative deprivation and equity theory in the areas of social psychology and sociology in the 1950s and 1960s. In the first conceptualizations, the notion of justice was associated with exchange relationships that were empirically studied at a micro level, and a possible relation to the issue of the legitimacy of inequality in a society was an area still out of sight. It was only with the beginning of public opinion studies about social inequalities in the 1970s and especially in the 1980s that topics such as distributive rules and justice ideologies as

---

[28] The arguments of Rawls in *A Theory of Justice* have generated a series of criticism, mostly dealing with the universal character of the principles that have been debated by the communitarians as an imposition of the values of the occidental culture in different situations or spheres that would require different distributive principles (Mulhall & Swift, 1996; Sandel, 1998; Walzer, 1983; Müller-Planterberg, 2001).

characteristics of societies started to appear in the empirical social science vocabulary (Cook, 1987; Cook & K. Hegtvedt, 1983; Huber & Form, 1973; Hochschild, 1981; Kluegel et al., 1995; Kluegel & Smith, 1986; Markovsky & Younts, 2001; Montada & Lerner, 1996; Wegener, 1992).

Empirical justice research based on public opinion surveys, particularly from the 1990s onwards, introduces the discussion about the complementation between normative and empirical approaches. Nevertheless, despite the arguments that have called for a cooperation between both perspectives (Elster, 1995; Liebig, Lengfeld, & Mau, 2001; Miller, 1992; Soltan, 1982; Swift, 1999; Swift, Marshall, Burgoyne, & Routh, 1995), the two traditions so far have mostly developed in parallel (Frohlich et al., 1987; Hegtvedt, 1992; Liebig & Lengfeld, 2002; Sabbagh, 2001; J. Scott, Matland, Michelbach, & Bornstein, 2001). The exchange between the traditions has been stimulated in the last two decades by the launching of comparative public opinion studies on justice such as the International Social Justice Project (ISJP) (Kluegel et al., 1995). Such comparative research projects have raised the issue of the extent to which people's justice conceptions are related to the principles that characterize distribution in a particular society. The comparison between normative justice principles and empirical justice principles –along the line of the *reflective equilibrium* discussed above – has also brought the issue of the legitimacy of distribution in different societies to the fore (Gijsberts, 1999; Kelley & Evans, 1993; Verwiebe & Wegener, 2000; Wegener, 1992).

The link between the empirical study of social justice and the concept of legitimacy emerges in the two broad categories in which empirical approaches are classified according to Wegener (1995, 1999), called *principle related* and *reward related*:

i. *Principle related* justice theories refer to the empirical study of general justice judgments that people hold about the distribution of goods and rewards in society. For instance, the level of agreement with statements such as 'the state should redistribute from those who have more, to those who have less', or 'people should get rewarded for their efforts'. The term *justice ideologies* is usually applied in this research area to characterize the distributive principles that predominate in a society (Wegener & Liebig, 1993, 1995a). Most empirical studies distinguish between two justice ideologies[29]: on the one hand *individualism*, related to distribution based on personal achievement criteria such as merit of effort, and on the other hand *egalitarianism*, which privileges an equal allocation of shares and an active role of the state in the distributive process (Aalberg, 2003; Gijsberts, 1999; Kluegel, 1989; Shepelak, 1989; Wegener, 1992). The study of justice ideologies has been associated with legitimacy in part of the empirical literature that contrasts people's support for ideologies with distributive principles of the society, i.e. attending to the contextual dimension of legitimacy. For instance, if a society is mostly organized according to market mechanisms and is at the same time accompanied by an ideology that supports such distribution based on individual merit or effort, this is usually interpreted as if this distribution were legitimized in this society (Shepelak, 1989). Legitimacy of economic inequality in this area is usually studied under the label *legitimacy of distributive rules*.

ii. *Reward related* theories refer to justice evaluations about concrete distributions of rewards to individuals, in the sense of expressions such as 'it is just that person A receives X'. Theories aimed at explaining what is considered a just reward for someone with specific characteristics encompasses relative deprivation theory (Runciman, 1966), equity theory (Adams, 1963; Homans, 1961), status value (J. Berger, Fisek, & Norman, 1989; J. Berger et al., 1972) and the justice evaluation theory (Jasso, 1978, 1980, 2007; Jasso & Wegener, 1997). Most of the empirical studies based on *reward related* theories are focused on one particular 'sphere of justice' (Walzer, 1983), dealing with the distribution of monetary rewards in the form of income, salary and/or earnings according to occupations (Arts, Hermkens, & Wijck, 1989; Gijsberts, 1999; Kelley & Evans, 1993; Lippl, 1999; Verwiebe & Wegener, 2000). Empirical research in this tradition has usually considered the term legitimacy by analyzing differences in earnings considered just for occupations with different status, and then comparing the just differences with the actual

---

[29] An alternative conceptualization in the area of justice ideologies is the one proposed by Wegener & Liebig (Wegener, 1999, 2001) which, based on the grid-group theory of Mary Douglas, points out the existence of four different ideologies (individualism, egalitarianism, ascriptivism, fatalism).

differences in earnings in the stratification system. In this research area, evidence of legitimacy is when the just earning differences are similar to the current earnings differences (Gijsberts, 1999). The analysis of rewards considered just for occupations of different status allows one to establish a subjective measure of the amount of economic inequality considered just in a society. It is actually this perspective of empirical justice research, called the *justice of earnings*, on which I will focus to propose an empirical assessment of the justification of economic inequality.

Table 5 summarizes the empirical areas in the study of social justice, the main object of study in each case, and the link with legitimacy research:

Table 5: Empirical justice, objects of study and legitimacy

Empirical justice area	Main object of study	Standard for legitimacy
Principle related	Justice ideologies	System distributive principles
Reward related	Justice of earnings	Earnings inequality in the occupational structure

The empirical study of social justice connects with the study of legitimacy when justice conceptions are analyzed with regard to some standard. In the *principle related* justice reward, the concept of legitimacy refers to the analysis of justice ideologies in relation to distributive principles that characterize the political system or the political culture (Mason & Kluegel, 2000), whereas in reward related, the justice of earnings associated with occupations is contrasted with the actual level of earnings inequality existent in the society. Making the relationship with the multidimensional concept of legitimacy, what appears in empirical social justice research so far is the analysis of the so-called contextual legitimacy (conformity with context standards), but the area of consensual legitimacy is still largely absent in empirical justice research at a macro level. In this research I advance the incorporation of the consensual dimension for the analysis of legitimacy at the macro level, and also propose a way of assessing the justification of economic inequality based on the literature of the *justice of earnings*.

3.2 THE JUSTIFICATION OF ECONOMIC INEQUALITY

Determining what people regard as a just distribution is not a simple task, especially when the possibilities are restricted to specific questions in a public opinion questionnaire. This section is aimed at analyzing the possibilities of tackling this problem, building on approaches from reward related empirical social justice research. I start by focusing attention on theories and proposals from the literature on the justice of occupational earnings, from which I highlight two formulations that allow an empirical approach to the study of the legitimacy of inequality: the status value formulation and the justice evaluation function. Based on both theories, in a following part, I present two strategies dealing with measuring the justification of economic inequality: the just reward components and the just earnings gap.

3.2.1 Defining the justice of occupational earnings

What is a just reward? Jasso & Rossi (1977) and Kelley & Evans (1993) refer to general perspectives in the literature regarding this question. The first one can be called *idiosyncratic*, which means that there are no common norms about distribution and therefore the public has no coherent views about justice. It follows the maxim of "justice is in the eye of the beholder" of Walster, et al (1975), and it finds empirical support in authors such as Converse (2004[1964]), who points out that public opinion is disorganized and random. The second is a *utopian* vision that assumes a consensual belief in equality as the main criteria and the ideal of justice, usually linked to a Marxian normative proposal on the communist society (Marx & Engels, 1932). The third one affirms that there is no consensus in equality, but there is some common ideal of earnings distribution characterized by a *certain degree* of inequality (d'Anjou, Steijn, & Van Aarsen, 1995). It is this last area where we can find most of the empirical developments oriented to determine the *certain degree* of inequality that is considered just, under the concept of the *justice of earnings*.

The empirical approach to the justice of earnings begins with research on promotions in the US Army by Stouffer (1949) in "The American Soldier", a large scale social psychological study carried out during World War II. One of the surprising findings

97

of this study was that the level of satisfaction with promotion policies was higher in groups where opportunities for promotions were actually comparatively poor[30]. This finding can be considered a starting point in research on distributive justice, where the main conclusion was the lack of a direct relationship between objective characteristics of a reward (such as promotion opportunities) and people's evaluation of it in terms of justice. Concepts such as *relative deprivation*[31] appear as a proposal to explain such counter intuitive findings, stating that "a person who is 'relatively deprived' need not be 'objectively' deprived in the more usual sense that he is demonstrably lacking something" (Runciman, 1966, pp. 10-11). Relative deprivation introduced explanatory mechanism processes of comparison and reference groups which, applied in the case of the American Soldier results in that the group with more promotion opportunities compared themselves with their own group, feeling more *relatively deprived* than those of the group with fewer opportunities (Crosby, 1979; Tyler, 1997; Wegener, 1991).

From here on, processes of comparison have played a central role in explaining the justice of rewards. The main concern in this area becomes the identification of the criteria used in the comparison process as well as determining the group or reference for the comparison. Formulations such as *equity theory* (Adams, 1963; Cook, 1975; Leventhal, 1976) further elaborate on comparison and exchange processes as basic in the determination of a just reward. In the equity-research framework, "effort has a certain exchange value in the sense that its amount or quality will elicit reward from others. Reward, too, has a certain exchange value in the sense that it elicits effort from others" (J. Berger et al., 1972, p. 121). The evaluation of this exchange process is performed according to a criteria or proportionality between efforts and rewards, and an exchange is considered just by the actors if rewards (or more generally, the output of the process) are in line with efforts (input). This evaluation of

---

[30] The compared groups in this regard were the Air Corps (many promotion opportunities) and the Military Police (few promotion opportunities).

[31] "A is relatively deprived of X when (i) he does not have X, (ii) he sees some other person or persons, who may include himself at some previous t expected time, as having X (whether or not this is or will be in fact the case), (iii) he wants X, and (iv) he sees it as feasible that he should have X. Possession of X may, of course, mean avoidance of or exemption from Y" (Runciman, 1966, p. 10).

proportionality between input and output requires a comparison process with others' ratios of input/output.

Nevertheless, equity theory presents a series of limitations for the study of the justice of rewards. *Status value* and *justice evaluation theory* emerge partially as alternatives to the predominant previous research perspectives in the 1950s and 1960s, which were mostly centered on equity theory (Markovsky, 1985). Both theories are of central relevance for this research, since they provide a framework for the study of the justification of inequality at the macro level (i.e. based on public opinion studies in large societies). In the following I introduce some basic concepts of each theory, which will be considered in the next section regarding the measurement of the justification of economic inequality.

a) The status value theory (J. Berger et al., 1972) builds on two main critics of the equity theory, referred to as (i) the distinction between local and referential comparisons, and (ii) the issue of the status value of a reward:

i. The first point establishes that comparisons can be of two types: *local comparisons* occur when one individual compares himself with another particular individual, and *referential comparisons* are performed with regard to a wide category or groups of similar individuals (for instance, with blue collar workers), for whom Berger et al. suggested the term *generalized other*. The authors propose that the equity formulation is only related to local comparisons, which "is not sufficient to produce a distributive justice process" (J. Berger et al., 1972, p. 122). A frame of reference – such as the generalized other – is needed to give meaning to the local comparisons in term of justice or injustice. This means, justice evaluations occur based on *referential comparisons*. An example to illustrate this situation could be two skilled workers who obtain a similar reward for the same investments (equity situation in a local comparison), but however their salary is quite below what they believe a skilled worker (generalized other) obtains on average in that society, leading to a situation of injustice despite equity. Therefore, "to make useful predictions about distributive justice, careful thought will have to be given to the nature and function of referential structures in comparisons" (J. Berger et al., 1972, p. 124).

ii. The second point refers to rewards that not only have a *consumatory value* in terms of the goods that they enable to be obtained, but also a *status value*. The status value of a reward means that they have significance in terms of social standing, worth and respect in society, and not only in terms of the quantity of the reward itself. Besides, there are status characteristics (for instance being female or white) that are significant in terms of evaluating the justice of a reward, but that in equity formulations would be considered mere investments together with other elements such as personal effort. *Referential structures* contain information about the status significance of the rewards, the characteristics of the subjects, and how characteristics are associated with goal objects in society, creating normative expectations about distribution. Actual distribution of goal objects are tested against the referential structure: a coincidence with expectations is considered just, and a difference is evaluated as unjust (J. Berger et al., 1972). Therefore, from the status value formulation, inequality would be considered just when congruent with the expectations of the referential structure. The empirical study of the referential structure becomes the key to explaining justice judgments, a point on which I elaborate further in the next section, after reviewing the proposal of the justice evaluation theory.

b) The justice evaluation theory is an alternative approach to that of status value, focused on the concrete measurement of the experience of justice and injustice in individuals and societies (Jasso, 1978, 1980, 1981, 1989, 1999, 2000, 2007; Jasso & Rossi, 1977; Jasso & Wegener, 1997). Jasso draws the attention to some limitations of the definition of justice according to the status value formulation, for which justice would be based on the following term:

(1) $$Justice\ evaluation = actual\ earning - just\ earning$$

A first critique of Jasso (1978) towards this formulation is that the result of such justice evaluation is expressed in units of the reward instead of what she calls *justice units*, which should have a meaning independent of the concrete reward under consideration. This is especially relevant at the moment of comparing justice evaluation of different subjects. A second related weakness is that a similar monetary value can have different meanings in terms of justice evaluation. For instance, a value of $200 certainly has a different meaning when is it the result of $400-$200 than when compared with the result of $20,000-$19,800. Besides, "the human experience that deficiency is felt to be more unjust than a comparable excess" (Jasso, 1978, p. 1403) is also sidelined by Berger et al. in their formulation. Based on these critical points, Jasso proposes a new specification of the *justice evaluation* function that attempts to overcome previous shortcomings and that in its basic formulation looks as follows:

$$(2) \qquad \text{Justice evaluation function} \quad = \quad \ln\left(\frac{\text{actual earnings}}{\text{just earnings}}\right)$$

This proposal for a justice evaluation is defined as the logarithmic function of the ratio of actual earnings to just earnings. Such formulation attempts to reflect that a) the judgment of fairness of an individual income involves a ratio procedure, where the equivalence of both terms represents perfect justice, and b) the logarithmic term quantifies being under rewarded as felt more intensely than being over rewarded. The result of the function is expressed in justice units where 0 expresses perfect justice, positive values represent unjust overreward, and negative values unjust underreward.

Even though justice evaluation theory is mostly concerned with defining the experience of justice regarding one's own earnings (called reflexive justice judgments), several lessons can be extracted to be applied in the measurement of the justification of economic inequality. Some of these lessons are the idea of defining a function that summarizes the information in quantitative terms, the proportion between quantities that allow comparisons among subjects (since they are expressed in 'justice units' and not absolute units) and the consideration of the just rewards with regard to the actual rewards.

Based on the concepts and proposals from status value and justice evaluation theory it is possible to point out two main ways of dealing with the measurement of the justification of economic inequality: the *just reward components* and the *just earnings gap*. Both are based on justice evaluations regarding occupational earnings, but they imply different emphasis and methodological strategies.

3.2.2 Measuring the justification of economic inequality

a) Just rewards components[32]

Status value theory gives a central role to the referential structure in explaining justice judgments. The referential structure is characterized by (i) certain elements or components that people take into account when defining what a just reward would be for a rewardee with particular characteristics, (ii) an order among the components in terms of priority for evaluating a reward (Cook, 1975; McCranie & Kimberly, 1973). The process of rewards evaluation based on the referential structure can be illustrated based on the following scheme:

Figure 4: Referential structure and determination of a just reward

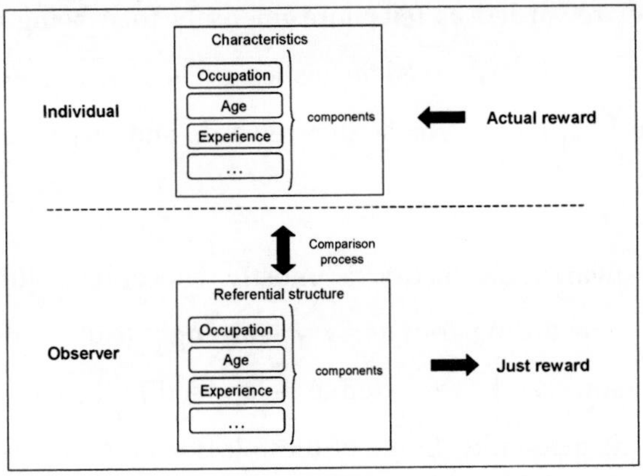

The figure represents an individual X that possesses a series of characteristics, and an observer or evaluator. From the individual we know that he performs a certain occupation associated with a salary (actual reward), but we also have information

---

[32] Even though the literature in this area refers mostly to dimensions, I use the term components to avoid confusion with the dimensions of the legitimacy model.

about other characteristics such as age, experience and education of this individual. With this information the task of the observer is to determine what a just reward would be for the individual X. According to status value theory, in performing this task people compare the actual situation of the individual with that of the referential structure, where several components are related to a certain status value. Based on the comparison between the actual situation and the referential structure, it is possible to perform a judgment in terms of a just salary for the individual X. For instance, if I had the information of someone who is a corporate manager, male, 35 years old, white, and who earns $2,500, I would compare this information with that of my referential structure (how much a male corporate manager, 35 years old and white *should* earn), and based on the comparison between the information of the individual and the value that I assign to each of the components (male, white, etc.) in my referential structure, I propose what I think would be a just salary for the corporate manager.

At this point it is possible to specify the association between the status value formulation and the measurement of the justification of economic inequality. By having information about the referential structure of representative individuals in a society (i.e. based on public opinion surveys), it would be possible to determine whether people justify economic inequality among individuals or not, to what extent occupational status is a criteria for justifying economic inequality, and also which other components besides occupation play a role in justifying inequality. In this sense, the *just rewards components* approach does not establish *a priori* that occupation is the most relevant element in justifying inequality, but leaves this assumption open to empirical test.

Even though research on the justice rewards components offers a comprehensive framework for research on the justification of inequality, one of its difficulties is its empirical implementation. It is not enough to ask in a survey what kind of criteria or components are considered relevant, but to assign a specific value for each component of the referential structure in economic terms, i.e. in monetary value. A survey methodology that is suitable for assigning a specific value to each component, and therefore to quantify the influence of each component in justifying inequality, is the factorial survey research (Alexander & Becker, 1978; Alves & Rossi, 1978; Alves, 1982; Headey, 1991; Jasso, 1978, 2006a; Schrenker, 2007; Steiner & Atzmüller, 2006; Wallander, 2009).

Factorial survey research is a specific methodology first developed by Peter Rossi for the study of the latent dimensions (components) behind a justice judgment regarding a determinate object[33]. The empirical research in this area started at the end of the 1970s with a series of papers from Jasso, Alves and Rossi (Alves & Rossi, 1978; Jasso & Rossi, 1977), who concluded that justice judgments are not random or of idiosyncratic character, rather they are performed against certain standards that are shared in society. Therefore, "people share with each other latent principles that govern which attributes of such objects are relevant and how such attributes should be weighed in coming to a summative judgment" (Rossi & Nock, 1982, p. 10). To uncover the attributes (components) that contribute to a judgment and their weight, Rossi proposed the *factorial survey research*. Instead of asking for the importance attributed to each component separately, the proposal from Rossi consists of presenting the respondent with a series of fictitious situations (called "vignettes"), in which all the components in study are expressed at once[34]. An example of a vignette could be: "Mr. Smith is a manager in a large corporation, has a university degree, and his monthly salary is $ 5,000". In such a vignette, the components gender, occupation, education and actual salary are present. Different vignettes represent combinations of the components. Based on the analysis of the respondent's proposal of a just earning for each vignette, it is possible to establish the differential contribution of each component to the just reward (Hermkes & Boerman, 1989; Shepelak & Alwin, 1986). In this sense, factorial surveys not only allow one to answer the question as to whether inequality in earnings is justified among occupations of different status, but also shed light on the specific income that each occupation deserves, i.e. the just earning differences among occupations. Further details in the

---

[33] This methodology is not restricted to the study of justice judgments. There are a series of applications to other research fields such as family status, prison reform, child abuse, among others (Rossi & Nock, 1982).

[34] For a specific description of the factorial survey design, see the data section of Chapter 4.

empirical part of this work will give additional information about this methodology, since the abstract formulation described so far makes sense in its concrete implementation.

Despite the fact that the factorial survey methodology was already proposed more than three decades ago, its use is still very restricted. The reasons are that the principles at the base of the survey, the design of the questionnaires and the analysis techniques entail a certain degree of complexity when compared with regular public opinion surveys. Still, with the factorial survey it is possible to answer some questions regarding the legitimacy of economic inequality that are only partially covered by other questionnaires. This was the motivation for designing a factorial survey questionnaire for the study of the justice of occupational earnings in Chile, in the framework of this research. From my knowledge, this is the first time that such methodology has been implemented in a country that does not belong to the industrialized world. However, the study is considered exploratory since it was applied to a small sample, as specified in the data description in Chapter 4. Therefore, the analysis of the justification of economic inequality based on the factorial survey corresponds only to a partial aspect of the empirical research. The major part of the analysis will be performed based on the second approach to the study of the justification of inequality, namely the just earning gap.

b) The just earnings gap

The *just earnings gap* represents a second approach to measuring the justification of economic inequality. Instead of analyzing different components of the referential structure based on status value theory, the just earnings gap builds on the approach of the justice evaluation theory (Jasso, 1978; Jasso & Wegener, 1997), which looks for ways to mathematize people's experiences of justice and injustice. In this tradition, the main objective is to define a function that accounts for the justification of economic inequality, which can be implemented in public opinion surveys and is comparable among individuals. Research along this line considers the occupational position as the main characteristic related to economic inequality (Evans & Kelley, 2006; Kelley & Evans, 1993; Gijsberts, 1999; Hadler, 2005; Kuhn, 2005; Osberg &

Smeeding, 2006; Verwiebe & Wegener, 2000). The idea behind it is that occupation to a large extent determines people's chances in life and thereby the income they can earn (Gijsberts, 1999). The methodological strategy to follow in this case commonly selects the extreme ranks of the occupational status dimension (a high and a low status occupation), and then compares the values of a just reward for these extreme ranks with regard to the actual (or perceived) reward. The objective is to obtain a measure of what people believe is a just amount of economic inequality in society based on judgments about occupational earnings.

It is possible to find different empirical perspectives regarding the comparison of just occupational earnings. Pioneer work on this subject started with the assessment of just occupational earnings in small scale studies by Rainwater (1974) in Boston, Szirmai (1988) in the Netherlands, and Headey (1991) in Melbourne. Further analysis of justice in occupational earnings has been based on the two major comparative public opinion research projects in the area of justice and inequality: the International Social Survey Program (ISSP) and the International Social Justice Project (ISJP). The consideration of research based on both datasets is not only important because most of the empirical study of legitimacy of inequality in large societies is based on them, but also because Chile has participated in both survey programs and most of the analysis of this research is based on these datasets. Research linked to the ISJP has been characterized by the use of the justice evaluation function (Jasso, 1978; Jasso & Wegener, 1997) applied to high and low status occupations, and then comparing the differences among them under terms such as the *absolute amount of injustice* (Lippl, 1999) or the *justice gap* (Verwiebe & Wegener, 2000). Even though the focus of these terms is more oriented toward assessing the experience of injustice than the justification of inequality, these studies are regarded as a precedent for this research in the consideration of the justice of occupational earnings in relation to legitimacy. On the other hand, researchers associated to the ISSP such as Kelley and Evans (1993) and Gijsberts (1999) compared just earnings for low status and high status occupations, as well as the proportion among them, i.e. how much an individual in a high status occupation should earn with regard to one of a low status occupation. They draw relevant conclusions for this research, such as that people have coherent views about just earnings for low status occupations and also about the hierarchy of earnings across nations, but they found no consensus about the just earning for high status occupations nor for the amount of inequality among different occupations. Despite country variations, equality of earnings is universally rejected by the public in industrial, communist and capitalist societies. Further empirical research along this line (Aalberg, 2003; Austen, 2002; Hadler, 2005; Osberg & Smeeding, 2006) has confirmed the tendency that in international comparison the hierarchy of just earnings is consensual across countries.

Based on the theory and the research reviewed in the area of the just earnings differences, I propose a term that will serve as the main dependent variable of this study regarding the justification of earnings inequality. The term is called the *just earnings gap*, and is represented in the following figure:

Figure 5: Just earnings gap

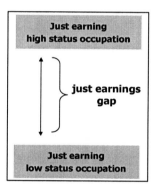

The just earnings gap is based on the occupational earning differences considered just between high status and low status occupations. It considers the proposal of a just earning in monetary terms for both occupations from the part of the respondent of a survey. The difference between both terms is expressed as a proportion, as illustrated in the following formula:

(3)   Just earnings gap = $\ln\left(\dfrac{\text{just earning}_{\text{ high status occupation}}}{\text{just earning}_{\text{ low status occupation}}}\right)$

This operationalization attempts to reflect the differences in earnings considered just for a high and a low status occupation, i.e. a measure of the justification of economic inequality. Concretely, the differences are expressed as a ratio of the earning considered just for a high status occupation, divided by the earning considered just for a low status occupation. The basic idea of the ratio is to express how much it is considered just what a high status occupation earns in relation to a low status occupation. Besides, the use of a ratio permits abstraction away from currency units, allowing cross national comparability and focusing directly on the relative income hierarchy (Kelley & Zagorski, 2004). The natural logarithm applied to the term follows the elaborations of Jasso regarding income magnitudes, since the difference in income in the upper extreme of the income continuum have a lower weight than those at the lower end. It is assumed that people think more in terms of percentages or proportions than in absolute differences (Kelley & Evans, 1993), i.e. an increase of $10 for someone who earns $100 means much more than for someone who earns $10,000,000.

The *just earnings gap* and the *just reward components* constitute the two alternatives for the empirical analysis of the justification of economic inequality, corresponding to the dependent variables in the multidimensional model of legitimacy. To reinforce again the argument of this thesis, the just earnings gap and the just reward components do not constitute a measure of the legitimacy of inequality, but they are only one of the dimensions in the analysis of legitimacy. Legitimacy of economic inequality will be evaluated according to two criteria defined in the last chapter, namely consensus regarding the justification of inequality and the congruence with regard to the actual stratification system of the society. The formulations of the specific hypotheses regarding the justification of inequality are delivered at the end of this chapter. Before presenting the hypotheses, I will discuss two additional concepts coming from social justice research literature that play a key explanatory role in the justification of inequality, namely the *perception of inequality* and the *justice ideologies*. The introduction of these two concepts takes place in the framework of the discussion about the utopian or existential determination of justice judgments.

3.3 EXPLAINING THE JUST EARNINGS DIFFERENCES: UTOPIAN OR EXISTENTIAL DETERMINATION?

In the previous presentation of the status value formulation, I mentioned the referential structure as an explanatory concept for what people evaluate as just. According to the status value approach, people's formulation of a justice judgment is based on a comparison process between an actual situation of distribution (an individual X that receives a reward Y), and personal standards regarding distribution as represented in the referential structure (J. Berger et al., 1972). Therefore, if we aim at understanding and explaining what people think about just earning differences, we need to tackle which standards have an influence on the referential structure (Alwin, Gornev, & Khakhulina, 1995; Berger et al., 1972; Kluegel, Csepeli, Kolosi, Orkeny, & Nemenyi, 1995; Shepelak & Alwin, 1986). *Existential* and *utopian* standards represent the two main explanations regarding judgments about earnings. According to Shepelak, "in order to understand the justice evaluation process, it is important to disentangle the role of existential standards – what *is* defines what ought to be – from the role of non-existential or utopian standards" (Shepelak & Alwin, 1986, p. 31). Disentangling both standards acquires relevance in the context of this research since they lead to different explanations of the legitimacy process:

i.   The *utopian* perspective refers to the fact that, at the moment of elaborating a justice judgment, people take normative ideals or principles into consideration about how goods and rewards should be distributed. For instance, if I am faced with a situation in which a high status occupation earns 50 times more than a low status occupation, I evaluate this distribution according to a normative principle that I support, say egalitarianism, and consequently my proposal for a just salary would be oriented to reduce the current income differences. Such a perspective has its roots in normative formulations about the existence of universal principles of justice (Rawls, 1971), and in empirical literature aiming at uncovering the supported principles in particular societies (Frohlich et al., 1987). Literature in social psychology that reacted against the universality of the equity formulation has also pointed out alternative normative standards in the utopian sense, such as equality and need (Deutsch, 1975). In sociological research based on public opinion, the utopian standards relate to the concept of *justice ideologies* (Wegener, 1992, 1998, 2003; Wegener & Liebig, 1995b, 1993) which represent an order-related approach to empirical justice, as discussed in the section 3.1 of this chapter. Justice ideologies are general normative standards about distribution, and they have been directly related to the issue of the legitimacy of inequality by literature contrasting support of different ideologies in political systems characterized by particular distributive policies (Lippl, 2003; Mau, 1997). In this research I will consider justice ideologies as representing general utopian standards that explain individual variation regarding preferences for just earnings inequality. Nevertheless, the sense of considering utopian standards is mostly a counterpoint to the existential ones, where the theoretical explanation of the legitimacy hypothesis in the context of high inequality actually lies.

ii. The *existential* determination refers to that, instead of appealing to general normative principles, what people consider as just is mostly based on the elements that characterize their existence, i.e. in their day-to-day reality (Kluegel et al., 1995; Mueller & Landsman, 2004; Shepelak & Alwin, 1986). In terms of Homans, "What is, is always becoming what ought to be" (1976, p. 244). Berger argues along this line regarding the referential structure, pointing out that an individual "believes he should possess what he believes others like him do possess" (J. Berger et al., 1972, p. 139). This idea has been highlighted by authors that refer to the role of perception as a framework that determines justice judgments (Hegtvedt, 2006; Markovsky, 1988). In this view, the proposal of a just earning is not guided from a utopian ideal of justice, but from the actual salaries that people perceive that others get on average in the labor market. Therefore, a central aspect to consider in evaluating this perspective is the *perception of occupational earnings*, since the existential determination implies a positive relationship between perceived and just earnings. Applying this rationale to the study of the justification of inequality means that perceived earnings differences have a positive influence on the just earnings differences.

The existential determination of the just earning differences constitutes a key element for the central argument of this thesis. So far we have discussed research areas regarding income inequality, the concept of legitimacy and the measurement of legitimacy, but the issue of why a high level of income inequality can be considered legitimate has not yet been tackled. At this point I am able to formulate the argument in a conceptual way: <u>what people consider a just distribution is most of all existentially determined</u>. Based on this proposition, I argue that the level of economic inequality of a society, reflected in the earnings of the occupational structure, has a decisive influence on what people finally consider just, and therefore societies with high inequality (such as Chile) would consider larger inequalities justified. The formulation does not discard the influence of utopian standards. In fact, the proposal is to test the influence of both utopian (justice ideologies) and existential (perception of inequality) on the just earnings inequality, and to argue that perceived inequality based on context standards has the most decisive effect. That *context matters* is certainly not a new idea in social research (Coleman, 1986; Hofstede, 2001; Triandis, 1995; Wiley, 1988). What is new in this formulation is the consideration of context influences in the particular area of the legitimacy of economic inequality, in addition to its empirical test. Actually, the empirical test of context-individual relationships in the area of comparative research is something that has acquired growing development recently by using statistical procedures such as multilevel models (Adamopoulos, 2008; Vijver et al., 2008), an approach that will be implemented in the empirical part of this research.

With the discussion on the existential/utopian determination of the just earnings inequality, I conclude the presentation of the theoretical concepts that are at the basis of the explanatory model of legitimacy. In the next and final theoretical section, I introduce the explanatory relationships of the model in the form of research hypotheses.

3.4 RESEARCH HYPOTHESES: EXPLAINING THE LEGITIMACY OF ECONOMIC INEQUALITY

This section is aimed at integrating the different aspects presented so far for the study of legitimacy of economic inequality in a unified explanatory framework. These aspects are threefold: the multidimensional legitimacy model, the justice of occupational earnings, and the utopian-existential discussion about the determination of justice judgments. In the last chapter I presented an explanatory model of the legitimacy of economic inequality, which includes three dimensions: subjective, consensual and contextual, and in which legitimacy is evaluated based on the relationship among the dimensions. The most relevant dimension corresponds to the subjective one (topic of this chapter), which entails people's justifications of economic inequality. The basic assumption is that in society there are shared standards about what a just salary for different occupations should be, and based on proposals of just salaries for occupations with different status, it is possible to have a measure of legitimacy of inequality in the subjective dimension. Therefore, the main aspect to explain in the model becomes the justice of occupational earning differences, in short *just earnings differences*. Two methodological approaches considered in this research for assessing the *just earning differences* are the just rewards components (via the factorial survey methodology) and the just earnings gap (via direct questions about just occupational earnings). The hypotheses are formulated in a general way taking the *just earnings differences* as the main dependent variable in order to simplify the presentation[35].

Figure 6 depicts a general explanatory model on which the research hypothesis are based:

---

[35] As it will be explained later in Chapter 4, the explanatory model is operationalized based on data of three different surveys. One of them corresponds to the just rewards components (factorial survey) and the other two to the just earning gap. Instead of defining hypotheses for each case, for the time being both approaches are encompassed under the general umbrella of the *just earning differences*, and the specification of the hypotheses corresponding to each dataset is discussed at the moment of the empirical analysis.

Figure 6: Extended multidimensional legitimacy model for the study of economic inequality

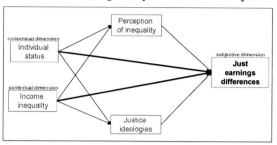

Figure 6 resembles the multidimensional model of the last chapter (Figure 3) but now adds two new elements. The first one is that the subjective dimension, previously named under the general label *justification of economic inequality* now appears specified as *just earnings differences*. The second addition corresponds to the concepts of perception of inequality and the justice ideologies. Both represent correspondingly the existential and the utopian determination of the just earnings differences.

An additional element that appears highlighted (in bold) are the two arrows that represent the two main hypotheses of this study. The rest of this chapter is based on these two hypotheses, called the *consensual legitimacy hypothesis* and the *contextual legitimacy hypothesis*. In the presentation of each hypothesis it is specified the role that perception and justice ideologies play in explaining legitimacy of economic inequality.

3.3.1 Consensual legitimacy

Hypotheses concerning consensual legitimacy refer to individuals within a particular society, and they will focus on the case of Chile. The consensual dimension of legitimacy is represented in the explanatory model by individual status. At first sight it seems paradoxical that an individual variable is oriented to measure consensus in a society, but the rationale behind this formulation is to test the degree of consensus despite differences in individual status (see section 2.3). Since this research looks for evidence of legitimacy of inequality in the Chilean case, the hypothesis to this regard is:

H₁: There are not significant differences between status groups regarding the just earnings differences in Chile

Figure 7 is based on the general model presented in Figure 6, but it includes the specification of the consensual hypothesis H₁ as a 0 (zero), indicating the expected lack of significant association:

Figure 7: Consensual legitimacy

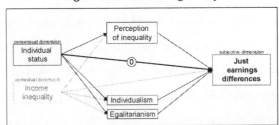

The figure omits the contextual dimension (to be considered in the next section) and details the two justice ideologies into study: individualism and egalitarianism. Perception and ideologies in the model are considered *mediators*. Mediators are variables that explain the relationship between two or more variables (Baron & Kenny, 1986; Frazier, Tix, & Barron, 2004; Mühleck & Wegener, 2002), and setting the predictors in this position in the model will enable testing of their contribution to explain consensus in just earnings differences. The question to answer can be formulated as: to what extent is the amount of earning differences considered just, as explained by existential (perceptions) or utopian (ideologies) standards of justice? The argument of this thesis in this regard is that existential standards play a stronger role than the utopian in the determination of justice judgments, i.e. *what is* determines to a great extent *what ought to be*, and that is why it is expected to find legitimacy of inequality in societies with high inequality, such as Chile. The hypothesis in this regard is:

H₁.₁: There is a larger contribution from the perception of inequality than from justice ideologies in explaining just earnings differences

In order to understand the mediator role of the perception and ideologies, we need to take into consideration the causal paths depicted in Figure 7 for both concepts:

a) Perception of inequality. Even though perception of inequality has been previously related to the study of legitimacy (Gijsberts, 1999; Headey, 1991; Kelley & Zagorski, 2004; Mühleck & Wegener, 2002; Wegener, 1999), the link between both concepts remains by and large sidelined in empirical research. Perception of inequality in this case refers to inequality in occupational earnings, i.e. perceived occupational earnings differences. Figure 7 depicts two explanatory relationships associated with inequality perceptions: the first between individual status and perception, and the second between perception and just earning inequality. Both need to be taken into consideration to understand the mediator role of perception in explaining the legitimacy of inequality. Starting with the first explanatory relationship (status → perception), previous empirical research has pointed to the *status dependency* of inequality perceptions (Groß, 2003; Wegener, 1987, 1990). Perception of reward hierarchies does not mirror reality adequately, but it is relative to the location an observer occupies within these hierarchies: low status observers tend to reduce the status continuum, leveling down perceived earning differences, whereas high status observers tend to polarize them. Explanations of this phenomenon are related to the available information in which the perception is based (Tversky & Kahneman, 1974), since the information about high status salaries in low status' environments is scarce and probably leads to a downward bias. An additional explanation is related to self-perceptual biases (Wegener, 1990), by which people tend to assume that their own earnings are near the average earnings. As a consequence, low status observers perceive high status earnings closer to their own earning, stretching down the status continuum. Therefore,

$H_{1.2}$: *People of low status perceive less earnings inequality than people of high status*

The status dependency of inequality is the basis to understand the second explanatory relationship linked to perception in the model (perception → just earning differences) and the mediating role of perception regarding consensual legitimacy. Previous empirical evidence has given support to the positive association between perception and justice judgments (Burgoyne, Routh, & Sidorenko-Stephenson, 1999; Castillo, 2009; Gijsberts, 1999; Kelley & Evans, 1993). Such a relationship means in general that a perceived earning is taken as a referential standard for a just earning, along the line of the existential determination pointed out before. The link between perception and justice judgments has also been associated in the area of social cognition to the *anchoring effect*. An anchor is "an arbitrary value that the subject tends to consider before making a numerical estimate" (Jacowitz & Kahneman, 1995, p. 1161). This means, a piece of information that the respondent takes as a reference for a judgment in situations of indeterminacy. Markovsky (1988) proposes this effect as a possible explanation for the determination of justice judgments, since "a just reward estimate should be biased toward a 'reward anchor' when that anchor is on the same scale as a potential just reward response" (Markovsky, 1988, p. 215). When asking the observer for a just reward, the indeterminacy of the task leads the respondent to search for some referent to perform the judgment (anchor), which is given by previous questions[36] about perceived earning. Then, the just earning is *anchored* in the perceived earning, and as a corollary:

H₁.₃ Perceived earnings inequality have a positive influence on the just earnings differences

Considering the last two hypotheses together it is possible to further elaborate on the *mediator role* of perceived inequalities, i.e. how perceived inequality explains consensual legitimacy. If the status dependence hypothesis is correct, low status observers perceive less inequality, and if the anchoring hypothesis is correct, this leads to a preference of less inequality. Therefore, low status people do not prefer less inequality because of a utopian principle of equality, but because they actually perceive less inequality. Therefore, along the line of consensus, people of low and high status would consider just a similar level of inequality with regard to the amount of inequality they perceive. As Wegener points out under the concept of the *illusion of distributive justice*, "we believe the distribution of goods to be just because we misperceive the distributions of these goods themselves" (Wegener, 1987, p. 1).

---

[36] In the datasets to be analyzed the questions regarding the perceived occupational earnings are previous to the just occupational earnings.

b. <u>Justice ideologies</u>. The inclusion of justice ideologies in the legitimacy model reflect the influence of utopian standards on the just earning differences (Shepelak & Alwin, 1986), serving as a counterpoint to the existential standards expressed in the perception of inequality. Research on justice ideologies is more frequent than research on perceived inequality, and most of the hypotheses presented here are based on previous findings in this area. Justice ideologies are principle related justice judgments based on general statements about how goods and rewards should be distributed in society (see section 3.1). Two justice ideologies that commonly appear in empirical research are individualism (distribution according to personal achievement and abilities assuming the market as the main allocator) and egalitarianism (distribution of equal shares, the state as the main allocator). Both ideologies are included in the model represented in Figure 7, in which each of the arrows depicts an explanatory relationship. Starting with the influence of individual status on the justice ideologies, the hypotheses are:

$H_{1.4}$: *Individual status has no influence on the support for individualism*

$H_{1.5}$: *Individual status has a negative impact on the preference for egalitarianism*

Consensus regarding individualism in the first hypothesis is related to the expected *primary* character of this ideology in the Chilean case. Primary ideologies are those that predominate in a particular society and are related to cultural values (Wegener, 1999). Assuming that the strong market reforms implemented in the country have had an impact in preferences for distribution, individualism should acquire a predominant character. On the other hand, egalitarianism would be of a *secondary* character, i.e. influenced by the position in the stratification structure, leading low status people to a higher support for this ideology. As pointed out by Kluegel (1989), such a situation could be associated to phenomena of *split consciousness* particularly in the low status groups who, besides support for the justice ideology of egalitarianism can at the same time endorse the primary ideology of individualism (as described in section 2.2.2).

As expressed in the model of Figure 7, *justice ideologies* are also expected to have an influence on preferences for earnings distribution, as supported by previous evidence (Lippl, 1999; Mühleck & Wegener, 2002; Verwiebe & Wegener, 2000; Wegener & Steinmann, 1995). Along this line, I propose that:

$H_{1.6}$: *Individualism has a positive effect on the just earnings differences*

$H_{1.7}$: *Egalitarianism has a negative effect on the just earnings differences*

Both hypotheses attempt to test the congruence between general utopian justice standards and particular preferences for earnings distribution. This means, people who support an individualistic ideology should support larger differences in occupational earnings, whereas egalitarians should tend to reduce them. In this sense, individualism should have a more decisive influence as explanatory of consensual legitimacy (i.e. as mediator) when compared to egalitarianism. This means that the high expected support for individualism in Chile should play a role in explaining the consensus across status groups regarding differences in occupational earnings.

3.3.2 Contextual legitimacy

Besides consensus, the consideration of contextual elements or standards in relation to people's beliefs about just earnings differences constitutes the second criteria for evaluating legitimacy. As pointed out by Beetham (1991a) (see sections 2.1 & 2.3) legitimacy is related to some norm or rule that people endorse. These rules are considered part of the context in which people are immersed, such as laws and conventions. In the case of economic inequality, there is not one written norm about how rewards should be distributed, but it is possible to trace back distributive rules by their effects in macro economic indicators. In this sense, it is possible to point out the level of *income inequality* in a society as an indicator of the distributive standards that characterize a society. The causal path from income inequality to just earning differences as represented in

Figure 6 depicts the second major hypothesis of this research, called the *contextual hypothesis of legitimacy*:

H₂: *Income inequality has a positive influence on just earnings differences*

This means, the higher the level of income inequality, the larger the occupational earnings differences considered just. As in the case of consensual legitimacy, contextual legitimacy also has a counter intuitive element, since from a rational point of view it would be expected that in societies with comparatively higher inequality people would find larger occupational earnings differences as unjust (Meltzer & Richard, 1981). But arguing within the existential determination of justice judgments, I expect that people's preferences for inequality are shaped by contextual factors, and therefore the explanatory relationship expressed in H₂. The empirical analysis of this hypothesis requires counting on information of several societies with different inequality levels, and therefore the contextual hypothesis of legitimacy makes sense with international comparative datasets. In this framework, the analysis of Chile is performed in relation to other countries that have different (usually lower) levels of income inequality.

The explanation of contextual legitimacy is also based on the mediator variables perception of inequality and justice ideologies. Similar to the presentation of the consensual legitimacy, the next figure represents the hypotheses to be tested for the contextual legitimacy:

Figure 8: Contextual legitimacy

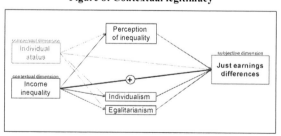

The figure highlights the contextual dimension instead of the consensual, and signals with a positive sign the main hypothesis (H₂) in this framework. The following hypotheses are an extension of those presented before to an international comparative scenario.

Starting with the utopian and existential determination of beliefs about just earnings, I expect that the predominance of the existential determination (i.e. by perceived inequality) is reflected in the countries in study. This means that, even though countries can endorse justice ideologies, first and foremost the occupational earnings considered just are expected to be influenced by the perceived inequality, therefore:

$H_{2.1}$: *There is a larger contribution from perception of inequality than justice ideologies in explaining country variations regarding just earnings differences*

The detail of the explanatory paths depicted in Figure 8 is presented separately for perception of inequality and justice ideologies.

a) Perception of inequality. The perceived amount of inequality plays a central role in explaining contextual legitimacy. A first element to consider is the influence of income inequality on perceived inequality at an aggregate level. The argument in this regard is that, despite misperceptions of inequality associated with individual status ($H_{1.2}$), on average societies with high inequality perceive more inequality (Castillo, Gerlitz, & Schrenker, 2008; Gijsberts, 1999). As Gijsberts points out, "people perceive greater inequality of income simply because more income inequality exists" (Gijsberts, 1999, p. 61), which leads to the hypothesis:

$H_{2.2}$: *In societies with higher income inequality people perceive higher inequality*

Hypothesis $H_{2.2}$ it is the basis for the following prediction that refers to the paradoxical sense of the contextual hypothesis. As discussed in the previous section, judgments about earnings take as a standard the perception of earnings, referred to as the *anchoring effect*. Markovsky already anticipated that such an effect could have relevant consequences beyond laboratory settings, proposing that it "provides a mechanism for maintaining economic stratification systems", and since "estimates of a just reward [...] will be biased toward those actual reward levels; thereby the status quo will be maintained" (Markovsky, 1988, p. 223). Translating this effect to an aggregate level, in societies with high inequality people perceive high inequality ($H_{2.2}$), and due to the positive association between perception and justice judgments:

$H_{2.3}$: Societies in which higher inequality is perceived, larger earning differences are considered just

This hypothesis represents one of the central quests of this thesis. Accordingly, the Chilean case should show a comparatively higher justification of earning differences when compared to other countries with less inequality, a central criterion for assessing the legitimacy of economic inequality.

b) Justice ideologies. Attending first to the impact of income inequality on justice ideologies at a country level, previous research in social justice has proposed that justice ideologies are comparable across societies (Castillo, 2007; Haller, 1989; Haller, Mach, & Zwicky, 1995; Lippl, 2003; Mason & Kluegel, 2000; Wegener, 1992; Wegener & Liebig, 1995). This means that it is possible to identify a common structure of justice ideologies (such as individualism and egalitarianism) in different contexts, but that their support varies according to the general structural situation of the society and its political culture (Berman & Murphy-Berman, 1996). Applying the previous micro level arguments to the macro level, it is expected that support for individualism is influenced by different aspects of political culture (such as market oriented societies, post-socialist countries, welfare state regimes). Nevertheless, globalization of the market economy has produced convergence towards values regarding distribution (Inglehart & Baker, 2000), such as the importance of criteria of personal achievement and individual abilities (i.e. individualism), being relatively independent of economic conditions. On the other hand, higher levels of inequality are expected to exert an influence on the justice ideology of egalitarianism, since by definition in countries with high inequality the majority of the population benefits less from the distributive system, leading to pressures for redistribution. Following these arguments, it is possible to point out that:

$H_{2.4}$: The level of income inequality does not influence support for individualism

121

H$_{2.5}$: Societies with higher inequality present a larger preference for the justice ideology of egalitarianism

It is relevant to mention that the hypotheses for justice ideologies must be considered in the context of hypothesis H$_{2.1}$, i.e. that despite some evidence for redistributive pressures such as in the case of egalitarianism, this is not enough to counterweight the greater influence of existential standards expressed in the perceived inequality.

Finally, along the line of the congruence between general distributive preferences and concrete justice evaluations (Mühleck & Wegener, 2002; Verwiebe & Wegener, 2000), I expect that justice ideologies have a consistent effect on earnings differences considered just:

H$_{2.6}$: Societies with higher individualism, consider on average larger earning differences as just

H$_{2.7}$: Societies with higher egalitarianism, consider on average smaller earning differences as just.

With these two last hypotheses, I cover all relationships depicted in the explanatory framework. Still, the hypotheses presented are formulated in an abstract way, referring to concepts more than to concrete variables. This abstract character has the objective of counting with a unique model of analysis that can be applied to different operationalizations and datasets. As I will detail in the next section, the empirical analysis will be based on the analysis of three surveys with different characteristics, which cover partial aspects of the multidimensional explanatory model of the legitimacy of economic inequality.

3.5 SUMMARY

The present chapter was aimed at completing the multidimensional legitimacy model introduced in chapter two with the specification of the subjective dimension of legitimacy, associated with the justification of economic inequality. The first section pointed out that studies in the area of distributive or social justice are aimed at conceptualizing and measuring people's experiences of justice and injustice, particularly those associated with the distribution of economic rewards. A particular research area within the social justice tradition is concerned with the *justice of occupational earnings*, i.e. with the earnings considered just for one's own occupation, as well as with the earnings of the occupations of other individuals. The justice of occupational earnings provides a way of addressing the justification of inequality in the subjective dimension of legitimacy, by estimating the amount of earnings inequality considered just for occupations with different status in the stratification structure.

The second section of this chapter dealt with different approaches regarding the conceptualization, evaluation and explanation of just earning differences. Two theoretical traditions are the most relevant in this regard. The first one is the status value formulation, focused on explaining the process of evaluating earnings in terms of justice. Scholars in this tradition propose the *referential structure* as an explanatory construct, which consists of a series of standards based on the actual social context about what constitutes a just reward for an individual with particular characteristics. On the other hand, the justice evaluation theory is concerned with specifying the experience of justice and injustice in quantitative terms, based on the proposition of the justice evaluation function. Based on the two theoretical traditions, I distinguish between two main strategies of evaluating the just earning differences in empirical terms in large societies: the just reward components (via factorial survey) and the just earnings gap. Both strategies are at the base of the public opinion surveys considered for the analysis of the legitimacy of economic inequality in the Chilean case.

Two contesting approaches regarding the explanation of just earnings differences were the topic of the third section, namely the *utopian* and the *existential* determination. Whereas the utopian position points out the predominant influence of general normative standards of distribution in justice judgments, the existential position argues that the standards for justice judgments reflect the reality of the distribution in a given context. The existential position is the cornerstone of the hypothesis about the legitimacy of inequality in contexts with high inequality such as the Chilean case, and therefore the integration of this perspective in the explanatory model acquires relevance. The empirical evaluation of the role of existential standards considers people's *perceptions of inequality* in occupational earnings. The contrasting position (utopian standards) will be reflected by the consideration of general preferences for distribution under the label of *justice ideologies*.

The fourth and last section of this chapter included the concepts discussed in the framework of empirical social justice into the multidimensional model of legitimacy, which allows the description of the specific research hypotheses. The *justice of occupational earnings differences* constitutes the main dependent variable of the model, located in the subjective dimension of legitimacy. Two main explanatory relationships are the basis of the model: the hypothesis of *consensual legitimacy*, by which it is not expected that individuals vary significantly according to individual status regarding the earning differences considered just (in the case of Chile), and the *contextual legitimacy* hypothesis, whereby societies with higher levels of economic inequality (such as Chile) should endorse larger just earning differences at an aggregate level. Perceived inequality and justice ideologies are integrated into the model as explanatory of both main hypotheses, in order to test the existential or utopian determination of earning differences considered just.

Chapter 4

DATA, VARIABLES AND METHODS

4.1 DATA

The explanatory model of the legitimacy of economic inequality requires some special considerations at the moment of its empirical analysis. It is a model that involves a series of predictions at the country level and in international comparison, assuming that it is possible to find information for all the variables in a unique dataset. But as commonly happens in empirical research, at the moment there is not one *ideal* dataset that fulfills the requirements for testing all research hypotheses at once. Facing this situation, the options are on the one hand to consider the available data at the moment, and on the other to design and implement new surveys that provide additional information for the variables in study. In the case of the present research, I am considering three different datasets, each of them covering partial aspects of the legitimacy model. Actually, two of the three datasets considered are based on surveys implemented in the framework of this research project, given the need for specialized data in testing some of the research hypotheses. Working with more than one dataset certainly makes the presentation and the analysis less straightforward, since in fact with the analysis of each dataset we obtain only partial pictures of a single phenomenon in study. Nevertheless, the effort invested in the analysis is considered a trade off for gaining greater validity in the empirical approach by considering different information sources.

The existence of three datasets that contain information about the variables in study for the case of Chile is a particular situation. Typically, less developed countries do not participate in comparative public opinion studies, mostly due to the reduced financial capacity to implement them and also to the lack of connections with international academic research networks. This started to change with the growing incorporation of developing countries in the comparative survey **International Social Survey Program (ISSP)**. Actually, in the ISSP 1999 dataset (focused on the topic of social inequality) three countries with higher poverty and inequality indexes are present: Chile, Brazil and the Philippines. The inclusion of these countries opens the opportunity to study people's perceptions and beliefs in contexts with different levels of income inequality. A second dataset to be considered is the **International Social Justice Project (ISJP)**, a comparative research project that started in 1991 and in which Chile participated in 2006. The participation of Chile in this specific and comprehensive survey was motivated by the development of the present doctoral research, and the data acquisition constituted an important part of the first two years working on this project. Finally, the third dataset is the **Factorial Survey of Occupational Earnings (FSOE)**, a specific survey designed for the Chilean case that delivers in depth information regarding the different components that influence judgments about occupational earnings.

4.1.1 Factorial Survey of Occupational Earnings (FSOE)

The Factorial Survey of Occupational Earnings was applied together with the ISJP questionnaire in Chile to a reduced sample in the city of Santiago in 2007[37]. The objective of this survey was to provide complementary information to the ISJP regarding the research hypotheses, since factorial surveys allow a more

---

[37] Even though the official year of the ISJP survey is 2006, the data was collected in Chile in the year 2007.

comprehensive study of judgments about occupational earnings (Alves, 1982; Jasso & Rossi, 1977). The methodological problem that this survey aims at solving is related to determining what are the criteria or *components*[38] that people take into account at the moment of performing a justice judgment about earnings, as well as to assess the importance (or weight) given to each of them. A component could be the occupation, age, sex or experience of an individual *X*, and the factorial survey enables one to see which of these individual characteristics take priority in judging the earning that the individual *X* obtains, as well as if these priorities are consensual throughout the population under study.

Since the objective is to determine the priority of the components of a just reward, direct questions in public opinion studies do not deliver appropriate information. By asking for the relevance of different components one at a time, we rule out the relative importance of each component with regard to other components. Factorial research enables one to overcome this constraint, since it presents all components at once in fictitious situations called vignettes. As mentioned earlier, the vignettes are descriptions of a person with a number of characteristics that represent the components in study. An example of a vignette is: "*Mr. Rojas has been the manager of a big corporation for 10 years, he does not have children and his wife currently does not work. He completed high school and his monthly income is $1,000,000 (pesos)*". The respondent is asked to evaluate the fairness of the monthly earning of several vignettes, and in case the income is considered unjust (over or under rewarded), the respondent is asked to propose a just income. As in the example, several components that appear in the vignette are assumed to influence the justice judgment (such as occupation, gender and educational level, among others), which later in the analysis enable to estimate the relative weight given to the vignette components regarding the income that is considered just.

The design of the FSOE was performed by the researcher with the assistance of the German research team of the ISJP at Humboldt University in 2007, using the factorial

---

[38] Factorial surveys literature refers to *dimensions* instead of *components*. I use the term components in this research to avoid confusion with the dimensions of the legitimacy model.

survey of the German ISJP 2006 as a model[39]. Three aspects must be considered in the description of this survey: the definition of the vignette components, the design of the questionnaire, and finally the data collection.

i. Components' definition. The total possible number of components to be included in the survey is limited, taking into account the amount of information that people are able to handle in evaluating a vignette (Jasso, 2006a; Steiner & Atzmüller, 2006). It is recommended not to exceed eight or nine components. The FSOE is based on eight components, and each of them contains a number of categories or levels as represented in the following table:

Table 6: Components and levels of the factorial survey

	Component	Levels	Nr. of Levels
1	Occupation	Unskilled worker, sales clerk, technician, teacher, lawyer, own private business, middle manager, high level manager	8
2	Actual earning	From $100,000 pesos to $1,500,000 pesos, in 10 categories.	10
3	Educational level	Elementary incomplete, elementary complete, high school ("educacion media"), technical and university education.	5
4	Years in occupation	From five to forty (5, 10, 20, 30, 40).	5
5	Last name	Mapuche, Spanish, Vasco-Castellano, European	4
6	Sex	Male, female	2
7	Marital status	Single, married with partner in labor market, married with partner not in labor market	3
8	Number of Children	From zero to five children	6

Occupation is the central component in study. Eight occupations were selected based on categories of other surveys such as the ISSP and the UNDP survey in Chile (UNDP, 1998, 2004), attempting to reflect different positions in the status continuum. Actual earning is a value in Chilean pesos corresponding to the salary of the individual presented in the vignette. The rest of the components attempt to reflect different justice criteria that are proposed in the classification of Morton Deutsch (1975): equity, equality and need. The components of education and the number of years in occupation relate to the consideration of equity according to merit as a criteria for just earnings. Sex and last name are categories associated with actual differential earnings based on discrimination in the labor market, which enables consideration of the justice criteria of equality (by the compensation of actual inequality in just

---

[39] Germany applied a factorial survey together with the ISJP questionnaire in 2006, but the topic in study was the justice of pensions.

income). *Last name* requires further explanation since it is particular to the case of Chile. As presented in the first chapter, empirical studies have shown that in Chile the type of last name, associated to different social status, produce discrimination in the salaries obtained in the labor market (Núñez & Gutiérrez, 2004a). In the FSOE, last names were categorized in four groups according to status: Vasco-Castellano, European, Spanish and Mapuche. High status last names are the Europeans and especially the Vasco-Castellano, associated with the traditional aristocracy in Chile. Spanish last names are difficult to classify in terms of status since they represent the majority of the population, but they tend to be associated with the middle class. Indigenous groups are generally characterized by a low status, and the last names selected are mostly from the Mapuche ethnic group (which is about 5 percent of the total population of the country). Finally, the components of *marital status* (in terms of having a dependent partner) and *number of children* echo the number of people dependent on a salary as a possible influence in a just salary, which is related to assessing the influence of <u>need</u> as justice criteria.

ii. <u>Questionnaire design</u>. Given the number of dimensions and levels, the total number of possible fictitious situations or vignettes results from the multiplication of the number of levels in each component, in this case:

| Total number of vignettes | = | 4(last name) x 2(sex) x 5(educational level) x 3(marital status) x 6(number of children) x 5(years on occupation) x 8(occupation) x 10(actual income) | = | 288,000 |

Given the large number of possible vignettes, it is not possible to consider all of them in a single questionnaire. To solve this problem, in a first step a representative sample of the vignette population is taken as part of the final questionnaire, which in this case adds up to 250 vignettes[40]. In a second step, the vignettes are randomly distributed into 10 different questionnaires, called *decks*, with 25 vignettes each. The respondents finally receive only one of the decks, which are randomly assigned.

iii. <u>Data gathering</u>. The factorial survey was administrated together with the ISJP in Chile in a restricted sample corresponding to the capital, Santiago. This restriction is

---

[40] The final sample was obtained after checking the representativity of the dimensions in several vignette samples.

due to budget reasons and also to the consideration of this part of the study as exploratory, especially given the lack of experience with factorial survey research in the country[41]. As in other studies where the factorial survey is secondary to the other questionnaire, the respondent is asked to take part voluntarily in the study (taking into account that in this case individuals have already been interviewed for about an hour with the ISJP questionnaire). If accepted, the questionnaire was left with the respondent and then collected in person later on by the interviewer. The time to fill out the questionnaire was estimated to be 15 to 20 minutes. Of the total samples corresponding to Santiago (266), 72% agreed to answer the survey, reaching a final sample of 189 subjects for the factorial survey. With this number it is possible to calculate the total (maximum) amount of vignettes evaluated:

$$\text{Vignette sample} \quad = \quad 189(\text{respondents sample}) \times 25(\text{vignettes per deck}) \quad = \quad 4,725$$

Both the respondents and vignette samples constitute the two aspects or levels considered for the analysis.

4.1.2 International Social Justice Project (ISJP)

The *International Social Justice Project* is a collaborative research based on public opinion surveys with a special focus on distributive issues and cross country comparisons. It includes specific research topics such as the preference for different justice ideologies, justice evaluations of one's own income and also others' incomes, perception of social inequality, and attributions of poverty and wealth. The project started in 1991 with 12 countries agreeing to fill in a common questionnaire in national representative samples (Alwin & Wegener, 1995). Countries participating in this first version of the project were Germany (considering East and West separately), Great Britain, the Netherlands, Japan, the United States, Russia, Poland, Slovenia, Estonia, Hungary and the former Czechoslovakia. The research agenda of this project has been characterized by the comparison between occidental countries and eastern European transformation societies, analyzing to what extent people's conceptions about distribution differ in post communist and market societies, as well as the

---

[41] Actually, from the author's knowledge this is the first factorial survey research performed outside countries of the western industrialized world.

legitimation of capitalism in the post communist bloc (Kluegel et al., 1995; Mason & Kluegel, 2000). A replication of the project in 1996 with six of the original members (East and West Germany, Estonia, Russia, the Czech Republic and Hungary) has made it possible to analyze the change in justice conceptions over time (Christoph, Jardin, Lippl, Stark, & Wegener, 1998). The year 2000 was the third wave of the project, implemented only in Germany and with a specific focus on time variations with a panel design (Hauss, Mika, & Wegener, 2000). The last version of ISJP was planned for the year 2006, replicated by the old-members Germany, Hungary and the Czech Republic, and including two newcomers: Israel and Chile. The representatives of the five countries participating in this last wave met in December 2005 at the Humboldt University, agreed on the questionnaire items to be replicated, and proposed new items for a new section on the topic *intergenerational justice* (Legewie, Gerlitz, Mühleck, Scheller, & Schrenker, 2006). In this meeting the country representatives also settled on the working principles for this version of the ISJP. A master questionnaire was written in English, and translated later into the languages of the participating countries.

The participation of Chile in ISJP 2006 is closely linked to this doctoral research. The proposal for this dissertation was presented to the international coordinator of the ISJP at the Faculty of Social Sciences of the Humboldt University in the year 2005. Part of the proposal consisted of the implementation of the ISJP survey in Chile, since it is the most specialized survey in distributive justice issues, and the topics presented in the survey were akin to the research hypotheses. Since ISJP is a collaborative research project, each country was expected to fund their own surveys. Several proposals were written to universities and research centers in Chile during the first semester of 2006. The sociology department of the University *Academia de Humanismo Cristiano* (in short Academia) from Santiago de Chile manifested interest in being the country partner institution for the ISJP in June 2006, agreeing to implement the survey and to collect the data by the end of 2006. The survey and ISJP working principles were introduced to the research group of the Academia by the author on a field trip to Chile in September 2006. In several meetings the Spanish translation of the survey was checked and it was decided that some questions regarding intergenerational justice would be left out, since the topic was not considered of main relevance at that time in the country[42].

A final version of the questionnaire was finished in October 2006. Nevertheless, due to some problems in the first implementation of the survey[43], the final fieldwork was performed in July-September 2007. The survey covered people over 18 and it was representative of 75% of the population. For practical reasons (costs and deadline for obtaining the data) some regions of the country were excluded, such as two administrative regions of the south end (regions XI and XII) as well as Eastern Island and Juan Fernández Islands. The survey was stratified and multi-staged according to PPS (Probabilities Proportionate to Size), and applied in a face-to-face interview. The completion rate was 41.2%, and the final number of questionnaires for the analysis was 890. Even though the sample number was less than the minimum proposed in the working principles of the project (1000 cases), the survey was accepted and merged with the ISJP database, which has been available for analysis since November 2007[44].

The ISJP is the most up to date survey regarding distributive justice in Chile, containing precise variables regarding the measurement of justice ideologies and the justice of income, which are key elements in the explanatory model of legitimacy. Even though ISJP is a comparative dataset, for the present analysis only the Chilean case is considered. The reason is that the small number of countries does not allow modelling the influence of context level characteristics such as income inequality, as explained later in the section on multilevel models.

---

[42] The interest in intergenerational justice in Germany focuses on the issue of the pensions system in a framework of a welfare state, in which pensions are at least partially financed by the younger generations. Several items in the questionnaire took this context for granted, which did not make sense in Chile, where the pension system is mostly based on private contributions.

[43] The first version of the survey was declared invalid, associated with a lack of control measures in the supervision of the interviewers. Given this situation, the University Academia proposed to finance a second implementation of the survey, which actually provided the data used for the present analysis.

[44] There was a previous version of a merged dataset with Germany, Israel and the Czech Republic. A final version was ready in January 2009, including also data from the ISJP in Hungary of 2008.

4.1.3 International Social Survey Program (ISSP)

The ISSP is an annual international collaborative project on surveys covering a broad range of relevant topics for the social sciences. It started in 1983 with four founding members (Germany, the United States, Great Britain and Australia), and up to now it has grown to 43 countries. Given its collaborative character, each country member must look for their own funding sources to implement the survey, and usually the ISSP questionnaire is administered as an extension of existing national studies (Braun & Uher, 2003). Each year the survey covers a particular topic which is repeated a few years later, allowing time comparisons. The topics are decided by a sub-committee formed by country representatives, and then a master questionnaire is written in English to be translated later into country specific languages. Once the information is collected and provided by each country, the data is archived at GESIS in Germany[45], supported in the processing of the data by the ASEP[46] (Análisis Sociológicos Económicos y Políticos) in Madrid.

Social inequality was the research topic in the modules of the ISSP 1987, 1992 and 1999. This survey includes a series of attitudinal items regarding income distribution, perception of inequality, distributive principles, expectations about the role of the state regarding social inequality, as well as questions concerning the perception and evaluation of occupational income. For the present research I analyze the dataset of the ISSP 1999, the last version of the module on social inequality in which for the first time Chile participated. In the official dataset of ISSP 1999, the number of participant countries reached twenty seven[47], which implemented the field work during the years 1999-2001. In this official dataset the data of Brazil is not included, since they finished the fieldwork later in 2002. Given that Brazil is an important reference for Chile in the analysis regarding inequality as a context level variable, its dataset was

---

[45] www.gesis.org

[46] www.jdsurvey.net

[47] Even though there are 28 country codes, they consider East and West Germany as separate countries, and therefore the number of countries is actually 27 (www.issp.org). The denomination of the participants as *societies* is more accurate than *countries*, but still in this analysis I will use both terms as synonymous.

merged with the official dataset, amounting then to 28 countries. The final list of the countries present in the dataset is shown in the following table:

Table 7: ISSP 1999 participating countries, sample size and year of fieldwork

Country	Sample size	Year of fieldwork
Australia	1672	1999/2000
Austria	1016	2000
Bulgaria	1102	1999
Brazil	1500	2002
Canada	974	1999/2000
Chile	1503	2000
Cyprus	1000	1999
Czech Republic	1834	1999
France	1889	1999
Germany (West)	921	2000
Germany (East)	511	2000
Great Britain	804	1999
Hungary	1208	1998
Israel	1208	1999
Japan	1325	1999
Latvia	1100	1999
New Zealand	1108	1999
Northern Ireland	830	1999/2000
Norway	1268	1999
Philippines	1200	1999
Poland	1135	1999
Portugal	1144	1999
Russia	1705	1999
Slovakia	1082	2001
Slovenia	1006	1998
Spain	1211	1999
Sweden	1150	1999
USA	1272	2000

Source: GESIS-ZA.

The implementation of the surveys is documented for each country, describing the sampling procedures, fieldwork methods, language(s) of the questionnaires and weights (when available). A specific report of the ISSP 1999 (Harkness, Klein, & Scholz, 2003) depicts to what extent the countries vary in the central aspects considered in the survey. Samples are in most cases probability multi-stage cluster samples, and by and large representative of the whole country territory. In the majority of the countries, questionnaires are carried out face-to-face with people older than 18, and in almost half of the countries the ISSP is administered as part of another larger survey study.

Despite the efforts of this research program to gather the data in the best conditions, there are still some shortcomings that affect its analysis. Missing data in some key variables results sometimes in a whole country being left out of the analysis, losing an important part of the cases[48]. Additionally, the codification of some variables differs from country to country, such as with the variable personal income that in some countries is only categorical (income deciles) instead of continuous. Another problem with the design of the questionnaire is that there are few items tapping common dimensions, affecting the extraction of latent variables with procedures such as factor analysis.

In spite of the above-mentioned shortcomings, the ISSP offers a unique possibility for empirical research given the variety of topics covered, the number of countries and the possibility of time comparisons. Specifically in the case of this research, ISSP 1999 is the only available dataset that considers variables about the perception and evaluation of occupational income and that at the same time includes a large number of societies. This last characteristic is highly relevant since it enables testing the influence of country level predictors (such as income inequality) on variables at the individual level (such as perceptions and beliefs), which is one of the key elements in the explanatory model of legitimacy.

4.2 VARIABLES

The variables in this study are directly related to the legitimacy model presented in chapter three. This section has the objective of describing how the different elements of the legitimacy model are expressed in the form of variables in the three datasets introduced.

4.2.1 Dependent variables

The main concept to be explained in the multidimensional model of legitimacy is the *justification of economic inequality*. As discussed in chapter three, there are two main

---

[48] Due to missing data in key variables, the cases of Northern Ireland and Israel are not considered into the analysis.

approaches to operationalize this construct: the *components of a just reward* and the *just earnings gap*, as illustrated in the following table:

Table 8: Conceptual approaches to the justification of inequality, datasets and dependent variables

Approach	Dataset	Dependent variable
Components of a just reward	FSOE	Just reward
Occupational earnings	ISJP - ISPP	Just earnings gap

The first approach is implemented in the analysis of the FSOE, whereas the second characterizes the analysis with the ISJP and ISSP data.

i. <u>Components of a just reward</u>. In the analysis of the FSOE the dependent variable corresponds to the *just reward*. The just reward is the salary in Chilean pesos proposed by the respondent after each vignette, in answer to the question: *In your opinion, what would be a just salary for Mr./ Mrs. X?*, in which X is the name mentioned in the vignette. As we will see in the analysis, with this information it will be possible to determine the specific contribution of each vignette component to the just reward in Chilean pesos, and therefore to observe which component has the largest influence in justifying economic inequality.

ii. <u>Just earnings gap</u>. The just earnings gap is an approach to measuring the justification of economic inequality based on earning differences considered just between high and low status occupations. Building on principles of the justice evaluation theory, as well as in previous research in international comparison, in the last chapter I proposed that the just earnings gap can be operationalized as the logarithmic ratio between the just salary for a high status occupation and a low status occupation. The use of a ratio generates a relative term which is internationally comparable, overcoming the problems of having answers in different currencies (Gijsberts, 1999). A situation of absolute equality is represented in the ratio as 0 (logarithm of 1), positive values indicate that the high status occupation should earn more than the low status one, and negative values the opposite. The higher the value, the higher the salary of the high status occupation should be in relation to the salary of the low status occupation, and hence the more the earning inequality is considered just.

Both ISJP and ISSP include questions for income considered just for a manager (high status occupation) and an unskilled worker (low status occupation). The specific questions of the ISJP and ISSP questionnaires are presented in Table 9:

Table 9: Questions about just occupational earnings in ISJP and ISSP surveys

	ISJP	ISSP
High status occupation	[Now] tell me what you think a just and fair average monthly income for a chairman or managing director of a large corporation would be?	About how much do you think the chairman of a large national corporation should earn a month/a year?
Low status occupation	[Now] tell me what you think a just and fair average monthly income would be for an unskilled worker, such as a factory line worker?	About how much do you think an unskilled worker in a factory should earn a month/a year?

Questions in both datasets refer to the same occupation, but there are some differences to take into account. ISSP asks about what "should be", something less specific than the "just and fair" question of the ISJP. Answers to the questions are in local currency, and in some countries monthly income is asked about whereas in others, yearly income. Since the just earnings gap is a ratio term, differences in currencies and in monthly/yearly earnings do not affect the interpretation of the variable.

4.2.2 Predictors

I use the term *predictors* (or covariates) instead of independent variables since some of the variables described here are also dependent on other predictors in the model. Therefore, predictors are classified into two types: exogenous and endogenous. Exogenous variables are those without predictors within the model, whereas endogenous variables have predictors within the model. In a path diagram, endogenous variables are distinguished by having an arrow pointing to them, expressing a causal relationship. Thinking in terms of the multidimensional model of legitimacy, justice ideologies and perceptions of inequality are considered endogenous predictors, since they are predictors of the justice gap, but at the same time they are expected to be influenced by other variables such as individual status and income inequality. Such distinction is relevant not only conceptually but also for methodological reasons, since ignoring causal relationships in the model can lead to spurious associations. This issue will be discussed in the methods section at the moment of presenting structural equation models (SEM).

The discussion about the comparability of predictors between surveys is restricted to the ISJP and ISSP, since the FSOE was applied together with the ISJP and therefore have the same predictor variables for the survey respondents.

i. Exogenous predictors

Exogenous predictors in the model are classified into three types: status, economic inequality and socio-demographic controls, as illustrated in the following table:

Table 10: Exogenous predictors

Type	Variable name	ISJP Chile	ISSP
Status	Net equivalent income	Total family monthly income / number of people in the household	Family income deciles Number of people in the household
	Educational level	1) Basic incomplete 2) Basic complete 3) Middle education 4) Technical education 5) University education	Casmin 1 (basic) Casmin 2 (intermediate) Casmin 3 (advanced)
	Subjective social position	Self attributed social position on a scale from 1(low social standing) to 10 (high social standing)	Self attributed social position on a scale from 1(low social standing) to 10 (high social standing)
Income inequality	Gini index	-	0 to 1 index of economic inequality
Socio-demographic controls	Sex	Female=1, ref. male=0	Female=1, ref. male=0
	Age	In years	In years
	Employment status	Unemployment=1, ref. other employment situation=0	Unemployment=1, ref. other employment situation=0
	Religion	Catholic=1, ref. other religions/no religion=0	Catholic=1, ref. other religions/no religion=0
	Ethnic group	Yes=1, ref. no=0	

- *Status*. Several standard comparative measures of status are based on the occupation of the respondent, such as EGP, ISEI and SIOPS[49] (E. Hoffman, 2003). Nevertheless, being based on occupation these variables left out a considerable part

---

[49] EGP (Erikson Goldthorpe & Portocarrero) class schema, ISEI (the International Socio Economic Index of occupational status) and SIOPS (Standard International Occupational Prestige Scale) are based on the description of occupation according to ISCO (International Standard Classification of Occupations) (Ganzeboom & Treiman, 1996, 2003).

of the sample cases, leading to consider alternative options. One of them is individual income, which in modern societies is related to the acquisition of goods and status symbols, and that influences the position in the stratification structure (Warner & Hoffmeyer-Zlotnik, 2003). Income variables are considered in the context of the household size in order to obtain a closer approach to the status situation. ISJP includes information from several sources of family income which, divided by the number of people in the household, constitute the *household equivalent net income*. In the case of ISSP, income questions are asked differently in each country, and the dataset only provides a common variable with the family income deciles. In this case, the number of people in the household is incorporated separately to control for net income[50]. A second variable related to status is the *educational level*. In the case of the analysis of the ISJP data, the educational levels reflect the Chilean educational system. For the international comparison with the ISSP data, the educational levels are operationalized in the CASMIN[51] categories (Brynin, 2003; Hoffmeyer-Zlotnik, 2003; W. Müller, Lüttinger, König, & Karle, 1989), distinguishing between primary, secondary and tertiary education. A final status variable is the *subjective self position*, which consists of a rating scale usually from one to ten in which the respondent positions himself from low to high status[52].

- *Income inequality*. Several indexes of income inequality as the Gini, Atkinson and Theil are alternatives to express the amount of income inequality in a society (Moran, 2003). The selection of the Gini index for this research is related to its wide consideration in previous research in income inequality, and also regarding the availability of information about it. The Gini index is based on the Lorenz curve of

---

[50] More precise measurements as the household net equivalent income are not possible since there is no information about the age of the household members in ISSP and this information is missing in ISJP Chile.

[51] The CASMIN (Comparative Analysis of Social Mobility in Industrial Nations) classification "has been developed within the social stratification framework in the 1970s in order to capture the effects of different educational systems on processes and patterns of inter- as well as intergenerational mobility" (Brauns, Scherer, & Steinmann, 2003, p. 221).

[52] It can be argued that this status predictor is not exogenous since it is an attitudinal variable. Taking this into consideration, in the model parameter estimation this variable is considered as endogenous, but was located exceptionally in this section to simplify the description of the legitimacy model with only two types of endogenous predictors (perception and ideologies).

distribution[53], and varies between 0 and 1: zero (0) is the point of absolute equality (equal shares), whereas inequality increases the closer the index approaches 1. This variable is obtained from third sources that have published rankings of countries to this regard, such as the UNDP (United Nations Development Program) and the LIS (Luxembourg Income Study), which have been previously summarized for the ISSP data (Lübker, 2007). The Gini index will be considered in the analysis of the ISSP data, since its influence as predictor can only be assessed in international comparison.

- *Individual control variables*. Some individual variables as age, sex, employment status and religion are usually considered in sociological research as controls, i.e., their possible influence is assessed even tough there are not specific hypotheses to this regard. These variables are measured similarly in both datasets, as described in Table 10.

ii. Endogenous predictors

Perception of inequality and justice ideologies are the two predictors in the legitimacy model that are considered endogenous. Many of the hypotheses regarding these two concepts assume this endogenous character, since according to the model they act as *mediators* between the effect of other (exogenous) variables and the dependent variable.

- *Perception of inequality*. This variable is operationalized in a similar way as the just earnings gap, but instead of just earnings it considers questions regarding perceived occupational earnings. Both ISSP and ISJP include questions about perceived occupational earnings for low and high status occupations (managers and unskilled workers), described in the following table:

---

[53] The Lorenz curve plots cumulative income shares against corresponding population shares. When all incomes are equal, the Lorenz curve follows a diagonal of perfect equality (45°). The curve approaches the axes to the extent that the distribution deviates from equality. The Gini index is defined as the ratio between the Lorenz curve and the diagonal to the total area under the diagonal (Moran, 2003).

Table 11 : Questions about perceived occupational earnings

	ISJP	ISSP
High status occupation	What do you think a chairman or a managing director of a large corporation earns per month on average?	About how much do you think the chairman of a large national corporation earns a month/a year?
Low status occupation	And how about an unskilled manual worker, such as a factory line worker? What do you think an unskilled worker earns per month on average?	About how much do you think an unskilled worker in a factory earns a month/a year?

Based on these questions it is possible to build a function reflecting the perceived earnings inequality, called the *perceived earnings gap*:

$$(4) \qquad \text{Perceived earnings gap} \quad = \quad \ln\left(\frac{\text{perceived earning}_{\text{high status occupation}}}{\text{perceived earning}_{\text{low status occupation}}}\right)$$

Properties of the ratio and the logarithm have the same characteristics as in the just earnings gap. The higher the value of the term, the higher the perception of earnings inequalities between occupations in the extremes of the status continuum.

- *Justice ideologies*. ISSP and ISJP datasets include a series of questions about general normative orientations regarding the distribution of goods and rewards in society. With such questions it is possible to tap different underlying dimensions that represent the justice ideologies, which in the case of this research are classified into two: individualism and egalitarianism. Underlying or latent dimensions means that these two variables (individualism and egalitarianism) are not measured directly from a single question, but they represent an aspect that is common to different questions in the surveys (in statistical terms, they correspond to a factor). Both ISSP and ISJP have questions that are related to the concepts of individualism and egalitarianism, but both questionnaires are not comparable in this regard. ISJP is more specialized and counts with variables that widely cover justice ideologies, whereas in ISSP we find fewer items. Still, it is possible to classify a series of questions in both datasets covering both ideologies, as described in the following table:

Table 12: Items corresponding to justice ideologies in ISJP and ISSP

	ISJP	ISSP
Individualism	• People who work hard deserve to earn more than those who do not • The responsibility held by the employee on the job should influence pay • The employee's individual effort should influence pay	Is it just or unjust – right or wrong – that people with higher incomes can: • Buy better health care than people with lower incomes? • Buy better education for their children than people with lower incomes?
Egalitarianism	• The government should place an upper limit on the amount of money any person can make • The fairest way of distributing wealth and income would be to give everyone equal shares • Government should redistribute income from the better-off to those who are less well-off	• It is the responsibility of the government to reduce the differences in income between people with high incomes and those with low incomes • People with high incomes should pay a larger share of their income in taxes than those with low incomes • People in wealthy countries should make an additional contribution to help people in poor countries

The items are rated on a scale from 1 (strongly agree) to 5 (strongly disagree)[54]. As it is possible to observe, items for each ideology differ in character across the datasets. Individualism in ISJP is more specifically centered on the working environment and the role of individual characteristics influencing pay, whereas in the case of ISSP it is referred to the evaluation of outcomes that follow and unequal distribution. In this sense, individualism in ISJP could be referred to as *meritocratic individualism* (Davey, Bobocel, Son Hing, & Zanna, 1999) whereas in ISSP we could speak of *market individualism*, in line with the concept of market justice of Lane (1986) and Mason & Kluegel (2000). The case of egalitarianism is more homogeneous in both datasets, underlining the principle of equality and redistribution. Still, with the available information it is not possible to test statistically whether the ideologies in the different datasets are tapping the same latent dimension. In this regard, ISJP justice ideologies count on more empirical support than those of ISSP, and therefore including ISSP ideologies with this operationalization can be regarded as exploratory. The extraction of the factors from the items is presented in the empirical analysis.

---

[54] Items are reverse coded previous to the factor analysis.

4.3 METHODS

Two main characteristics of the multidimensional model of legitimacy are, on the one hand, that it entails a series of causal relationships among variables, and on the other, that it considers individual and context level variables (in the case of the ISSP data). A traditional approach to multivariate causal models is regression analysis, particularly OLS (Ordinary Least Squares) regression for continuous variables. Nevertheless, common OLS regression presents some limitations in facing situations such as testing models with multiple causal relationships, the presence of latent variables, and the analysis of datasets with hierarchical (multilevel) structure. Such situations can be better addressed by alternative analysis methods such as *structural equation models* and *multilevel models*. Even though literature and software about these methods has been available for already more than 20 years, their use in the analysis of public opinion data is still a growing endeavor, facilitated in recent years by the availability of new software. In this section I will briefly describe the basic characteristics of both analysis methods as well as the indexes used for their interpretation.

4.3.1 Structural equation models (SEM)

SEM is a general approach to the analysis of multivariate data that is specially suitable for models with a series of causal relationships and/or models with latent variables (Bollen, 1989; Jöreskog, 1970; B. Muthén, 2004; B. Muthén & L. Muthén, 2007). In general terms, the structural equation model is divided into a *measurement model* and a *structural model*.

The *measurement model* is the part of the structural equation model that deals with the relationships between observed measures or *indicators* and latent variables or *factors* (Bollen, 1989; Raykov & Marcoulides, 2006). The measurement model indicates the number of factors, how the indicators are related to the factors, and the relationship among the indicators' errors. Confirmatory factor analysis (CFA) is the procedure performed in the SEM framework to extract the latent dimensions oriented by a

143

theoretical construct which is tested against the data[55]. Unlike other methods dealing with latent variables (such as exploratory factor analysis), the shared variance among the indicators is operationalized as true score variance adjusting for measurement error[56] (Brown, 2006). Additionally, CFA offers an analytical framework for measurement invariance, testing the equivalence of measurement models across groups, which is an important feature for international comparison (Dimitrov, 2006).

The *structural model* specifies how the factors and other variables present in the model (called covariates) are related to one another[57]. These relationships form a structural regression model that can be represented as a path diagram. One special advantage of this analysis is that it allows testing of both direct and indirect effects: the direct effects are those that go directly from one variable to the other, whereas the indirect effects are between two variables that are *mediated* by one or more intervening (endogenous) variables (Raykov & Marcoulides, 2006)[58]. Of particular relevance for this research are the indirect effects of status and inequality variables on the just earnings gap mediated by the endogenous predictors justice ideologies and perception of inequality. Instead of testing these effects sequentially (and therefore incorporating measurement error), in SEM the complete model (measurement and structural) is tested at once against the data based on an estimation method, and then evaluated according to a series of fit indexes:

- *Estimation and fit.* In SEM framework it is estimated to what extent the proposed model is capable of reflecting causal relationships in the data. The model is expressed in a *model implied covariance matrix*, which is tested against the sample covariance matrix, expressed in the following way:

---

[55] CFA is usually contrasted with EFA (Exploratory Factor Analysis), in which the factor structure cannot be specified in advance.

[56] The classification of true score also makes reference to EFA, in which a score procedure can also be implemented through regression, but in this case the variable generated for each case of the dataset contains the measurement error.

[57] Models of CFA with covariates are called MIMIC models (Multiple Indicators Multiple Causes).

[58] "Although regression analysis can also be used to estimate indirect effects – for example by regressing the mediation on the explanatory variable, the effect variable on the mediator, and finally multiplying pertinent regression weights – this is strictly appropriate when there are not measurement errors in the involved predictor variables. Such an assumption, however, is in general unrealistic in empirical research in the social and behavioural sciences" (Raykov & Marcoulides, 2006, p. 7).

(5) $$\sum(\theta) = S$$

in which θ is a vector containing the parameters of the model, $\Sigma(\theta)$ is the covariance matrix derived as a function of the parameters contained in the vector θ, and S is the sample covariance matrix (Ruiz, 2000). The process of fitting a model to the data can be conceived as a repeated insertion of values for the parameters in the model implied covariance matrix until a certain optimality criterion is satisfied (Raykov & Marcoulides, 2006). If the model is correct, the population covariance matrix could be reproduced exactly from the parameters of the model, meaning a perfect fit. Since this is usually not the case, evaluating the goodness of fit of a model means measuring the extent to which both covariance matrices differ. Defining the matrix distance as a fit function, the closer the value of this function to zero, the more the two matrices involved are identical. Several methods of parameter estimation in SEM are aimed at minimizing this fit function, from which the Maximum Likelihood (ML) is the most commonly used for continuous variables (assuming normal distribution) (Andreassen, Lorentzen, & Olsson, 2006). The assumption of normality can be considered too restrictive when analyzing attitudinal items of five categories as those of the indicators of justice ideologies, leading to a consideration of alternative estimation methods. A more flexible estimator recommended in such cases is the robust weighted least squares WLSMV (Weighted Least Squares Mean and Variance adjusted). Flora & Curran (2004) have shown that this estimator produces accurate test statistics, parameter estimates and standard errors under a variety of conditions. Estimation with WLSMV is currently possible with the software Mplus (B. Muthén & L. Muthén, 2007), which is used for the model testing in this research.

- *Fit indexes*. Estimation is followed by the evaluation of goodness of fit (Hu & Bentler, 1998). In SEM there are different fit indexes that summarize the quality of the model, and each of them is a source of limited and complementary information. Based on the authors that have analyzed the different indexes (Hu & Bentler, 1999; MacCallum & Austin, 2000; Raykov & Marcoulides, 2006; Yu, 2002), in reporting the results of the estimation I describe three indexes[59]: Chi-square, CFI and RMSEA. Roughly, Chi-square test produces a p-value that suggests the retention of the model when it is higher than the significant level; that is, when it is not significant[60]. Nevertheless, this statistic tends to produce spurious small p values in large samples, leading to consider alternative indexes. The CFI (Comparative Fit Index) is less sensitive to sample size and compares the null model with the observed covariance matrix, estimating the percent of lack of fit which is accounted for by going from the null model to the proposed model (Raykov & Marcoulides, 2006). It varies between 0 and 1, and closeness to 1 indicates good fit. Finally, the use of RMSEA has been encouraged in recent years, given its sensitivity to model misspecification and also because a confidence interval is available (MacCallum & Austin, 2000). It is suggested that a value less than .05 indicates that the model approximates the data.

4.3.2 Multilevel models

Multilevel models have been developed for the analysis of hierarchically structured data, characterized by the presence of variables describing individuals and variables describing groups (Greenland, 2000; Hadler, 2004; Hans, 2006; Kreft & de Leeuw, 1998). In hierarchical data the lower or *micro* level observations are nested within higher or *macro* levels. Taking into account the structure of the data in different levels allows the consideration of the issue of the *contextual dependency* of the observations. This is a relevant aspect to take into account since it influences the estimation of the error variance in traditional linear models, producing biased estimates in simple OLS regression (smaller standard errors and spurious significant results) since OLS assumes no covariance in the error terms. The group or contextual dependency of the observations is reflected in the *intraclass correlation*, defined as "the proportion of the variance in the outcome variable that is between the second-level units" (Kreft & de

---

[59] Traditional goodness of fit indexes such as GFI and AGFI have been questioned by authors such as Hu & Bentler (1998) since they are inconsistently sensitive to model misspecification and strongly affected by sample size.

[60] Chi-square is a fit index that acquires significant values when the compared matrixes statistically differ. In this case, the objective is to demonstrate that the model covariance matrix does not differ from the data covariance matrix, and therefore the non-significance of Chi-square is an indication of good fit.

Leeuw, 1998, p. 9)[61]. The presence of *intraclass correlation* leads us to consider alternatives to common OLS, such as multilevel models. In the case of this research, some of the hypotheses relate to the influence of belonging to a particular country (context level) in the perceptions and beliefs about inequality (individual level). It is actually expected that the variations in perceptions and beliefs about inequality are context dependent, and that this contextual dependency is related to variables such as income inequality. In the same sense, the data of the factorial survey has a hierarchical structure, in which the judgments about the vignettes are nested into the respondents (Schrenker, 2007; Steiner & Atzmüller, 2006).

Characteristic of multilevel models is that the regression coefficients (intercepts and slopes) are able to be estimated as random, that is, they are allowed to vary across context units. *Random intercept only models* assume that the mean of the predictor variable varies across context units, but the influence of the variable (slope) remains the same. On the other hand, *random slope models* relax this last assumption and the effect of the predictor variable is allowed to vary across context units (Gelman & J. Hill, 2007). Even though the advantage of this kind of model is that all parameters are estimated at once (and not single regression for each context unit), it is still possible to estimate means of intercept and slopes. This kind of estimation is performed mostly for descriptive analysis and also for specific predictions within units, and is called empirical Bayes estimation[62].

Different procedures have been proposed in a multilevel framework to take into account the amount of explained variance with predictors at different levels. The objective is to obtain an indicator analogous to R^2 in ordinary linear regression for each of the levels, for which there is not absolute consensus in the literature (Hans, 2006). In general, measures of the explanatory power are based on the comparison of a given model with the *null model*, a model without predictors and only with a random intercept (Bryk & Raudenbush, 1992a). Regarding the overall significance of

---

[61] The intra class correlation represents the maximum part of the variance that can be explained with characteristics at the context level (Hans, 2006).
[62] Empirical Bayes estimation is based on prior means which are estimated from the data, also named the Best Linear Unbiased Predictor (BLUP) (Skrondal & Rabe-Hesketh, 2005).

the model, the *Likelihood Ratio Test* or *deviance* test appears as a recommended alternative (Hans, 2006). The *deviance* consists of comparing the log likelihood of two different models in which the difference in the number of the predictors is expressed as degrees of freedom. In this sense, this test delivers information about the extent to which the model with additional parameter estimates has an influence on the improvement of the overall fit.

Finally, multilevel models have been also used in combination with SEM models in recent years, so called multilevel-SEM (Cheung, Leung, & Au, 2006; Dyer, Hanges, & Hall, 2005; Heck & Thomas, 2009; B. Muthén & L. Muthén, 2007; Selig, Card, & Little, 2008). The combination of both methods is appropriate in cases that include latent variables and endogenous predictors in a hierarchical dataset. Some of the features of multilevel-SEM are implemented by the end of the empirical analysis, when assessing the effect of mediator variables in international comparison.

Chapter 5

EMPIRICAL ANALYSIS I:
LEGITIMACY OF ECONOMIC INEQUALITY IN CHILE

The empirical analysis of public opinion data is organized into two parts. The first part corresponds to this chapter and considers Chile as a case for the study of legitimacy of income inequality. The second part is presented in the next chapter, extending the analysis of legitimacy to international comparison. Presenting the analysis in this order follows the intention of first testing the explanatory model of legitimacy in a particular context (taking Chile as a case study), and then in a second step to consider how this explanatory model works in an international comparative setting. This particular-to-general approach has been suggested for social research especially when testing explanatory models (J. Berry, 1999; Helfrich, 1999; Sabbagh & Golden, 2007) - based on the concepts of *emic* and *etic*. The *emic* perspective "adopts the viewpoint of a cultural insider and attempts to understand the culture in its own frame of reference" whereas the *etic* perspective "focuses on the universal aspects of human behavior, namely general laws and causal explanations, by imposing on it a general knowledge structure created by the researcher" (Sabbagh & Golden, 2007, p. 2). By considering only Chilean data first, I will focus the analysis on an *emic* sense, and only in a following step the generalization of the model (i.e. *etic* perspective) will be tested in international comparison.

A second reason to present the analysis divided into two parts is related to the consideration of the two central research hypotheses in a stepwise approach. The hypothesis of *consensual legitimacy* (H_1) is the central topic of the present chapter, particularly based on the analysis of the ISJP data, and the next chapter considers the hypothesis of contextual legitimacy (H_2). This sequential approach is illustrated in Table 13:

Table 13: Organization of empirical chapters

	Research approach	Datasets	Dependent variable	Legitimacy hypothesis
Chilean case (Chapter 5)	Emic	FSOE Chile	Just reward	(Exploratory)
		ISJP Chile	Just earning gap	Consensual legitimacy (H_1)
International comparison (Chapter 6)	Etic	ISSP	Just earning gap	Contextual legitimacy (H_2)

The table summarizes the main elements concerning the organization of the empirical section: research approach, datasets, dependent variable and legitimacy hypotheses. For the analysis specifically focused on the case of Chile, I consider two datasets: the FSOE and the ISJP. The analysis of the FSOE allows a comprehensive approach to the area of justice of earnings in the *emic* sense, attending to the particularities of the justice judgments about earnings. Nevertheless, the analysis is considered exploratory given the restrictive character of the sample (N=189). Exploratory means in this context that I will not direct the analysis to the hypothesis testing, but discuss some of the assumptions regarding the use of just earnings variables in the study of legitimacy. In this sense, the analysis of the FSOE represents a trade off by losing in the generalizability of the results but gaining in addressing the complexity of the subjective dimension of legitimacy and in exploring areas for future research. With the ISJP Chile, I take into consideration the hypotheses related to consensual legitimacy (H_1) and with the ISSP, those concerning contextual legitimacy (H_2).

5.1 LEGITIMACY AND COMPONENTS OF THE JUST EARNINGS: A FACTORIAL SURVEY APPROACH

People's evaluations regarding just earnings certainly constitute a complex research object, a complexity that is usually constrained to the analysis of some standardized questions by conventional public opinion surveys. Conventional surveys consider direct questions about just salaries, usually for low and high status occupations, assuming occupation as the only determinant of just earnings. Even though this approach offers several advantages in terms of simplifying the respondent task and the empirical analysis of the data, it has also been criticized for attempting to elicit normative preferences in a *social vacuum* (Finch, 1987), as if beliefs and values were not affected by potential additional considerations. The use of factorial surveys in the study of judgments about earnings is specifically aimed at introducing additional considerations in this social vacuum, by which the respondent evaluates a situation (described in a vignette) instead of an occupation. Figure 9 depicts a schematic comparison of conventional surveys and factorial survey approaches regarding the justice of earnings:

Figure 9: Comparison of conventional surveys and factorial surveys in justice of earnings

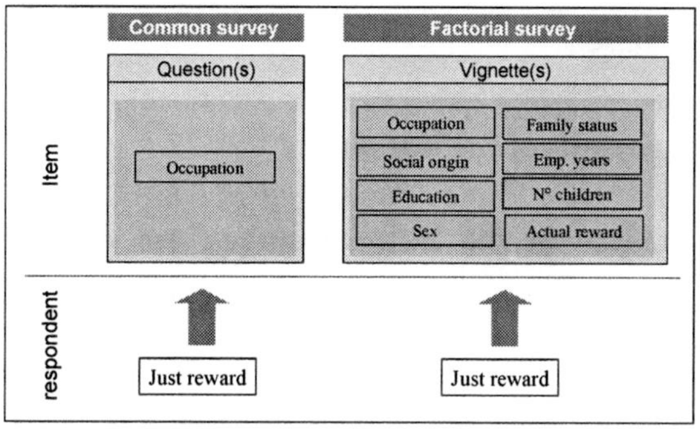

Common to both approaches is the respondent task of assigning a just reward, in one case to the occupation and in the other to the vignette. Since the vignette includes other components besides occupation (in total eight, as represented in Figure 9), with this approach we are able to open the *black box* of conventional surveys and to find out which components play a role in people's minds while performing a normative judgment about occupational earnings (Jasso, 2006a).

Since factorial surveys enable assessing the importance (or weight) of different components in the assignation of a just reward, a <u>first objective</u> in the analysis of the FSOE will be to establish to what extent occupation is a central character when compared to other components. This aspect is relevant for discussion at this initial point since the analyses of the other considered datasets (ISJP and ISSP) are based on this assumption. In other words, testing the centrality of occupation as a component of justice judgments supports the use of a "simplified" version of people's beliefs based only on occupation – as proposed with the *just earnings gap* for conventional public opinion studies. A <u>second objective</u> of this section is to introduce the discussion on the relationship between beliefs about distribution and legitimacy of inequality. As proposed in the multidimensional concept of legitimacy inspired by David Beetham (1991a), beliefs are only one aspect to be considered in the analysis of legitimacy, namely the subjective dimension. For an encompassing evaluation of the legitimacy we need to include two additional dimensions into the discussion: the consensual and the contextual. With factorial survey it is possible to introduce both dimensions in an explorative way, which will serve as a referent for further analysis with the ISJP and ISSP datasets.

5.1.1 Exploring the components of the just reward

The basic units of analysis in the factorial survey are *components* and *levels*. *Components* are the aspects that are supposed to have an influence on the just reward, and *levels* are the categories that constitute each component (for instance, the component *sex* has two levels: male and female). The aim of factorial survey analysis is to establish an explanatory model of the just reward in which the components are the determinants or independent variables. As expressed by Jasso, by the analysis of factorial survey the objective is "to ascertain the equation inside-the-head for each person" (Jasso, 2006a, p. 338). This equation has been expressed in the following way: (Rossi & Nock, 1982):

(6) $$Ji = b_0 + b_1 X_{i1} + \ldots + b_k X_{ik} + e_i$$

Equation (6) is a general expression of the explanatory model of the just reward, in which J is the value of a just reward for an individual i, predicted by a series of variables (components) X with a residual e. In order to get a clear picture of the idea behind this model, I start the analysis in a descriptive way, assessing the influence of one component at a time on the just reward. This part of the analysis is a illustration of what will later be tested in the explanatory multivariate models.

Starting with the central component in study, the following graph represents the unadjusted mean just earning (in Chilean pesos) for each of the eight types or levels of *occupation* presented in the vignettes:

Graph 2: Mean just earnings according to occupation

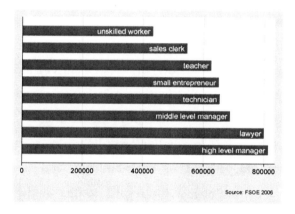

Source: FSOE 2006

In comparative terms, we see that on average it is considered just that high status occupations (such as high level managers or lawyers) obtain superior earnings when compared to low status occupations (such as unskilled workers and sales clerks). This is consistent with other public opinion studies in other countries regarding the justice of earnings (Aalberg, 2003; Evans & Kelley, 2006; Gijsberts, 1999; Kelley & Evans, 1993), as well as with sociological research in the areas of status and prestige of occupations (Ganzeboom & Treiman, 1996; Ganzeboom et al., 1991). Actually, when comparing this result to conventional status measures they appear to be highly correlated: with ISEI (Socio-Economic Index of Occupational Status) the correlation coefficient reaches 0.73 ($p<0.01$) and with SIOPS (Standard International Occupational Prestige Scale) 0.74 ($p<0.01$). Such findings support the general assumption that a certain level of earnings inequality among occupations is considered just in the Chilean society, or in other words, that equality in earnings for different occupations is not a supported justice criteria. Furthermore, the greatest difference in just incomes occurs between the occupations of unskilled worker and the high level manager. This endorses the assumption that these two occupations represent extremes of the status continuum in terms of just earnings (at least among the presented occupations), and consequently that the range of inequality considered just could be summarized in a ratio term as the just earning gap.

The close relationship between occupational status and just earnings has sometimes been interpreted as related to the existential determination of justice judgments: people's normative preferences reflect the reality, and what is becomes what ought to be (Hadler, 2005; Homans, 1976; Shepelak & Alwin, 1986). Nevertheless, it might well be that occupation is not the main referent for just earnings, and that people take into account some alternative criteria. Therefore, the factorial survey includes additional components related to different distributive principles in order to test this assumption. Following the classical distinction of Deutsch (1975), the three main distributive principles are equity (distribution according to personal contributions), equality (redistribution independent of contributions), and need (distribution compensating personal constraints). With regard to the equity principle, two components related to personal contributions or merits have been included in the FSOE: educational level and years in the work force. Graph 3 and Graph 4 illustrate the average influence of education and working years on the just earning:

Graph 3: Mean just earnings by education   **Graph 4: Mean just earnings by working years**

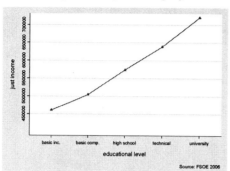 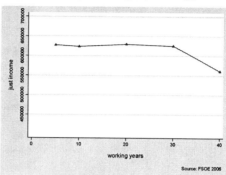

As in the case of occupation, educational level was also expected to influence the just salary and we actually see almost a linear relationship between both variables. Hence people do consider additional components besides occupation when performing judgments about earnings. As far as work experience is concerned, there are no big variations besides the lowest salary considered just for people with the largest number of years working.

As indicative of the distributive *principle of need,* the survey considers the number of persons that are potentially dependent on the income, as the number of children and the existence of a dependent partner. On the other hand, characteristics such as sex and last name were associated with the *principle of equality* as lower earnings are statistically ascribed to these specific group characteristics. As mentioned in chapter 1, there is empirical evidence in Chile that the type of last name affects people's occupational earnings, since association of some names to social origin leads to discrimination in the labor market (Núñez & Gutiérrez, 2004a). On the other hand, sex is also a dimension that influences earnings worldwide, and in the specific case of Chile this gap amounts to 30% between men and women (M. Valenzuela, 2007).

Table 14 summarizes the results of the just earnings for each of the previously mentioned vignette components:

Table 14: Just earnings for vignette components related to principles of equality and need

Distributive principle	Vignette component	Levels	Just earnings* (in Chilean pesos)
Need	Marital status	Single	-517
		Married, working partner	9,636
		Married, partner without job	-9,119
	Number of children	None	-29,945
		One	3,773
		Two	34,363
		Three	5,626
		Four	-22,997
		Five	9,180
Equality	Last name	Mapuche	-17,969
		Spanish	-14,086
		Vasco-Castellano	14,313
		European	17,742
	Sex	Female (in reference to male)	24,167

* As deviation from group means

Just earnings are expressed in the table as deviations of each component mean[63]. For instance, regarding marital status it is considered just that single persons earn -516 pesos below the average just salary. In the dimensions of marital status and number of children, people without potentially dependent family members (single / no children) are evaluated as deserving a lower salary. Nevertheless, this criterion that could be associated with the distributive principle of need (Deutsch, 1975) does not apply consistently throughout the respective dimensions: cases with dependent partners receive lower earnings than those with working partners, and the just earning does not increase proportionally to the number of children. Regarding the components associated to equality, we find support to previous empirical evidence in Chile regarding discrimination based on last name, whereby for indigenous Mapuche people the just earnings are the lowest, and the highest are for European and aristocratic Vasco-Castellano last names. On the other hand, this result contrasts with the revindicative character of the just salary for women, since it is higher than for a man and therefore shows a tendency to equalize current earning differences.

---

[63] The significance of the differences within each component is analyzed in the next section in multivariate models.

Summing up the descriptive results of this first part of the analysis, we have seen that occupation is indeed regarded as a relevant dimension for evaluating a just earning, giving preliminary support to one of the central assumptions of this study. At the same time, there is evidence that besides occupation other components appear to have an influence on just earnings, revealing the complex and multifaceted character of justice judgments. Nevertheless, the influence of other components does not appear to reflect a straightforward influence of alternative distributive criteria for distribution as equality or need. Still from this descriptive analysis we do not know what component exerts the greatest influence in the just reward, for which we need to consider the influence of all components at once in a multivariate framework.

5.1.2 Components of just earnings and legitimacy of inequality

In this section I present a series of multivariate models aimed at determining the relative weight of each component of the *just earning*. The independent variables correspond to the levels of each vignette component. Since most of them are categorical, they are coded as dummies and interpreted with regard to the reference category. Regression coefficients are unstandardized, i.e. represent the contribution of the component's levels to the just reward in Chilean pesos. The coefficients are estimated with maximum likelihood multi level models, as recently suggested by several authors for the analysis of this kind of survey (Jasso, 2006a; Schrenker, 2007; Steiner & Atzmüller, 2006). In multilevel frameworks, model's parameters are estimated according to the clustered nature of the data, since each respondent represents a cluster in which the vignette judgments are nested, whereas the vignettes are clustered in different questionnaires (decks). Furthermore, these models relax the assumption of an equivalent intercept for all respondents, setting it as a random parameter. Therefore, besides the respondent-specific vignette model presented above in equation (6), there is a random intercept model between respondents that, following Steiner & Atzmüller (2006) and Schrenker (2007), can be expressed as:

(7) $J_{div} = \gamma_{00} + \beta_1 Name_{div} + \beta_2 Sex_{div} + \beta_3 Couple_{div} + \beta_4 Children_{div} + \beta_5 Yearsworking_{div} + \beta_6 Education_{div} + \beta_7 Occupation_{div} + \beta_8 Actualreward_{div} + \zeta_d + \zeta_{di} + \varepsilon_{div}$

J_{div}	just earning of the v vignette by the i respondent in the d deck
γ_{00}	general intercept
$\beta_1\text{-}\beta_8$	regression coefficients
ζ	error component at higher levels
ε	residual

The model considers a random intercept, a series of slopes that corresponds to the vignette components, and error terms at the different levels. Based on this equation, a series of multilevel regression models are estimated and presented in Table 15. The vignette's components are incorporated sequentially in models 1 to 3, with the objective of comparing the relative importance of some components. The *actual reward* component is incorporated in all models for reasons to be detailed later.

The analysis of the explanatory models is organized into three points: (i) components' differential weights, (ii) the factorial survey and multidimensional legitimacy, and (iii) the influence of the actual reward on the just reward.

i. <u>Component's differential weight</u>. Model 1 of Table 15 illustrates the influence of those components that have been associated with the distributive principles of equality (last name and sex) and need (dependent partner and/or children). The coefficients reveal that people with an aristocratic last name should obtain greater earnings compared to those with a Mapuche last name, in the line of previous empirical evidence (Núñez & Gutiérrez, 2004a, 2004b). On the other hand, the sex variable indicates that women should earn more than men, a finding that acquires a redistributive character when compared to Chilean reality. Attending the components associated with the principle of need, having a dependent partner does not influence the just salary significantly, but having children generates a redistributive effect, raising the salary by \$9,085 for each additional child. This first model indicates only partial evidence regarding the influence of components related with the distributive principles of equality and need in the determination of the just salary.

158

Table 15: Multilevel regression models of the just reward on vignettes' levels

	Components	Levels	(1)	(2)	(3)
1)	Last name	Spanish	-1,179.83	-6,424.22	-14,511.15
	(Ref= mapuche)		(0.08)	(0.47)	(1.07)
		Aristocrat	34,633.24*	18,237.42	5,828.16
			(2.45)	(1.31)	(0.43)
		European	16,012.93	-3,138.60	957.58
			(1.14)	(0.23)	(0.07)
2)	Sex	Female	29,476.04**	-6,736.52	-17,334.72
	(Ref=male)		(2.86)	(0.66)	(1.73)
3)	Couple	Couple no job	1,140.27	13,958.25	-5,577.51
	(Ref= no couple)		(0.09)	(1.19)	(0.48)
		Couple work	24,810.72	30,379.22*	-9,321.37
			(1.91)	(2.41)	(0.74)
4)	Children	N° Children	9,085.43**	13,631.35**	15,102.15**
			(3.00)	(4.58)	(5.11)
5)	Working years	N° Years (log)		5,638.72	13,030.49*
				(0.88)	(2.07)
6)	Educ. level	Basic complete		32,206.97	23,153.19
	(Ref= basic inc.)			(1.47)	(1.09)
		High school		69,427.23**	40,270.67*
				(3.67)	(2.12)
		Technical		144,286.33**	88,468.21**
				(7.76)	(4.72)
		University		256,442.52**	197,229.60**
				(13.79)	(9.64)
7)	Occupation	Sales			73,888.11**
	(Ref= unskilled)				(4.56)
		Technician			115,933.84**
					(5.61)
		Teacher			56,146.37
					(1.78)
		Small bus. owner			184,697.31**
					(11.59)
		Middle manager			153,695.94**
					(8.42)
		Lawyer			241,714.13**
					(5.03)
		Upper manager			291,259.19**
					(13.98)
8)	Actual income	Income	0.33**	0.34**	0.33**
			(25.28)	(26.33)	(26.43)
		Constant	383,355.04**	244,749.64**	169,158.28**
			(20.68)	(7.97)	(5.46)
		N (respondents)	178	178	178
		N (vignettes)	4,421	4,421	4,421
		R² (level 1)	0.14	0.20	0.25
		Log Likelihood	-62,556	-62,339	-62,264

Unstandardized coefficients, maximum likelihood estimation, absolute z statistics in parentheses, * $p < 0.05$, ** $p < 0.01$. Intraclass correlation (rho) null model=0.05. R^2 based on a comparison of the error variance of the null model with the error variance of the calculated model (Bryk & Raudenbush, 1992a). Deck's effects controlled as an additional level (not displayed).

When incorporating *education* and *working years* in model 2, most of the previously mentioned effects are no longer significant, a result that remains stable in model 3 with the inclusion of occupations. Therefore, there is a predominant determination of the just reward by those components related to personal achievement and equity according to individual contributions.

Model 3 confirms what was anticipated in the descriptive section, i.e. the just salary increases with occupational status (with the only exception of the teacher[64]), whereas the greater just earning difference is between the highest and lowest status occupation (manager and the unskilled worker). We also appreciate an important increase in the explained variance when incorporating occupation, but we still need to test its relative contribution to the just reward as presented in Table 16:

Table 16: Contribution of vignette components to explained variance of the just reward and model fit

Component	R^2	Log Likelihood	Deviance	df
(Null)	0.000	-62,872.22		
Name	0.004	-62,864.38	15.68**	3
Sex	0.004	-62,863.21	18.03**	1
Couple	0.000	-62,871.90	0.63	2
Children	0.000	-62,871.87	0.71	1
Work	0.002	-62,868.42	7.60**	1
Education	0.060	-62,728.51	287.41**	4
Occupation	0.100	-62,660.19	424.07**	7

** $p < 0.01$.

In the table it is possible to observe the results of tests based on comparing the null model with models that include each of the components, the so-called *deviance test* (Hans, 2006). Even though several components appear to have a significant effect on the just reward, occupation comparatively explains most of the variance (R^2=0.10) and also presents the highest deviance value as compared to the log likelihood of the null model[65]. From this first point of the analysis we can conclude that, even though several components significantly contribute to the evaluation of a just reward, the occupation is the one that to a larger extent explains variation in just earnings. This finding can be considered as supporting the consideration of occupational status as a central element for the justification of economic inequality, the assumption behind the formulation of the just earnings gap – the main dependent variable in the

---

[64] This can be explained since, by definition, all teachers have a university education in the vignettes, and their salaries have to be adjusted by education in the model. So in analytical terms an unskilled worker with a university title would earn the same as a teacher. Still it is a comparatively low salary for the university educated, which actually reflects the reality of this occupation in the Chilean labor market (Mizala & Romaguera, 2005).

[65] This analysis excludes the actual reward component, which is discussed later on in this chapter.

analysis of further datasets. But besides this methodological aspect, the influence of occupation in just earnings constitutes a finding along the line of the *existential determination* of justice beliefs (J. Berger et al., 1972; Shepelak & Alwin, 1986), i.e. that just earning differences reflect actual differences in the stratification structure, which bring us to the issue of the legitimacy of earning differences.

ii. Exploring the legitimacy of earnings inequality with the factorial survey. Up to this point I have focused on the analysis of justice beliefs regarding earnings without mentioning the issue of legitimacy. This is because the argument of this research is actually that justice beliefs alone are not enough to evaluate the degree of legitimacy of a distributive system – even though they are a key component. Even though the explorative character of the factorial survey bears some limitations for a multidimensional analysis, I will now comment on the exploratory approach to both dimensions with the factorial survey and about how some of the restrictions of this survey are tackled with the analysis of the further datasets included in this study.

- *Consensual dimension.* The idea of this dimension in the legitimacy model is to consider the degree of consensus in the population regarding beliefs about distribution. In this framework, consensus means the general normative agreement despite calculations of expediency, i.e. self interest (Dornbusch & W. Scott, 1975). This aspect is operationalized in the legitimacy model by including status variables of the respondents, whereby the agreement in just earning despite status differences is interpreted as a sign of consensus. The inclusion of respondent variables in the analysis of factorial surveys requires some technical specifications, since the FSOE dataset is characterized by a hierarchical structure of the data, in which the vignettes are clustered or nested in respondents. In multilevel terms, the respondents are considered *level 2 units* whereas vignettes correspond to *level 1 units*. Taking this into account, Table 17 illustrates the effect of respondent status predictors on the just earning:

Table 17: Multilevel regression model of the just reward on respondent's status predictors

	Just reward
Income (hh equivalent)	0.12
	(1.59)
Educational level (Ref= basic incomp.)	
Primary complete	-28,869.36
	(-0.88)
Secondary complete	-52,297.60
	(-1.79)
Technical superior	41,800.43
	(0.96)
University	-35,020.88
	(-0.79)
Subjective standing	-5,587.08
	(-1.52)
Constant	219,742.40
	(4.57)
N level 2	162
N level 1	4,021
Log likelihood	-56,728
R^2 level 2	0.00

Unstandardized coefficients, maximum likelihood estimation, absolute z statistics in parentheses, * $p < 0.05$, ** $p < 0.01$ Intraclass correlation (rho) null model=0.05. R^2 based on a comparison of the error variance of the null model with the error variance of the calculated model (Bryk & Raudenbush, 1992a). Deck's effects controlled as an additional level (not displayed).

The model of Table 17 already contains the vignette components as in model 3 of Table 15, but they are not displayed here again since their significance remains stable. As observed, none of the predictors expresses a significant influence on the just income, which means that differences in the just reward are not explained by status characteristics. In other words, people of different status support similar differences in occupational earnings, giving preliminary support to the consensual legitimacy hypothesis. The adjective of preliminary attends to the reduced number of cases in the sample, which additionally becomes even smaller when introducing level 2 predictors, due to missing data. The search for further evidence of this kind will be the central topic in the analysis of the ISJP data.

- *Contextual dimension*. This dimension points to the consideration of justice beliefs in reference to an external standard of the society – in this particular case in assessing to what extent just earnings depart from real earnings in Chile. It is possible to explore this dimension with the FSOE in a descriptive way, by comparing the just salaries estimated by the previous models with the current salaries that characterize the labor market in Chile. Since the main interest in this research is on the just earning differences, I will center this descriptive comparison on the higher and lower status occupations. Starting with the lower status occupation, an external standard in this regard is the minimum salary in Chile, which at the time of the interview corresponded to $159,000 pesos (about €206). On the other hand, the *just minimum salary* (Bay & Pedersen, 2006) would be defined by the salary considered just for the lowest status category of each component of the vignettes (such as unskilled worker, single, no children, and incomplete basic education). Since the lowest status category of each component is used as a reference for the estimation of regression coefficients in Table 15, the coefficient of the constant (intercept) in model 3 is equivalent to the just minimum salary, which reaches $169,158 pesos. In descriptive terms, this means that the current minimum salary and the just minimum salary differ by about 6%, which could be interpreted as a relative *conformity* with the situation or the external standard (Beetham, 1991a). Looking now at the *highest just salary*, this is obtained from adding the regression coefficients from model 3 that correspond to the high status levels (such as a manager with a university education), which rises to $ 779,747 pesos. Unfortunately, there are no clear standards for contrasting this figure with real salaries in Chile, mainly due to the great dispersion of salaries under this category. Nevertheless, the difference between higher and lower just salaries in proportional terms (4.6) appears smaller than the current salary differences in Chile between high and low status occupations (7.3) based on a report of the International Labor Organization (ILO, 2008b). According to this preliminary descriptive analysis of the contextual dimension, it would be considered just to reduce current earnings differences, but diminishing from the top instead of leveling up from the bottom.

iii. <u>The role of actual earnings in determining the just earning</u>. Up to this point we have not made reference to the vignette component *actual reward*, since this requires additional remarks and its analysis has significant consequences for the empirical study of legitimacy. The actual earning is a vignette component which is randomly assigned to each fictitious case. Given its arbitrary assignation, from common sense it would not be expected that such a component has an influence on the just earning. Nevertheless, the actual reward is the component with the greatest explanatory power in the multilevel models of the just reward, accounting for 12% of the explained variance. Such a finding has also been reported in previous vignette studies (Schrenker, 2007), associated to the interpretation that people consider first and foremost the salary that someone actually earns as a standard for justice judgments. In other words, there is a tendency to lean responses towards the actual salary, which is the source of the positive association among both terms, as represented in Graph 5:

Graph 5: Influence of the actual earning on the just earning

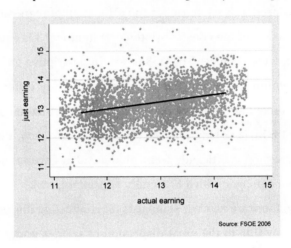

Source: FSOE 2006

Each point on this scatter plot represents the proposed just earning with regard to the actual earning. The line depicts the positive relationship between both, which refers us to the influence of *what is* on *what ought to be*. Such a relationship is based on two main sources: on the one hand a third of the respondents (34%) consider that the actual reward presented in the vignette is just (i.e. actual reward=just reward), and on the other hand when taking these cases out of the analysis, the rest of the respondents still let guide their judgments from the actual reward in a positive way ($z=7.88$, $p<0.01$). Positive means in this case that respondents tend to consider as just a higher income for those with high earnings, and a lower income for those with low earnings, irrespective of their other attributes. The term *anchoring* has been used in the literature to refer to this cognitive phenomenon by which justice judgments are dependent on or anchored in the rewards perceived by the respondent (Markovsky, 1988; Tversky & Kahneman, 1974). If we translate this cognitive interpretation in legitimacy terms, the perceived earnings are accepted as they are by a significant part of the respondents, whereas for others there is a significant tendency to what has been called the *Mathew effect* (Merton, 1988): giving more to those who have more, and less to those who have less. Such a finding delivers support to the hypothesis regarding the influence of existential standards in determining justice judgments (Shepelak & Alwin, 1986), which corresponds to the keystone for arguing legitimacy of inequality in contexts with high inequality. At the same time, it highlights the need to incorporate perception as a standard for justice evaluations in the study of legitimacy and distribution (Hegtvedt, 2006; Markovsky, 1988; Wegener, 1987), a point to be advanced further in the following sections of the empirical analysis.

5.1.3 Summary

The analysis of factorial surveys offers a comprehensive picture of the subjective dimension of legitimacy when compared to conventional public opinion surveys. Within this approach it is possible to test the weights that people assign to different components at the moment of performing a justice judgment, accounting for the complexity of them. Given this feature, a first objective of the analysis was to test the weight given to the occupation as a determinant of the just earnings, which appeared to be highly relevant. This finding supports the use of just earnings associated with occupations as dependent variables in studying the legitimacy of inequality. In addition, there is significant evidence regarding the role of perceived earnings on the earnings considered just, i.e. of what is on what ought to be. The analysis introduced the implementation of the multidimensional model of legitimacy in its consensual and contextual dimensions. Taking this preliminary evidence into account, the next sections are aimed at hypotheses testing now based on national representative data.

5.2 CONSENSUS IN EARNING DIFFERENCES: ANALYSIS OF THE ISJP CHILEAN DATA

This section is aimed at testing the hypotheses related to consensual legitimacy through the analysis of the ISJP Chilean data. Consensual legitimacy corresponds to the first of the two criteria for legitimacy based on the multidimensional model. The second criterion (i.e. contextual legitimacy) will be the topic of the next chapter. Figure 10 summarizes the research hypotheses based on the multidimensional legitimacy model:

Figure 10: Summary of the consensual legitimacy hypotheses

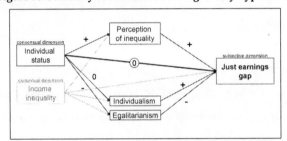

The scheme is based on the model introduced in chapter three, but now it specifies the dependent variable as the *just earnings gap* and the hypotheses are depicted as signs next to the explanatory paths. The contextual dimension of the model appears faded, since its analysis will not be performed until the next chapter. Summarizing the hypotheses, the central association of the scheme is the one between *individual status* and *just earnings* which, according to the consensual legitimacy hypothesis applied to the Chilean case, is expected to be non-significant: individuals would not diverge in the just earning gap despite their individual status. *Perception of inequality* is expected to be larger in higher status groups, and at the same time it would be positively related to the preference of just earning differences. Finally, the justice ideology of *individualism* is expected to be consensual (or primary) in different status groups, and to have a positive influence on the just earning gap. On the other hand, *egalitarianism* would have a challenging (i.e. secondary) character associated with the discontent of lower income groups, which would be reflected in a preference for lesser earning differences.

The analysis guided by the research hypotheses begins with descriptive results of the variables and relationship among them, followed by the presentation of explanatory multivariate models.

5.2.1 Descriptive analysis

- *Just and perceived earnings gaps.* The ISJP survey includes questions about the income considered just for an unskilled manual worker and a chairman or managing director of a large company, which constitute the main elements for the operationalization of the subjective dimension of legitimacy. In Graph 6 we observe the distribution of the mean responses for the salaries considered just in Chilean pesos, as well as the perceived salaries for the same occupations:

Graph 6: Mean perceived and just earnings

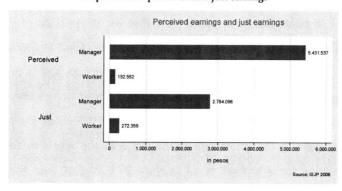

Graph 6 gives us a first approach to the distributions of the occupational earnings in the ISJP data. There are clearly greater differences between manager and worker in perceived earnings as compared to just earnings, i.e. respondents consider as just (on average) smaller differences in occupational earnings than the ones perceived, as reflected in the following table:

Table 18: Mean perceived and just earnings differences[66]

	Ratios	Proportion
Perceived	manager earning / worker earning (5,431,527 / 152,552)	35.6
Just	manager earning / worker earning (2,784,096 / 272,359)	11.3

---

[66] I use here the term "difference" to avoid confusion with the term "gap", used later for the logarithmic ratio.

According to Table 18, on average the perceived income of a manager is 35.6 times higher than that of an unskilled worker, whereas the proportion evaluated as just is about 11.3. This proportion is actually higher than the current salary average differences in Chile (7.3) according to the World of Work Report 2008, meaning that on average people prefer more inequality than that existing. This is certainly an interesting aspect regarding legitimacy that refers us to the descriptive approach to the contextual dimension. Still, it could be claimed that the selection of the external standard for comparison is arbitrary, and that different conclusions could be raised when selecting a source other than the World of Work Report. Such problem can be solved when analyzing the contextual dimension in an international comparative framework, as I will detail in the next chapter. For the time being, in the rest of this chapter I will focus my attention on the consensual dimension of legitimacy.

A relevant aspect to point out from Table 18 is that the proportion of just earning inequality is smaller than the perceived inequality. This so-called *tendency to equalize* or consider smaller income differences than that perceived as just is an empirical finding that appears in several public opinion studies about occupational earnings (Arts & van Wijck, 1989; Gijsberts, 1999; Kelley & Evans, 1993). Still, the proportions of increase or decrease in the salaries of managers and the workers are different: while the just earning for a worker is on average 37% higher than the perceived earning, the just earning of a manager should be decreased by 49%. There seem to be greater feelings of injustice regarding the earnings of the high status occupation than the low status occupation. In other words, justice seems more related to level down from the top than to level up from the bottom, as anticipated previously by the factorial survey research. This tendency expressed in direct questions about earnings contrasts to the results of indirect questions about the justice of the salaries of worker and manager, as shown in Table 19:

Table 19: Evaluation of actual incomes of manager and worker (percentages)

	Much less than deserved	Somewhat less	About deserved	Somewhat more	Much more than deserved	Total
Manager	3.30	2.73	41.98	13.65	38.34	100.00
Worker	68.18	19.71	11.10	0.68	0.34	100.00

Source: ISJP 2006, Chilean data. Answers to the question regarding perceived earnings: Do you think this is much less than a managing director /worker deserves to earn, somewhat less than deserved, about what is deserved, somewhat more than deserved, or much more than deserved? The original scale ranges from -5 to +5 and it has been recoded here in 5 categories.

Almost 42% of the interviewed think that the perceived salary of the manager is what he/she deserves, contrasting with the 11% regarding the unskilled worker. On the other hand, almost 90% consider a workers' salary to be less than they deserve, whereas about 50% think that the managers get more than they deserve. When comparing these results with the previous proposals for just salaries it is interesting to notice that, despite the overall consensus about the low worker's salary, this is not reflected in a proportional increase in questions regarding a just salary. In this sense, what is felt as unjust in a rating scale question does not necessarily reflect what is considered just in a concrete question about just salaries, which is one of the reasons why this research considers direct questions about earnings in the dependent variable.

Up to this point the descriptive analysis delivers information concerning people's perceptions and beliefs about occupational earnings, but how to interpret these results in terms of legitimacy? In other words, what does a just earnings difference of 11.3 mean? On the one hand it would be possible to say that, despite some variations in just earnings of low and high status occupations, the differences between just and perceived earnings indicate a lack of legitimacy: people prefer less inequality than they perceive. But on the other hand, though the perceived earnings inequality by far exceeds the just earnings inequalities, people in Chile clearly do not support the complete equality of earnings as criteria of justice (i.e. the just earning differences are not close to a ratio of 1). Therefore, different conclusions can be drawn depending on the standard of reference. Descriptive results based only on perceptions and beliefs give us a general picture of the subjective dimension of legitimacy, but they are certainly not enough to evaluate the degree of legitimacy of the economic inequality. Actually, one of the main problems in the public opinion debate about legitimacy is related to this issue, namely the definition of the *right* construct and/or indicator of legitimacy, as for instance with the case of diffuse support (Easton, 1975; Kaina, 2008; Muller et al., 1982; Seligson, 1983). A similar tendency has characterized the debate about the legitimacy of inequality in Chile, in which the discussion about what type of question or variable is the right indicator has led to different and contradictory interpretations (Cumsille & Garretón, 2000; Lehmann & Hinzpeter, 2001). In this regard, a central argument of this research is that an adequate approach to legitimacy should not be based on the definition of the right indicator, but on the inclusion of additional dimensions as for instance the degree of consensus regarding just earning differences.

- Consensual legitimacy, perception and ideologies. A central element to evaluate the legitimacy of inequality is the degree of consensus in the population regarding beliefs about the distribution of income. I refer to this as the consensual dimension of legitimacy. Translated into empirical concepts, consensus in this case means more than a simple measure of dispersion. We require testing consensus based on variables that reflect the instrumental interests on distribution, as the status variables of income. If people show a degree of consensus in the earnings considered just despite of income differences, this is considered as evidence of legitimacy. The following graph compares the perceived gap and the just gap according to income quintiles:

Graph 7: Mean perceived and just gap according to income

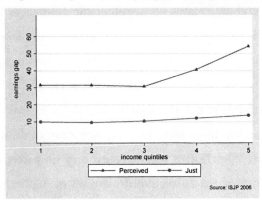

Source: ISJP 2006

The graph shows the income quintiles on the x axis and the earnings differences as a ratio term between manager and worker on the y axis. Two main observations can be derived from this picture. On the one hand, the different income groups show support for a similar just earning gap, in line with the consensual legitimacy hypothesis. On the other hand, people of higher income groups clearly perceive a wider earnings gap, also giving preliminary support to this hypothesis and confirming previous empirical findings concerning the status dependency of perception (Groß, 2003; Wegener, 1987). As a rather paradoxical result, since lower status people perceive less inequality, the distance between what is just and what is perceived appears to be smaller in lower income groups, a phenomenon that has received the label of the *value consensus paradox* (Wegener, 1990). The status dependency of inequality perceptions constitutes a central aspect in explaining legitimacy phenomena, and therefore the character of mediator that this variable occupies in the multidimensional legitimacy model.

Besides the perception of inequality, a second group of variables included in the explanatory model are the justice ideologies. In this study attention is given to two justice ideologies that have been considered previously in empirical justice research: individualism and egalitarianism. These ideologies are measured by several items in the dataset, which are rated on a five point rating scale from absolutely agree to absolutely disagree. The following graph shows the mean percentage of responses to the categories "absolutely agree" and "agree" in the items associated with both ideologies:

Graph 8: Preference for egalitarianism and individualism

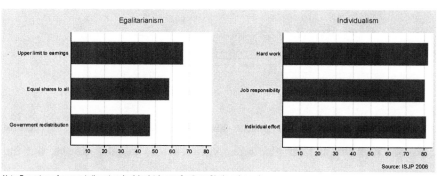

Note: Percentage of answers to the categories "absolutely agree" or "agree" in the rating scale.

At first sight, items of the individualistic justice ideology exhibit higher agreement and fewer differences in their means than those of egalitarianism. A great majority believes that hard work, responsibility and effort should influence earnings. In the case of egalitarianism, a majority agrees with the idea of an upper ceiling on occupational earnings, but on the other hand government redistribution is preferred less. Looking at both ideologies in comparative terms, the greater support for individualism can be related to the influence of free market reforms – which has characterized Chile for the last 40 years – on people's preferences for redistribution, an issue to reconsider later in the analysis of international comparative data. For now we focus our attention on the consensus regarding both ideologies, which are also expected to be affected for individual status variables. Following a rational argument, people at the lower end of the income continuum would be expected to show a higher preference for egalitarianism, whereas for individualism the opposite would be the case. On the other side, a legitimating effect has been attributed to ideologies that do not correspond to the instrumental interests of the individuals, which some authors associate with the Marxist concept of false consciousness (Jost & Major, 2001b). The following graph gives us some empirical information regarding this debate:

Graph 9: Individualism and egalitarianism by income level

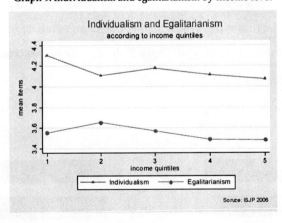

The graph shows the mean of the justice ideologies items according to income quintiles. We see that support for ideologies varies across income groups, but the pattern does not appear to follow the rational-instrumental logic. If this were the case, the line pattern would look like an X, in which individualism would be an ascending line whereas egalitarianism a descending one from bottom income groups to the top. Nevertheless, in the poorest quintile we observe the highest support for individualism, a scenario in which ideologies have been attributed to playing a legitimizing role (Glaser, 2005; Sidanius et al., 2001). On the other hand, egalitarianism does not appear with an extreme variation, specially when comparing the poorest and richest quintile. Such descriptive results contradict the hypothesis of the consensual (primary) character of individualism, opening a new front for discussing legitimacy, namely the situation where people at the bottom of the stratification structure show the strongest support for the distributive norms that shape the distribution (Jost & Major, 2001a).

In addition to the analysis that directly relates ideologies with legitimacy, one of the main interests in this work is to consider ideologies as a counterpoint to perception in the determination of the just earnings gap, in the context of the existential - utopian debate (see section 3.3). To analyze this point we need to move one step forward to the multivariate analysis of the multidimensional legitimacy model.

5.2.2 Multivariate analysis

As in the descriptive analysis, in this section I will proceed stepwise tackling the different aspects of the multidimensional model, i.e. the research hypothesis. First, I analyze the role of perception regarding consensus in the just earning gap, then I follow with the justice ideologies, and finally all the variables are incorporated at once in order to analyze the relative weight of perception and ideologies in explaining the just earnings gap.

a) Individual status, perception of inequality and the just earnings gap

Three variables constitute the operationalization of status: household equivalent income, educational level and self attribution of status (social standing). I will first focus on the influence of the status variables on the perceived earning gap, which according to the corresponding research hypothesis is expected to be positive, i.e. the higher the status, the higher the perceived differences between earnings of different occupations. In a second step I present evidence about the influence of status variables and the perceived gap on the just earnings gap.

Table 20 reports a OLS estimation of status variables and socio-demographic control variables on the *perceived gap*:

Table 20: OLS regression models for the perceived income gap

	(1)	(2)	(3)	(4)
Educational level				
(Ref=Primary incomplete)				
Primary complete	0.38*	0.34*	0.34*	0.34*
	(2.43)	(2.15)	(2.16)	(2.15)
Secondary complete	0.30*	0.21	0.20	0.17
	(2.43)	(1.66)	(1.58)	(1.31)
Technical superior	0.62**	0.51**	0.50**	0.53**
	(3.56)	(2.89)	(2.82)	(2.89)
University	0.68**	0.53**	0.52**	0.51*
	(3.62)	(2.72)	(2.67)	(2.53)
(log) Household income		0.13**	0.13**	0.16**
		(2.96)	(2.84)	(3.45)
Subjective social standing			-0.02	-0.01
			(-0.88)	(-0.54)
Female (Ref=Male)				-0.09
				(-1.00)
Age				-0.00
				(-0.67)
Employment status				
(Ref.= Employed)				
Unemployed				0.32*
				(2.17)
Pension / disabled				-0.05
				(-0.29)
Others				0.21*
				(2.05)
Religion (ref.= Catholic)				
No religion				-0.02
				(-0.25)
Other religions				0.06
				(0.59)
Ethnic background (ref=ethnic group)				0.04
				(0.18)
Constant	2.66**	2.79**	1.39**	1.03
	(23.5)	(17.7)	(2.67)	(1.82)
Observations	750	750	750	750
R^2	0.03	0.04	0.04	0.05

OLS estimator, unstandardized coefficients, t statistics in parentheses ** $p<0.01$, * $p<0.05$. Weighted data.

In general, results of the regression models deliver information about the positive relation between status variables and perception of inequality, particularly regarding income and education. Model 1 shows the positive influence of education on the perceived gap, which increases with higher educational levels. Household income is introduced as a second status variable in model 2 also with significant effect. Even though it produces some modification in the education coefficients (secondary education is no longer significant), superior educational levels are still related to perception of greater inequality.

Social standing does not demonstrate a significant effect on the perceived inequality when introduced in model 3. Separate tests showed evidence of an association between subjective standing and perception of inequality (t=-2.08), which surprisingly appeared to be negative.

Additional analysis showed that the effect of social standing on perceived inequalities is affected particularly by the income variable, since between both there is also a negative association (-0.07, $p< 0.05$). Individuals of low social status tend to overestimate their position in the social structure (and higher status people to underestimate it), moreover they perceive less income inequality. As a consequence, the effect of social standing vanishes in model 3 under control of household income. All in all the effects associated with social standing constitute an additional element that speaks for the role of perceptual biases regarding economic inequality. Finally, model 4 introduces socio-demographic controls depicting some significant effects, such as that of unemployment. Still, the incorporation of controls does not reflect a notorious increase in the explained variance, which actually remains rather low despite the significant influence of status variables on the perception of inequality.

- Status, perception and the just gap. So far we have empirical evidence in line with the hypothesis that people of lower status perceive less income inequality (in occupational earnings) than people of high status. Now we incorporate this knowledge in explaining the legitimacy of income inequality by analyzing the influence of the perceived inequality on the inequality considered just i.e. the just earnings gap, as illustrated in the following figure:

Figure 11: Structural path of status, perceived gap and the just gap

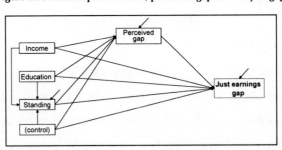

The path diagram represents the influence of the status and control variables on the perceived gap, which corresponds to the models of Table 20. Additionally, it includes the prediction of the just earnings gap by status variables and the influence of the perceived gap on the just gap. Standing appears as predicted by income, education and control since it is considered an endogenous status variable[67]. Given that the path model includes endogenous variables, an appropriate framework for the estimation of regression coefficients corresponds to structural equations models (SEM) (Bollen, 1989; Jöreskog, 1970; B. Muthén, 2004). Table 21 illustrates a series of regression models with the just earnings gap as a dependent variable, following a similar structure to the ones presented in the analysis of the perceived earnings gap. Models 1 to 3 show the effect of status variables on the just gap, and model 4 includes the perceived income gap as predictor. In model 1 the just earning gap is regressed on educational level, showing that higher educational levels prefer higher income inequalities. This effect is moderated by household income in model 2, meaning that keeping income level constant, only people with university degrees prefer higher inequality. Such results are in opposition with theoretical views that associate higher education with a preference for lower inequality, the so-called "Enlightenment thesis" (N. Davis & R. Robinson, 1991), but rather point in the direction of the influence of education on the embeddedness of core cultural values (Jackman & Muha, 1984; Weakliem, 2002). Social standing is introduced in model 3, again with no significant effect (as in the models for the perceived gap).

---

[67] The endogenous character of social standing is related to being an attitudinal variable that has predictors within the model, as discussed before when looking at the lack of significance of standing on the perceived earnings gap.

Table 21: Structural equation model of the just earnings gap on status variables and perceived earnings gap

	(1)	(2)	(3)	(4)
Educational level				
(Ref= Primary incomplete)				
Primary complete	0.14	0.10	0.09	-0.05
	(0.98)	(0.71)	(0.64)	(-0.45)
Secondary complete	0.15	0.07	0.04	-0.06
	(1.32)	(0.60)	(0.30)	(-0.62)
Technical superior	0.36*	0.27	0.25	0.00
	(2.26)	(1.64)	(1.51)	(0.01)
University	0.54**	0.40*	0.37*	0.11
	(3.18)	(2.30)	(2.01)	(0.74)
(log) Household income		0.13**	0.12**	0.06
		(2.95)	(3.26)	(1.50)
Subjective social standing			0.00	0.00
			(0.17)	(0.24)
Perceived gap				0.45**
				(11.98)
Constant	1.70**	0.44	0.41	0.02
	(16.1)	(1.01)	(0.82)	(0.05)
Observations	683	683	683	683
R^2	0.02	0.03	0.04	0.30

Maximum likelihood estimator. Unstandardized coefficients, z statistics in parentheses ** $p<0.01$, * $p<0.05$. Weighted data. Non-displayed control variables in models 4 and 5: sex, age employment status, religion, ethnic group. Chi 2 = 0.00 (saturated model).

Until this stage of the analysis we can preliminarily conclude that the consensus hypothesis of the legitimacy model only counts with partial evidence. High status individuals (higher income and educational level) actually prefer a larger just earnings gap. This is a sign of dissent among status groups with regard to preferences for inequality, which can be explained by rational economic interests: low status people prefer fewer differences in earnings than do high status people. Nevertheless, the lack of consensus radically changes when the perception of inequality is incorporated in model 4 as an endogenous variable: there is a positive influence of the perceived inequality on the just earnings gap, and there are no longer significant status differences. This finding – consensus in just earnings relative to perception of inequality - leads to further elaboration in two aspects:

i. The first aspect to consider is the positive effect of the perceived inequality on the just earnings gap. From the descriptive analysis we know that the just gap is smaller than the perceived gap; people on average prefer less inequality than they perceive. Hence, the positive effect of perception means that people consistently take the perceived inequality as reference for their preferences about just earnings (Hegtvedt, Clay-Warner, & C. Johnson, 2003). This is consistent on the one hand with the arguments inspired by processes of socialization, i.e. how people's perceptions about inequality are shaped – often unquestioningly – by what society teaches about the nature of physical and social reality (Kluegel & E. Smith, 1986). On the other hand, the influence of perception on evaluation in general has been related to cognitive mechanisms as the *anchoring effect* (Chapman & E. Johnson, 1999; Jacowitz & Kahneman, 1995; Markovsky, 1988; Tversky & Kahneman, 1974). As Markovsky points out, "the apparent fairness of specific reward levels can be affected by changes in socially constructed frames of reference" (Markovsky, 1988, p. 213). Then, judgments about inequality are framed or anchored in perception, which serves as orientation or a standard for justice judgments[68]. In other words, even though the just income gap is always *something less* than the perceived inequality, this *something less* is not random but quite consistent as reflected by the notorious increase in the variance explained by model 4 (R^2= 30%).

ii. The second aspect with regard to the effect of perception on preferences of inequalities is the so-called *mediator effect* (Baron & Kenny, 1986; Younts & Mueller, 2001). The introduction of perceived inequalities is considered as *mediator* of status effects, which in the last model appears as no longer significant. This means that status differences in the preference for inequalities are actually explained by differences in the perception of inequalities. To understand this statement we have to take into account the importance of perception for the legitimate level of inequality: what is considered just must be analyzed with regard to what people actually perceive in order to determine the level of legitimacy of the actual situation (Hegtvedt et al., 2003). This idea is represented in the following scheme:

---

[68] This is named by Markovsky (1988) as assimilation effect, which occurs when a judgment is biased towards an anchor.

Figure 12: Perceived and Just gap according to status differences

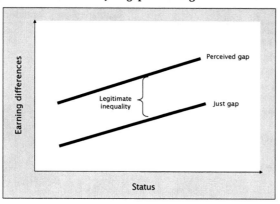

The figure depicts two lines that represent the relationships between status and earning differences (perceived and just). Low status people prefer less inequality than people with high incomes (just gap), but at the same time they perceive less inequality. If we agree with the argument that perception of inequality is an element that must be taken into account for justice evaluations (Markovsky, 1988), then consensus is produced across status groups since they do not differ in what is seen as *legitimate inequality* in the figure, that is, the distance between the perceived inequality and the just inequality. Again this interpretation reinforces the idea that legitimacy in this research is not conceived as an attitudinal variable or a belief, i.e. legitimacy is not the just earnings gap. Rather, legitimacy is a relationship among variables, in which individual status is a central component for evaluating consensus, and also the perceived inequality as mediator variable. An additional element that is expected to partially explain consensual legitimacy are the justice ideologies, which are considered in the following section.

b) Justice ideologies and status variables

As pointed out in the methods chapter, justice ideologies are measured in the ISJP as latent variables. Latent variables are conceptual constructs that are assumed to be tapped by several items i.e. indicators in a questionnaire (Bollen, 1989). The extent to which the items actually correspond to a latent variable is statistically tested by procedures of confirmatory factor analysis (CFA). The following table shows the results of a CFA for the ideologies of individualism and egalitarianism:

Table 22: Confirmatory factor analysis for justice ideologies in ISJP Chilean data

Items	Egalitarianism	Individualism	u2
• The government should place an upper limit on the amount of money any person can make	0.52	0.20	0.67
• The fairest way of distributing wealth and income would be to give everyone equal shares	0.54	-	0.71
• Government should redistribute income from the better-off to those who are less well-off	0.65	-	0.58
• People who work hard deserve to earn more than those who do not	0.17	0.39	0.81
• The responsibility held by the employee on the job should influence pay	-	0.71	0.50
• The employee's individual effort should influence pay	-	0.77	0.40

Model fit

Chi^2: 5.55, df(5) , P-Value=0.33. CFI: 0.99 RMSEA: 0.01

Correlation between factors: 0.07

WLSMV estimation. Standardized coefficients. Obs: 864. Non-depicted factor loadings fixed to zero.

The two factor model presents a good fit to the data as concluded from a non significant Chi^2 and a low RMSEA. Two loadings were allowed to vary freely in the non-intended ideology since this contributed to a better fit and their loadings are rather low (<0.3). The two ideologies extracted as latent variables present a low correlation, leading to the conclusion that they are independent constructs. This finding is in line with the split-consciousness thesis (Kluegel, 1989), which proposes that the support for one ideology does not necessarily imply rejection of the other, even though their contents seem to be logical opposites.

In the following the influence of status variables on justice ideologies is statistically tested. Table 23 shows the results of structural equation models with both justice ideologies as dependent variables. According to the hypotheses relating status and ideologies, it was expected that status variables would not have a significant effect on individualism and that they would show a negative effect on egalitarianism, which is only partially supported by these results. The hypothesis regarding the lack of a significant effect of status on individualism was based on the idea that this ideology is predominant in societies where the state plays a minor role in redistribution (Wegener, 1995), which characterizes the Chilean case (especially when compared to traditional welfare states). We actually do observe a great consensus with regard to individualism among different educational and income levels in model 1, with the only exception of the technical superior educational level. But this apparent consensus does not match the descriptive analysis of the ideologies in which individualism appeared to be highly supported by the lowest income group (quintile 1). To test this empirical finding I added a second model where the household linear income is replaced by household income quintiles.

Table 23: SEM of justice ideologies on status variables

	Individualism		Egalitarianism	
	(1)[a]	(2)[b]	(3)[a]	(4)[b]
Educational level				
(ref.= primary incomplete)				
Primary complete	0.04	0.05	0.01	0.00
	(-0.53)	(0.62)	(0.06)	(0.02)
Secondary complete	-0.01	0.01	0.01	0.00
	(-0.15)	(0.16)	(0.18)	(0.05)
Technical superior	0.19*	0.21*	-0.10	-0.12
	(2.01)	(2.25)	(-0.79)	(-0.96)
University	0.06	0.08	-0.27*	-0.28*
	(0.58)	(0.78)	(-1.96)	(-2.04)
Household (HH) income				
Log HH Income	-0.04		-0.07*	
	(-1.42)		(-2.16)	
HH Inc. quintiles (Ref.= Q.1)				
Quintile 2		-0.14*		-0.14
		(-2.28)		(-1.80)
Quintile 3		-0.14*		0.00
		(-2.10)		(0.01)
Quintile 4		-0.22**		-0.03
		(-3.40)		(-0.36)
Quintile 5		-0.16*		-0.20*
		(-2.27)		(-2.23)
Social standing	0.01	0.01	-0.01	-0.01
	(0.83)	(0.88)	(-0.58)	(-0.46)
Observations	747	747	747	747
R^2	0.05	0.07	0.04	0.05

Model fit

a: Chi[2]: 43.75, df(39), P-Value: .0.28. CFI: 0.99 RMSEA: 0.01

b: Chi[2]: 43.50, df(43), P-Value: .0.44. CFI: 0.99 RMSEA: 0.01

WLSMV estimator, unstandardized coefficients, z statistics in parentheses ** $p<0.01$, * $p<0.05$. Weighted data. Non-displayed control variables: sex, age, employment status, religion, ethnic group.

In model 2 we see that the income quintiles 2 to 5 actually show a lower level of individualism than quintile one, giving statistical support to the previous arguments of the descriptive section (see Graph 7). Paradoxically, the lack of consensus in individualism is mainly originated by the highest support for this ideology from the side of the poorest income group. This finding is related to empirical evidence in the framework of system justification theory (Jost, 2002; Jost & O. Hunyady, 2003; Jost & Major, 2001a) which predicts highest support for distributive norms from those that benefit the least from the stratification system.

In the case of egalitarianism we see in model 3 that in general people of high income and educational level exhibit a lower support for this ideology. This means that this ideology acquires a secondary character (Wegener, 1995), determined by demands associated to social position – especially in relation to income. Again, in model 4 the continuous income variable is replaced by income quintiles. In this model we see that there is not a constant effect of egalitarianism with growing income, but that the highest income quintile is the only one that significantly shows support for this ideology. The consensus with regard to the relatively higher egalitarianism of the quintiles 1 to 4 when compared to quintile 5 can be interpreted if we take into account the situation of income inequality in Chile: quintile 5 accounts for almost 50% of the total income (MIDEPLAN, 2006), and in this regard quintile 1 to 4 can be thought of as a single category whose earnings fall below the median. Therefore, the rational link between status variables and justice ideologies seems more straightforward in the case of egalitarianism, whereas individualism appears to be consensual and with generally higher support by the population – as we know from the descriptive analysis. The primary character of individualism and the secondary role of egalitarianism has been interpreted in the sense of legitimacy of inequality by the majority of the literature dealing with the link between socioeconomic status and support for ideologies (Castillo, 2007; Lippl, 2003; Sidanius et al., 2001; Wegener & Liebig, 2000; Wegener et al., 2000).

c) Integrating the perception and ideologies in the consensual legitimacy model

This last point of the analysis is about putting all previous pieces of information together in a single model: status variables, perception of inequality, justice ideologies, and the just earnings gap as the ultimate dependent variable. Figure 13 illustrates the interrelationships between variables to be later tested in a structural equation model:

Figure 13: Structural equation model of consensual legitimacy

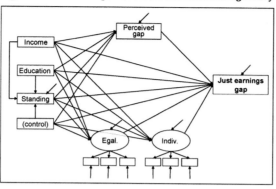

The different variables and paths represented in the figure correspond to the empirical operationalization of the consensual legitimacy model. It is similar to the previous illustration of the model including the perceived gap (Figure 11), but now incorporates the justice ideologies, each one represented as a latent variable based on three correspondent indicators. Both ideologies are predicted by status variables as analyzed before in Table 23, and at the same time this model considers the influence of the ideologies on the just earnings gap.

A possibility provided by the inclusion of perception and ideologies in one single model is to compare the contribution of both terms in determining the just earnings gap. Such an aspect is of particular interest in this research since these variables represent two different visions about the determination of justice judgments: the existential determination and the utopian determination (Shepelak & Alwin, 1986). As presented in Chapter 3, the existential position proposes that people orient their justice evaluations mainly based on already existing standards in the "real world", which in concrete terms means that people consider an income as just taking into account what is an average income for the corresponding occupation (J. Berger et al., 1972), i.e. what people perceive to be the case. Therefore, the existential determination is represented in the model by the perceived inequality (the perceived gap). On the other hand, ideologies represent normative-utopian orientations which are assumed to be consistent with values that are not necessarily influenced by existential constraints, at least in the case of dominant or primary ideologies (Kluegel, 1989; Wegener, 1998). Since the general hypothesis of this research is the existence of legitimacy of economic inequality in a context of high inequality as Chile, this is equivalent to saying that justice judgments about inequality are first and foremost existentially determined, and that perceived inequality acquires a predominant role when compared to justice ideologies.

Table 24 illustrates a summary of the results of the structural equation models:

Table 24: SEM of just gap on perceived gap, justice ideologies and status variables

	Perceived gap	Individualism	Egalitarianism	Just gap
	(1)	(2)	(3)	(4)
Educational level (ref.= primary incomp.)				
Primary complete	0.30	0.02	0.05	-0.04
	(1.48)	(0.28)	(0.49)	(-0.26)
Secondary complete	0.18	0.00	0.06	-0.03
	(1.06)	(-0.06)	(0.74)	(-0.26)
Technical superior	0.61**	0.16	-0.04	-0.05
	(2.81)	(1.65)	(-0.31)	(-0.32)
University	0.55*	0.05	-0.22	0.03
	(2.29)	(0.54)	(-1.48)	(0.18)
Household income	0.18**	-0.04	-0.08*	0.04
	(3.55)	(-1.42)	(-2.47)	(1.10)
Social standing	0.00	0.01	-0.01	0.00
	(-0.04)	(0.67)	(-0.56)	(-0.14)
Perceived gap				0.45**
				(18.15)
Individualism				0.25*
				(2.39)
Egalitarianism				-0.33**
				(-3.84)
Observations	669	669	669	669
R^2	0.06	0.04	0.05	0.34

Model fit

Chi²: 58.65, df(44), P-Value: .0.06. CFI: 0.97 RMSEA: 0.02

WLSMV estimator, unstandardized coefficients, z statistics in parentheses ** $p<0.01$, * $p<0.05$. Weighted data. Non-displayed control variables: sex, age, employment status, religion, ethnic group. Social standing, perceived gap, individualism and egalitarianism are set as endogenous variables in model 4.

The first three models replicate the ones that we have previously estimated for the perceived gap and the justice ideologies. The significant effects witnessed previously remain rather stable. This stability is associated with the lack of covariance of justice ideologies and perceived gap ($r=0.06$ with individualism and $r=-0.06$ with egalitarianism, both non significant) which means that the two concepts explain different aspects of the preference for inequality in occupational earnings.

184

The estimation of model 4 represents the ultimate objective of the analysis of the ISJP Chilean data, in which we are able to analyze the influence of both justice ideologies and the perceived gap on the just gap. Here again the advantage of structural equation models is the estimation of ideologies and perception as endogenous predictors of the just gap, whereas both ideologies are estimated as latent variables in one single model.

Two aspects are central in the analysis of model 4: (i) the effect of justice ideologies on the just gap, and (ii) the comparison of the influence of ideologies vs. perception of inequality in explaining consensual legitimacy:

i. We observe in model 4 that both justice ideologies show evidence of a significant influence on the just gap in the expected sense: individualism has a positive impact and egalitarianism a negative one. According to these results, preferences for general utopian standards about distribution do have an effect on preferences for the distribution of occupational earnings, confirming previous evidence (Gijsberts, 1999; Mühleck & Wegener, 2002; Verwiebe & Wegener, 2000).

ii. At the same time, in model 4 the influence of the perceived gap on the just gap (as analyzed before) remains highly significant. Making reference to the conceptual framework, this means that both utopian standards (ideologies) and existential standards (perception of inequality) play a role in explaining the just earnings gap. Nevertheless, the magnitude of influences (as expressed in the z values of the coefficients) suggests that perception is the most relevant determinant in the model regarding what people consider a just distribution of earnings. But besides the differentials in z values, a crucial aspect corresponds to determine to what extent perception and ideologies *explain* consensual legitimacy, i.e. act as *mediators* between the status variables and the just earnings gap. In order to test the differential contribution of perception and ideologies in explaining this relationship, the model presented in Table 25 reports direct and indirect effects of perception and ideologies, taking income as a central status variable.

185

Table 25: Direct and indirect effects on the just gap

	Just gap
Total effect of income	0.14 **
	(3.49)
Indirect effects	0.10 **
	(3.41)
By:	
Perceived gap	0.08 **
	(3.46)
Individualism	-0.01
	(-1.24)
Egalitarianism	0.03*
	(2.08)
Direct effect	0.04
	(1.10)

Model fit:
Chi^2: 58.65, df(44), P-Value: 0.06. CFI: 0.97 RMSEA: 0.02

WLSMV estimator, unstandardized coefficients, z statistics in parentheses ** p<0.01, * p<0.05. Weighted data. Non-displayed control variables: sex, age, employment status, religion, ethnic group.

The model attempts to determine the role of perception and ideologies in explaining the relationship between status (as measured by income) and the just earnings gap. The *total effect* of income refers to the influence of income on the just gap without the presence of mediator variables (perception and ideologies), which has positive sign. The *indirect effects* are the part of the total effect that is accounted for as mediator variables, in this case perception of inequality and justice ideologies. As we see, perception of inequality denotes a highly significant effect when compared to the ideologies, which is interpreted as a predominance of existential over utopian standards regarding preferences for inequality. As a final result of this model, the direct effect of income on the just gap is not significant, *which is interpreted as partial support for the consensual legitimacy hypothesis for the Chilean case.* The consensus does not appear as an *absolute consensus* but a *relative consensus*, since the effect of status variables on the just earnings gap appears as positive in principle, but this is later explained mostly by perceptual variables. Therefore, the relative consensus is mostly explained by the status dependency of inequality perceptions, since people of lower status, somehow paradoxically, perceive less inequality than those of high status.

5.3 SUMMARY

The analysis of the legitimacy of inequality with a focus on the Chilean case considered two datasets: the Factorial Survey of Occupational Earnings (FSOE) and the International Social Justice Project (ISJP). The first dataset offered an exploratory approach to the justice of occupational earnings in Chile, taking into account several aspects or *components* that people consider at the moment of performing a justice judgment. Occupational status appeared as the principal component in which people base their proposal for a just reward and also as the main criteria for justifying inequality in society. The lack of differences among status groups regarding just occupational earnings offered preliminary support for the *consensual legitimacy* hypothesis. On the other hand, the *just minimum salary* showed up to be similar to the current minimum salary in Chile, considered as evidence of *contextual legitimacy*. Additional analysis of the influence of the actual occupational earnings (as presented in the vignettes) on the just earnings called attention to the importance of perceptual standards. A just earning is strongly influenced by the information about the actual income that an individual obtains, highlighting the role of perception and existential standards in the legitimacy of inequality.

The second part of the chapter looked for evidence of the consensual hypothesis and the influence of perceptual and ideological variables. Assuming that status variables are proxies for rational interests, their lack of significance as predictors of the just earning gap was interpreted as a sign of consensus. This consensus is not considered absolute, since status groups actually vary in their preferences for income differences, but rather is a *consensus relative to perception of inequality*: differences between what is perceived and what is just do not significantly vary across status groups. Hypotheses related to perception are supported by the data, whereby it is confirmed that perception of inequality is status dependent. At the same time, inequality perceptions have a positive effect on the just gap, in other words, what is perceived influences what ought to be. Regarding justice ideologies, there is no support for the hypothesis regarding the primary character of individualism and only partial support for the secondary character of egalitarianism. Actually, individualism appeared not as consensual but surprisingly as strongly supported by the poorest income group. Even though ideologies do influence the just earnings gap, analysis of the explanatory power showed that the perception of inequality plays a stronger role. The predominant character of inequality perceptions in explaining consensual legitimacy is considered as evidence of the existential determination of justice judgments, which is a key argument for explaining the legitimacy of inequality in societies with high inequality such as Chile. Still, in this chapter the concept of *existential* is linked to perceptual variables, and perception actually does not necessarily mirror the current level of inequality. Therefore, a missing element in the analysis is the influence of the current level of inequality in individual's justice conceptions – the contextual legitimacy –, topic of the next chapter.

Chapter 6

EMPIRICAL ANALYSIS II:

LEGITIMACY OF ECONOMIC INEQUALITY IN INTERNATIONAL COMPARISON

The present chapter is centered on the analysis of the influence of income inequality as a contextual factor in people's beliefs about inequality, based on the international comparative dataset *International Social Survey Program* (ISSP) of 1999. The consequences of findings at this level go beyond the Chilean case and are an attempt to test the generalizability of the explanatory model of legitimacy in international comparison. In this sense, I focus on the *etic* dimension of cross cultural research (J. Berry, 1999; Jasso, 2006b; Sabbagh & Golden, 2007), attempting to develop general explanations for the legitimacy of economic inequality.

The hypotheses are based on the multidimensional model of legitimacy, as represented in Figure 14. The scheme emulates the one introduced before in the hypotheses section (3.4), but now the explanatory relationships associated with the *contextual dimension* appear as the highlighted dimension. The hypotheses corresponding to the *consensual dimension* are shaded to simplify the representation, even though they will be incorporated at the end of the chapter.

Figure 14: Summary of the contextual legitimacy hypotheses

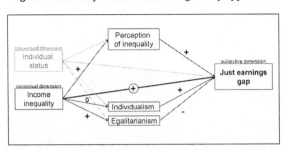

The central hypothesis in this section corresponds to the relationship between income inequality and the just earnings gap, called the contextual legitimacy hypothesis. As argued in chapter two, one of the central aspects of legitimacy is the *congruence* of people's beliefs with rules or norms (Beetham, 1991a), also referred to as *isomorphism* in neo-institutional and also cross cultural research (Adamopoulos, 2008; Deephouse, 1996). In terms of legitimacy of economic inequality, the congruence with the context means that people's justifications of inequality have a positive association with the current level of inequality, i.e. the higher the income inequality, the larger the differences in occupational earnings that are considered just. This is certainly one of the most provocative hypotheses of this research and it is based on theories that emphasize the influence of context characteristics in people's normative preferences, i.e. the existential determination of them (J. Berger et al., 1972; Homans, 1976; Shepelak & Alwin, 1986).

Besides this central hypothesis, Figure 14 also incorporates additional explanatory elements in the model that were already outlined in detail in chapter three and that are briefly summarized here. With regard to *perception of inequality*, it is expected that on average countries with high inequality are also characterized by a larger perceived earnings gap. At the same time, since judgments about earnings are expected to be framed (Hegtvedt, 2006) or anchored (Markovsky, 1988) in inequality perceptions, the perceived gap is expected to exert a positive influence on the just gap. As far as *justice ideologies* are concerned, countries with higher inequality are not expected to differ significantly in individualism and to express higher egalitarianism, given the corresponding primary and secondary character of these general normative preferences. Finally, the schema depicts the impact of ideologies at a country level: individuals of countries with higher individualism are expected to prefer on average a larger just earning gap, whereas those with higher egalitarianism to support less inequality, reflecting the influence of general normative orientations on inequality preferences. All in all it is expected that perception of inequality play a predominant role in explaining legitimacy instead of utopian standards of justice in the form of ideologies. If this is the case and the day-to-day reality is the main source of justice standards, countries with a high level of inequality such as Chile would support on average larger income differences.

As in the previous chapter, the analysis starts with a descriptive approach to the main variables of study, namely the just gap and the endogenous-mediator variables – perceived gap and justice ideologies. This preliminary analysis serves as input to the second section, in which the hypotheses are tested in a multilevel framework, considering the two-level structure of the data (individuals nested in countries). In the third section I combine all explanatory relationships of the model by introducing the perception of inequality and justice ideologies as predictors of the just gap. This task requires not only addressing the multilevel structure of the data but also the estimation of multiple causal relationships given the presence of endogenous variables. Therefore, the estimation of this final model is performed with a combination of multilevel and structural equation models (Heck & Thomas, 2009; B. Muthén, 1994).

6.1 DESCRIPTIVE ANALYSIS OF JUST EARNINGS GAP, PERCEIVED GAP AND IDEOLOGIES

A first issue to consider in the analysis is the country inter-variability regarding the just earnings gap, since with no variation at the country level units, there are actually no differences to be explained with the proposed model. As expected, countries display substantial variation as far as the preference for earnings inequality (just gap) is concerned, as depicted in the following graph:

Graph 10: Countries average just earnings ratio

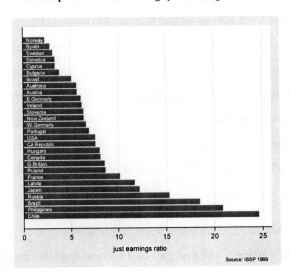

Countries in the graph are sorted according to their value in the just earning ratio (still not logarithmic to facilitate its interpretation); this means, the bars express people's judgments about how much a high status occupation should earn in proportion to what a low status occupation should earn. A first observation is that, despite the variability within countries, values of the ratio are higher than unity in all cases, which means that absolute equality in earnings is not seen as a criterion of justice in any of the countries of the dataset. A second aspect to highlight is that the three countries with higher income inequality included in this dataset (Chile, Philippines and Brazil) are the ones that prefer the highest differences in earnings, a finding that appears as paradoxical at least to approaches that expect redistributive pressures from the median voter in contexts of high inequality (Borge & Rattsø, 2004; Meltzer & Richard, 1981). This already hints at the relationship between inequality as a context level predictor and people's preferences for it, which is illustrated in Graph 11 considering the countries' Gini index as a measure of context level inequality:

192

Graph 11: Just earnings gap by income inequality

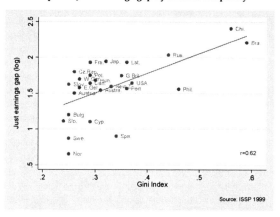

Source: ISSP 1999

The graph clearly illustrates a positive association of income inequality and people's preferences for inequality, in which the biggest preferences for inequality are accounted by the two countries with the highest income inequality in the dataset: Chile and Brazil. Although there are some antecedents in the empirical literature about the relationship between inequality level and attitudes towards inequality (Evans & Kelley, 2006; Gijsberts, 1999; Hadler, 2005; Osberg & Smeeding, 2006), it appears to be somewhat surprising that this specific aspect related to earning differences has not yet been addressed in previous empirical research in the area, despite the availability of this dataset for already more than seven years[69].

The positive association between inequality and preference for it is not considered as ultimate evidence in this research, but actually a starting point in search of explanations about this relationship. According to the explanatory model of legitimacy, perceptions of inequality and justice ideologies are concepts that are expected to shed additional light on the understanding of inequality preferences. Examining the association between inequality level and perceived inequality, Graph 12 reports the distribution of country means in the perceived earnings gap:

---

[69] A possible reason for this is that most people working with ISSP data are interested in time comparisons, and the countries with high inequality included here are participating in the survey for the first time. Besides, even though the topic could have been brought to attention particularly from research in these same countries, the large gap in research capacity has not enabled them to take advantage of the possibilities of this comparative project. Actually, in the Chilean case there are no publications with the ISSP data about social inequality, as reported by the documentation of ISSP (T. Smith, 2008).

Graph 12: Perceived earnings gap by income inequality

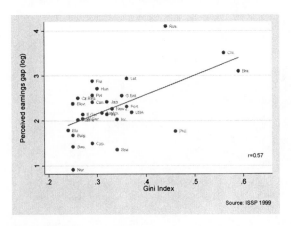

The medium to strong association between both variables denotes that on average people do perceive inequality according to the actual inequality level in comparative terms. It is relevant to consider the values on the y axis to compare with the previous graph, since the perceived inequality is in all cases higher than the just inequality. This means, there is a general tendency to strive for more equality with regard to inequality perceived, consistent with the previous analysis of the ISJP Chilean data. But as discussed before, these average differences between what is perceived and what is considered just is not regarded as a sign of illegitimacy of the distributive system. Rather, the multidimensional definition of legitimacy is based on relationships among a series of aspects expressed in the explanatory model. Again, legitimacy is not only a high average support of a certain belief, but the consensus regarding the belief and the congruence with a context rule or standard.

Following with the descriptive analysis, the ISSP includes a series of variables that are related to the justice ideologies of individualism and egalitarianism, from which it is possible to extract the correspondent latent variables or factors (even though with less specificity as achieved in the ISJP and therefore they are not directly comparable). Results of the factor analysis are presented later on in section 6.2, and for this descriptive analysis I use the country mean factor scores to illustrate their relationship with the income inequality level, as represented in the following plots:

Graph 13: Individualism and income inequality

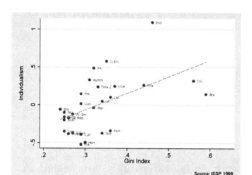

Source: ISSP 1999

Graph 14: Egalitarianism and income inequality

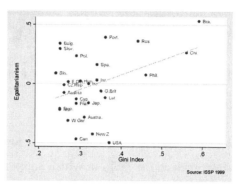

Source: ISSP 1999

Even though we observe a general positive relationship between inequality and individualism, this does not appear to be mainly caused by countries at the upper end of the inequality indicator, but mostly by a cluster of Anglo-Saxon countries (Great Britain, Australia, United States, Ireland and New Zealand). These countries, classified as a liberal type of welfare state regime by Esping Andersen (1990), have been traditionally associated with this ideology, confirming previous evidence in this research area (Haller et al., 1995; Lippl, 1999, 2003; Wegener, 1995). The Philippines appears as the country with the highest score in this ideology, whereas Chile and Brazil exhibit similar levels to those of the liberal countries. On the other hand, in the case of egalitarianism we see a different picture, in which countries with high inequality now share similar levels as those of former communist countries as well as Spain and Portugal, while liberal countries depict lower average values. In this sense, whereas most countries seem to be influenced by their political culture in the alternate preference for individualism and egalitarianism (Kluegel et al., 1999; Mason & Kluegel, 2000), in countries with high inequality we observe a relatively high support for both ideologies. This could be associated with different sources of influences regarding normative preferences: on the one hand a predominance of individualistic-meritocratic values that has been related to the cultural influence of the liberal market reforms (Gijsberts, 1999; Jost, Blount, Pfeffer, & G. Hunyady, 2003; Kluegel et al., 1999; Lane, 1986), and on the other the structural situation of inequality associated with redistributive demands which would be expressed in the egalitarian ideology. But before further elaborating on possible explanations of this

195

phenomenon it is necessary to go one step forward in the analysis and to establish whether individual and country differences are statistically significant or not, an analysis performed with multilevel models.

6.2 EXPLAINING LEGITIMACY AT THE INDIVIDUAL AND COUNTRY LEVELS: A MULTILEVEL FRAMEWORK

Multilevel models are especially suited for the analysis of data with a hierarchical structure such as the ISSP, in which some research units (individuals) are nested in second level units (countries) (Hadler, 2004; Kreft & de Leeuw, 1998; Skrondal & Rabe-Hesketh, 2005). With this approach it is possible to estimate the influence of context variables on individual characteristics while taking into account the interdependence of observations (i.e. correlated residuals) at the country level and its impact on the estimation of the standard errors.

The main interest in this section is to test the influence of the income inequality level on the main dependent variable (just earnings gap), as well as on the explanatory-endogenous variables of the explanatory model (perceived inequality and justice ideologies). Before starting to estimate model parameters, a prior step in multilevel framework consists of calculating the amount of variance of the dependent and endogenous variables that corresponds to the second level (country) units, the so-called *intraclass correlation* (*rho*). *Rho* can be interpreted as a measure of interdependence of the observations at the context level units and therefore as an indicator that encourages the use of multilevel models (Hans, 2006). Besides, *rho* corresponds to the maximum proportion of variance that can be explained by context level variables, and therefore it serves as a key reference for interpreting the influence of income inequality on peoples' perception and beliefs. The following table shows the variance components and the intraclass correlation for the dependent and endogenous variables:

196

Table 26: Variance components and intraclass correlation of dependent and endogenous variables

	Perceived gap	Individualism	Egalitarianism	Just gap
Country level variance	0.47	0.19	0.06	0.18
Individual level variance	0.82	1.06	0.33	0.66
Intraclass correlation (rho)	**0.37**	**0.15**	**0.15**	**0.21**
Average group observations	700	882	882	621
N level 2	26	26	26	26
N level 1	18,214	22,932	22,932	17,523

Maximum likelihood estimation.

Estimation of *rho* is found by dividing the country level variance through the total amount of variance, which is then transformed into a percentage. For instance, in the case of the perceived gap, 37% of the variance corresponds to country level differences. The *rho* of this and other variables presented in the table indicates that the observations have an important degree of contextual dependence, i.e. there is not only individual variation but also country level variation in the dependent and endogenous variables.

6.2.1 Multilevel analysis of the perceived gap

The last chapter referring to the Chilean case found evidence of a positive association between status and the perceived amount of inequality. Now the objective is to observe whether this association is also applicable in an international comparative scenario, to test the explanatory power of the income inequality level in people's perceptions, and to discuss the consequences of these results for the legitimacy of inequality. Table 27 shows the results for the estimation of multivariate models explaining the perceived gap. Models in the table add predictors in a hierarchical way, considering the status variables in model 1, while model 2 adds the demographic controls and model 3 introduces context level inequality. A first general overview reveals that status variables bear a positive relationship with perception of inequality, as expressed in the positive values of household income and education. The negative effect of the number of persons in the household is also in line with this argument, since the larger the number of people who depend on the family income the smaller the amount available for individual consumption.

Table 27: Multilevel regression models of the perceived earnings gap

	(1)	(2)	(3)
Status Variables			
Household income	0.04**	0.04**	0.04**
	(12.26)	(10.88)	(10.91)
Household size	-0.04**	-0.02**	-0.02**
	(8.16)	(4.30)	(4.35)
Education (Ref=CAS 1)			
CAS2	0.11**	0.17**	0.17**
	(5.54)	(8.61)	(8.64)
CAS3	0.21**	0.28**	0.28**
	(8.94)	(11.92)	(11.94)
Subjective standing	-0.02**	-0.02**	-0.02**
	(5.44)	(5.51)	(5.51)
Control Variables			
Female (Ref=Male)		-0.13**	-0.13**
		(9.50)	(9.50)
Age		0.02**	0.02**
		(8.02)	(8.04)
Age^2		-0.00**	-0.00**
		(5.49)	(5.50)
Unemployed		-0.03	-0.03
(Ref= other emp. status)		(1.05)	(1.04)
Catholic		-0.06**	-0.06**
(Ref= other religion)		(3.03)	(3.03)
Context variable			
Gini index			4.74**
			(4.09)
Constant	2.20**	1.68**	0.12
	(16.20)	(11.45)	(0.30)
R^2 individual level	0.02	0.04	0.04
R^2 country level	0.02	0.02	0.40
Log Likelihood	-23,892.86	-23,735.91	-23,729.44
N (individuals)	18,214	18,214	18,214
N(countries)	26	26	26

Unstandardized coefficients, maximum likelihood estimation, absolute z statistics in parentheses, * $p < 0.05$, ** $p < 0.01$. Rho null model=0.37. R^2 based on a comparison with the null model (Bryk & Raudenbush, 1992b).

Nevertheless, the self-attributed social position indicates a negative relationship with the perceived gap, contrasting with the other status indicators. A possible interpretation of this effect is related to the so-called *reference group hypothesis* (Evans & Kelley, 2004; Stouffer et al., 1949), which points out that people tend to consider themselves as part of the majority, generating a distorted image of the stratification system with a few at the bottom, the majority in the middle, and a few at the top. As a consequence, those who overestimate their position in the status structure (since other status variables are under control) shorten their distance from those at the top and therefore misperceive actual inequality (Wegener, 1990). An additional argument for the overestimation of one's own social status can be found in theories of self-evaluation (Della Fave, 1980, 1986a; Shepelak, 1987; Stollte, 1983; Taylor-Sutphin & Simpson, 2009), making people avoid identifying themselves as belonging to the poorest strata. Despite the negative effect of subjective status, the rest of the status variables support the idea that "perception of social status and reward hierarchies are relative to the location an observer occupies within these hierarchies" (Wegener, 1987, p. 2), i.e. perception of inequality is status dependent: the higher the status, the higher the perceived inequality. This finding gives additional support to the evidence obtained for the Chilean case with ISJP data.

Several control variables added in model 2 exhibit significant effects, which in general speaks for the socially embedded character of the perception of inequality. Perception is not a perfect reflection of reality, but is affected by a series of social characteristics as it has been stated by social cognition approaches (Hollander & Howard, 2000; Howard, 1994). Yet the influence of individual variables requires additional research by looking at specific country datasets, since this general model is only able to explain a restricted 4% of the variance.

The small amount of explanatory power achieved with individual variables contrasts with the 40% of explained variance at a context level when introducing the Gini index in model 3. This positive influence confirms the descriptive evidence of the previous descriptive section, in which we observed that people in countries with high income inequality on average perceive larger income disparities. But now we have an additional element in the analysis: that the relatively accurate perception of inequality occurs despite perceptual biases at the individual level. This means, *within* societies the perceptions are affected by the relative position in the status structure, but *between* societies the relative position of the country in the inequality continuum does not appear to be affected by this bias. However, it must be considered that at this point, from the models calculated we do not know the country variability regarding the status dependency of perceived income inequality. Such an inquiry will be tackled in the last section of this chapter (6.3), when discussing the variability of perceptions and consensus between countries.

6.2.2 Multilevel analysis of justice ideologies.

Cross national studies considering justice ideologies is characteristic of research comparing capitalist and post communist countries in their preferences regarding distribution, as well as in industrial countries according to their welfare state regimes (Delhey, 1999; Haller et al., 1995; Lippl, 2003; Märker, 2000; Mühleck & Wegener, 2002; Wegener, 1998; Wegener & Liebig, 2000; Wegener et al., 2000). Complementary to this research line, the particular focus of this study lies in country differences in justice ideologies as a corollary of overall inequality in society and also influenced by individual status.

Before explaining ideological preferences it is necessary to address the latent character of these constructs in the data, as presented in Table 28:

Table 28: Confirmatory factor analysis for justice ideologies in the ISSP data

Items	Egalitarianism	Individualism	u2
• It is the responsibility of the government to reduce the differences in income between people with high incomes and those with low incomes	0.69	-	0.52
• Do you think that people with high incomes should pay a larger share of their income in taxes than those with low incomes?	0.49	-	0.76
• People in wealthy countries should make an additional tax contribution to help people in poor countries.	0.39	-	0.85
• Is it just or unjust that people with higher incomes can buy better health care than people with lower incomes?	-	0.91	0.17
• Is it just or unjust that people with higher incomes can buy better education for their children than people with lower incomes?	-	0.88	0.24

Model fit

Chi^2: 242.6 df(4) , p=0.00. CFI: 0.99 RMSEA: 0.046

Correlation between factors= -0.26

ML estimation[70], standardized coefficients. Obs: 27,980, not displayed factor loadings are fixed to zero.

---

[70] Model parameters were estimated with Maximum likelihood instead of with the option WLSMV for categorical outcomes. The reason was due to computation problems with this option when fixing the factor loadings for measuring invariance.

Both ideologies are extracted through factor analysis (as in the case of the ISJP Chilean data), but now this procedure requires some additional specifications since a common factor structure needs to be asserted across contexts (Brown, 2006). Table 28 presents a common confirmatory factor solution that serves as a reference model for further estimations, which according to the model indexes and factor loadings shows a satisfactory fit to the data. Now in a second step the generalizability of this solution onto each country is tested, which in technical language is called *measurement invariance* across groups (Brown, 2006; Dimitrov, 2006). Measurement invariance consists of introducing additional constraints to the factor solution, whereby the factor loadings that appear in Table 28 are fixed to be equal across all countries. The fit indexes of the constrained solution appear to be satisfactory (CFI=0.98, RMSEA= 0.046), pointing out that the factor solution is applicable in the countries considered in the dataset. With this information we are able to advance to the multilevel modelling of the justice ideologies.

The explanatory models for both ideologies are presented in Table 29. As in the analysis of the perceived gap, I present three models for each variable: model 1 for status, model 2 adds controls and model 3 includes income inequality. An initial interesting aspect in model 1 for both ideologies is the differential impact of status variables, with a general positive effect in the case of individualism and a negative one for egalitarianism. Even though this result could lead one to postulate a rational base for the preference of some distributive norms (Wegener & Liebig, 1995b), we need to look at the amount of variance explained, which is much smaller in the case of individualism. Therefore, in general the preference for individualism appears to be less status dependent when compared to egalitarianism, an argument in the line of the general *primary* character of the former and the *secondary* of the latter (Wegener, 1999). That is, the general preference for distribution according to market rules (Lane, 1986) seems less influenced by structural factors than the one for egalitarian redistribution.

Table 29: Multilevel regression models for egalitarianism and individualism

	Egalitarianism			Individualism		
	(1)	(2)	(3)	(1)	(2)	(3)
Status Variables						
Household income	-0.03**	-0.03**	-0.03**	0.02**	0.05**	0.05**
	(17.96)	(16.98)	(16.98)	(5.39)	(4.83)	(4.82)
Household size	0.01**	0.01**	0.01**	-0.01**	-0.01	-0.01
	(4.49)	(5.40)	(5.38)	(2.99)	(1.79)	(1.83)
Education (Ref=CAS 1)						
CAS2	-0.06**	-0.05**	-0.05**	-0.02	-0.01	-0.01
	(6.04)	(4.24)	(4.23)	(1.27)	(0.38)	(0.30)
CAS3	-0.15**	-0.14**	-0.14**	-0.00	0.02	0.02
	(12.24)	(10.55)	(10.55)	(0.14)	(0.82)	(0.88)
Subjective standing	-0.05**	-0.05**	-0.05**	0.05**	0.05**	0.05**
	(20.80)	(20.33)	(20.32)	(12.73)	(12.49)	(12.54)
Control Variables						
Female (Ref=Male)		0.08**	0.08**		-0.11**	-0.11**
		(10.29)	(10.29)		(8.25)	(8.25)
Age		0.01**	0.01**		-0.00	-0.00
		(4.92)	(4.93)		(0.95)	(0.93)
Age²		-0.00**	-0.00**		0.00	0.00
		(3.74)	(3.75)		(1.48)	(1.47)
Unemployed		0.02	0.02		-0.02	-0.02
(Ref= other emp. status)		(1.13)	(1.13)		(0.64)	(0.64)
Catholic		0.01	0.01		0.05*	0.05*
(Ref= other religion)		(0.75)	(0.75)		(2.35)	(2.33)
Context variable						
Gini index			0.34			2.79**
			(0.80)			(3.51)
Constant	0.45**	0.21**	0.09	-0.33**	-0.29**	-1.21**
	(10.81)	(4.07)	(0.63)	(3.65)	(2.75)	(4.35)
R² individual level	0.07	0.08	0.08	0.01	0.02	0.02
R² country level	0.32	0.33	0.34	-0.04[1]	-0.04[1]	0.30
Log Likelihood	-19,027.60	-18,950.54	-18,950.23	-33,136.49	-33,094.77	-33,089.73
N (individuals)	22,932	22,932	22,932	22,932	22,932	22,932
N(countries)	26	26	26	26	26	26

Unstandardized coefficients, maximum likelihood estimation, absolute z statistics in parentheses, * $p < 0.05$, ** $p < 0.01$. Rho null model=0.15 both for individualism and egalitarianism. R² based on a comparison with the null model (Bryk & Raudenbush, 1992b).
[1] A negative R² is possible in this modelling framework given that the inclusion of an additional predictor can increase the magnitude of the variance components.

Adding control variables in models 2 does not produce substantial change in the previous parameter estimates. Considering control variables it is interesting to note that women express consistently less preference for individualism and more for egalitarianism, which is in part probably associated with socialization factors (given that the model is under control of status variables). In line with the cultural character of individualism, we see the influence of belonging to a particular religion (catholic) in the preference for this ideology.

A further argument along the line of the primary character of individualism refers to the role of individual-level variables in explaining country differences, as reflected in the R^2 for country level units. In egalitarianism 32% of country variation is explained by individual variables, whereas in the case of individualism this is close to 0%. This means, egalitarianism is to an important extent associated with structural intra-country characteristics, whereas individualism is significantly associated with between-countries' inequality level, raising the country-level explained variance to 30% in model 3 when including Gini. In other words, individuals in highly unequal societies are not comparatively more egalitarian, but actually more individualistic. Previous research in international comparison has considered such predominance of the individualistic ideology as legitimacy of inequality (Jost et al., 2003; Jost & Major, 2001a; Lane, 1986). With the empirical evidence presented here we can extend this idea to the cross country level, where we observe that countries with higher inequality – where by definition the majority is not benefiting from the distributive system – exhibit the most support for the distribution based on individual-meritocratic principles.

6.2.3 Multilevel analysis of the just earnings gap

Table 30 reports the corresponding estimation of multilevel models for the just earnings gap, following the hierarchical structure of the tables presented in previous sections. As noted in model 1, all status variables reveal a positive significant influence on the just earnings gap. The negative effect of household size is also considered as part of the general positive effect of income (as discussed before in the section on inequality perception), since it implies that a smaller proportional amount of income per household member is related to less preference for income inequality. The overall positive effect of status variables has a particular meaning in the context of this research, since the influence these variables on the just earnings gap represents the *consensual dimension* in the explanatory model of legitimacy. Since status variables depict a positive influence, the general consensus hypothesis does not hold at a cross national level. In preliminary terms, the lack of consensus can be interpreted as a sign of general debilitated legitimacy of inequality. But as previously pointed out, we still have to incorporate additional elements of the model (i.e. perceptions and ideologies) and then assess whether this lack of consensus still holds. As we saw in the last chapter, signs of consensus appeared in the Chilean case only when perceptual variables were incorporated, i.e. status differences regarding inequality preferences were explained by the status dependency of perception. The generalizability of this finding will be analyzed in the next section when introducing perception of inequality as a predictor of the just earnings gap.

Table 30: Multilevel regression models of the just earnings gap

	(1)	(2)	(3)
Status Variables			
Household income	0.04**	0.043**	0.04**
	(14.54)	(14.19)	(14.24)
Household size	-0.05**	-0.03**	-0.03**
	(11.10)	(6.49)	(6.57)
Education (Ref=CAS 1)			
CAS2	0.06**	0.13**	0.13**
	(3.61)	(7.09)	(7.15)
CAS3	0.13**	0.21**	0.21**
	(6.25)	(9.69)	(9.71)
Subjective standing	0.02**	0.01**	0.01**
	(3.95)	(3.66)	(3.66)
Control Variables			
Female (Ref=Male)		-0.14**	-0.14**
		(11.92)	(11.92)
Age		0.00	0.00
		(0.88)	(0.91)
Age²		0.00	0.00
		(1.83)	(1.81)
Unemployed		0.02	0.02
(Ref= other emp. status)		(0.59)	(0.59)
Catholic		-0.02	-0.02
(Ref= other religion)		(1.29)	(1.27)
Context variable			
Gini index			3.42**
			(5.02)
Constant	1.33**	1.13**	0.01
	(14.84)	(11.12)	(0.02)
R² individual level	0.03	0.05	0.05
R² country level	-0.08	-0.08	0.45
Log Likelihood	-20,985.561	-20,818.891	-20,810.092
N (respondents)	17,523	17,523	17,523
N(countries)	26	26	26

Unstandardized coefficients, maximum likelihood estimation, absolute z statistics in parentheses, * p < 0.05, ** p< 0.01. Rho null model=0.21. R² based on a comparison with the null model (Bryk & Raudenbush, 1992b).

Adding control variables in model 2 does not imply significant changes in status parameters. The explanatory power of the individual level variables reaches 5%, which means that despite significant predictors, most of the individual variance remains unexplained. In contrast to the individual level, including Gini in the last model raises the amount of country level explained variance to 45%, meaning that almost half of the variance in the just earnings gap is explained by differences in income inequality. This finding supports one of the main hypotheses of this research in terms of legitimacy, namely *that individuals of countries with high inequality in average prefer larger earnings inequality*. As argued in chapter three, this finding is grounded on theories that argue for the existential determination of justice preferences, i.e., justice preferences are to an important extent context dependent.

6.3 MULTIDIMENSIONAL LEGITIMACY IN A MULTILEVEL-SEM FRAMEWORK

This section constitutes the last part of the empirical analysis, aimed at testing the overall explanatory model of legitimacy. On the one hand, this means including perceptions of inequality and justice ideologies as explanatory variables of the just earnings gap, in order to establish their contribution to explaining legitimacy in a cross national scenario. On the other hand, it implies incorporating the consensual dimension into the analysis, i.e. including the analysis of consensual legitimacy across countries. This combination of theoretical constructs requires at the same time a combination of methodological approaches, since both the multilevel character of the data and the endogenous character of some variables in the model must be taken into account. Multilevel structural equation models (Curran, 2003; Longford & B. Muthén, 1992; B. Muthén, 1994; Mehta & Neale, 2005), in short M-SEM, are suited for the analysis of data under these conditions, since they permit considering relationships among a series of causal relationships in path models (addressing the endogeneity issue), and simultaneously tackle the contextual dependency of datasets with hierarchical structure. The use of this type of analysis is relatively new in comparative social research (Heck & Thomas, 2009), and to my knowledge there are no publications to date applying this methodology to cross national public opinion studies.

6.3.1 The influence of perception and ideologies on the just earnings gap at a cross national level

The idea behind M-SEM analysis applied to the multidimensional model of legitimacy can be represented graphically by decomposing the model into two levels, *within* and *between* countries, as depicted in the following schema:

Figure 15: Multilevel SEM of the explanatory model of legitimacy

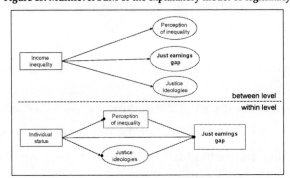

The schema depicts a simplified representation of the explanatory relationships in the two levels of analysis. Following the standards for graphical representation of SEM models (B. Muthén & L. Muthén, 2007), directly measured variables are depicted in a square form, whereas latent variables are circle shaped (such as the justice ideologies at the individual level). In the lower part of the figure we observe associations at the *within* (individual) level, which actually correspond to the model addressed in the previous chapter for the Chilean case with data from the ISJP. This *within* model is associated with the consensual dimension of legitimacy, whereby the objective is to measure the consensus with regard to the distribution of earnings despite the respondent's status differences. This consensus in the just earnings gap is evaluated in relation to perception of inequality and the justice ideologies of individualism and egalitarianism (which appear as a single variable to simplify the representation). The *between level* section incorporates income inequality as a predictor, which corresponds to the *contextual legitimacy* hypotheses. At this level the focus is on international comparison, i.e. to what extent income inequality can explain country differences in the dependent (and endogenous) variables: perception of inequality, justice ideologies and the just gap. The incorporation of income inequality as a predictor is actually what was presented in the previous section separately for each dependent variable, and that now is intended to be modeled altogether. At this level the dependent variables correspond to the intercepts of the regression models that are allowed to vary freely across countries, i.e. they are random intercepts in multilevel language. The variables are represented as latent (circles) since random intercepts are not directly measured but estimated based on variance components (Curran, 2003; Skrondal & Rabe-Hesketh, 2004).

Table 31 presents the results of the estimated multilevel structural equation models:

Table 31: Multilevel SEM models of the perceived gap, justice ideologies and the just earnings gap

	Perceived gap (1)	Individualism (2)	Egalitarianism (3)	Just gap (4)
Status Variables				
Household income	0.04**	0.02**	-0.06**	0.01**
	(6.33)	(2.96)	(-9.48)	(3.23)
Household size	-0.04**	-0.01	0.01**	-0.02**
	(-6.20)	(-1.40)	(3.31)	(-5.93)
Education (Ref=CAS 1)				
CAS2	0.10**	0.01	-0.14**	-0.02
	(4.79)	(0.40)	(-6.79)	(-1.09)
CAS3	0.20**	0.02	-0.27**	-0.03
	(6.88)	(0.58)	(-6.92)	(-1.18)
Subjective standing	-0.03**	0.06**	-0.08**	0.01*
	(-3.03)	(7.94)	(-9.02)	(2.01)
Context variable				
Gini index	4.61**	3.16**	0.59	3.36**
	(3.89)	(3.08)	(0.83)	(6.48)
Endogenous variables				
Perceived gap				0.50**
				(21.39)
Individualism				0.07**
				(7.76)
Egalitarianism				-0.21**
				(-8.53)
R^2 individual level	0.02	0.02	0.17	0.37
R^2 country level	0.38	0.32	0.02	0.48
N (respondents)	17,874	17,874	17,874	17,874
N(countries)	26	26	26	26

Model fit:
X^2: 510.9, df(41), P-Value=0.00. CFI: 0.95 RMSEA: 0.025

Unstandardized coefficients, MLR estimation, absolute z statistics in parentheses, * $p < 0.05$, ** $p < 0.01$.

The first three models depict the influence of status and inequality variables on the perceived gap, individualism and egalitarianism, correspondingly[71]. In general the significance of the coefficients and the explained variance replicate the models of the previous section, therefore the attention is focused on model 4 which represents the

---

[71] Control variables were excluded for reasons of parsimony and to avoid convergence problems.

influence of status variables, justice ideologies and perception of inequality on the just earnings gap, as represented in Figure 15. The influence of the perceived inequality on the just inequality that was reported for the Chilean case is also applicable in an internationally comparative framework: people that perceive higher inequality also prefer higher inequality in the different countries considered in this analysis. Justice ideologies also present similar influences on the just gap: individualists support larger income differences, whereas the opposite applies to egalitarians. Comparing the effects of ideologies and perception, the larger z value in the case of perception indicates its stronger influence as predictor, also similar to the analysis of the ISJP Chilean data.

A general conclusion from this cross national model is that the legitimacy of inequality in Chile is therefore not grounded on unexplained particularities in the society that lead people of this country to prefer higher inequality. Rather, it is influenced by a general tendency whereby the context level inequality influences the perception of it, whereas at the same time the perception has a positive impact on the preferences for inequality. In other words, context matters for justice standards, and this is reflected in the significant positive influence of the Gini index on the just earnings gap. Even a high level of income inequality as a context-existential determinant appears to be a stronger determinant than utopian standards of justice (i.e. justice ideologies), leading people of contexts with high inequality to prefer larger income differences, i.e. to a more extended legitimacy of economic inequality.

6.3.2 The consensual dimension of legitimacy in international comparison

This chapter has been focused so far on the influence of context level variables in the legitimacy of economic inequality, i.e. contextual legitimacy. The objective of this last part of the empirical analysis is to incorporate the consensual dimension of legitimacy in an international comparative framework. The consensual dimension was the main aspect of analysis in the chapter on the Chilean case, and now it will be extended to an international comparative level by analyzing the variations of consensus across countries. The starting point of the analysis is the final model of the last section (Table 31, model 4), where we observe that the effect of a status variable such as income (in combination with household size) is still significant. The significant influence of income means that there is no evidence of overall consensus regarding the legitimacy of inequality. Nevertheless, this model does not provide information regarding whether the lack of consensus is something that occurs in each country, or whether there are significant differences across countries in consensual legitimacy, i.e. variations of consensus. The following graph illustrates the variations of consensus based on the influence of income on the just gap in each country:

Graph 15: Country fitted regression lines of just gap on income deciles (empirical Bayes prediction)

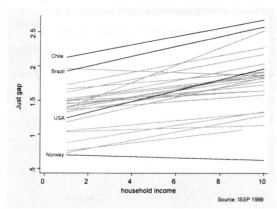

Each line on the plot represents the association between household income and the just earning gap in a particular country (some of them highlighted as reference), estimated by empirical Bayes prediction[72]. We observe that the regression lines have different intercepts, since they are allowed to vary across countries. The random intercepts represent what has been considered in the multilevel models of previous sections in this chapter, whereby the evidence indicates that the intercepts have positive covariation with income inequality, i.e. countries with higher inequality prefer a larger earning gap. But in previous models the assumption was that the slope(s) coefficient(s) was equal (or fixed) across countries. The influence of household income on the just gap was assumed to be the same in each country – in graphical terms, parallel regression lines. In this section I relax this restrictive

---

[72] Empirical Bayes prediction is an estimation of the Best Linear Unbiased Predictor (BLUPS) for the random effects in multilevel models (Skrondal & Rabe-Hesketh, 2005).

assumption and the slopes are allowed to vary, i.e. they are random slopes (Heck & Thomas, 2009; Kreft & de Leeuw, 1998; Skrondal & Rabe-Hesketh, 2005). As we observe in Graph 15 the fitted regression lines reveal some variation in their slopes. Still most of them depict a positive slope, i.e. from this image it appears that in most societies there is not consensus regarding the just earning gap across household income groups.

Two aspects derived from the previous descriptive observations constitute the inquiries for the analysis in this section: (i) whether variations of consensus are significant across countries, and (ii) to what extent variations of consensus are explained by income inequality level of the respective countries. This last point acquires relevance in reference to the analysis of the Chilean case, since it is still not clear whether consensus regarding earnings inequality in this country is something particular to this case, or whether consensus is somehow in general related to high levels of inequality. The empirical test of the variations of consensus according to inequality level is possible in a multilevel framework, by including two particular features in the model: random slopes and cross level interactions. Figure 16 is an illustration of the multilevel model including both features:

Figure 16: Variations of consensus across countries in multilevel SEM framework

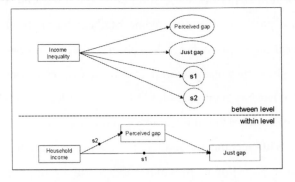

The schema is based on the previous version of the multilevel SEM diagram (Figure 15), but now includes random slopes, denoted as s1 and s2. The first random slope (s1) is added as a dot on the path from income to the just earnings gap representing variations of consensus. This means, this slope is no longer fixed but will be allowed to vary across countries. The random slope s1 also appears as a (latent) variable at

210

the between level predicted by income inequality, representing the influence of income inequality on the variations of consensus, so-called cross level interaction (Kreft & de Leeuw, 1998). An additional slope is allowed to be random in the path from household income to the perceived gap (s2), which is also predicted by income inequality at the between level model. Since perception of inequality constitutes a central variable in explaining legitimacy (as reported in the Chilean case), the objective of setting this additional slope as random is to explore the role of perception in explaining variations of consensus at cross national level[73].

I begin the presentation of the models attending first to perceptions of inequality (s2), and then I proceed to analyze how perception of inequality is related to the variations of consensus across countries (s1). Table 32 presents two models with the perceived earnings gap as the dependent variable. Model 1 introduces the household income as a random slope, bearing a significant increase in the fit of the model (as seen in the deviance test). This is interpreted as that the influence of income on perception significantly varies across countries. Model 2 tests to what extent country variations are explained by the level of income inequality by introducing a cross level interaction (Gini x household income).

Table 32: Random slope and cross level interaction in the perceived earnings gap

	(1)	(2)
Household income	0.04**	-0.02
(random effect)	(5.12)	(-1.10)
Gini index	4.10*	3.62**
	(2.56)	(3.10)
Cross level interaction		
Gini x income		0.16**
		(3.86)
Log likelihood	-26,761,91	-26,759,21
Deviance (df)	92.34 (1)**	5.40 (1) *
N (respondents)	19,529	19,529
N(countries)	26	26

Unstandardized coefficients, MLR estimation, absolute z statistics in parentheses, * p < 0.05, ** p< 0.01. Deviance test model 1 in reference to model with household income as fixed effect (LL -26,808.08).

---

[73] Justice ideologies are not considered in the analysis for parsimony reasons and also because of computation problems for parameter estimates when including latent variables in multilevel models with random slopes and cross level interactions.

The positive and significant value of the coefficient means that in countries with higher inequality there is a larger influence of status (represented by household income) on the perceptions of inequality. From previous models there was already evidence that perceptions of inequality are status dependent, but now model 2 additionally indicates that the status dependency of perceptions is even stronger in more unequal societies. In other words, poor people in Chile or Brazil perceive less inequality (relative to rich people) than poor people in Norway or Germany. Having considered the variations of inequality perception across countries, the second step of the analysis corresponds to the estimation of multilevel models for the variations of consensus across countries (s1 in Figure 16).

Table 33 presents three multilevel models with the just earnings gap as a dependent variable:

Table 33: Variations of consensus, cross level interaction and influence of inequality perceptions

	Just gap (1)	Just gap (2)	Just gap (3)
Household income	0.03**	0.04**	0.05**
(*random effect*)	(6.01)	(3.03)	(4.04)
Perceived gap	0.49**	0.49**	0.49**
	(20.97)	(20.90)	(21.02)
Gini index	3.11**	3.16**	3.23**
	(6.66)	(6.97)	(2.69)
Cross level interactions			
Gini x income		-0.03	-0.12**
		(-1.10)	(-2.62)
Gini x Perceived gap			0.48**
			(21.02)
Log likelihood	-47,519	-47,519	-47,455
Deviance (df)	38 (1)**	0 (1)	128 (2)**
N (respondents)	20,455	20,455	20,455
N(countries)	26	26	26

Unstandardized coefficients, MLR estimation, absolute z statistics in parentheses, * $p < 0.05$, ** $p < 0.01$. Deviance test model 1 in reference to model with HH income as fixed effect (LL -47,538).

Models 1 and 2 are similar to the ones presented for the perceived gap in Table 32. Model 1 adds a random slope to the household income variable, which according to the deviance test signifies an increase in the fit. In other words, the country variations in consensus represented in Graph 15 are significant. Nevertheless, country differences are not related to the level of income inequality, according to the lack of significance of the cross level interaction in model 2. This means, even though the influence of income on the just earnings gap differs from country to country, there is not evidence of higher consensus in societies with higher inequality[74].

The two first models are referred to what I have called the absolute consensus, meaning the direct influence of status variables on the just earnings gap. But as we know from the analysis of the Chilean case, consensus can also be considered as relative to perception of inequality, so-called *relative consensus*. Evidence from the ISJP Chilean data showed that there are not significant differences between status groups regarding what they consider just as relative to what they perceive. Model 3 translates the relative consensus to a cross national setting, introducing perceived earnings gap as a predictor of the variations of consensus across countries. Models of Table 32 indicated that perception of inequality (influenced by status) varies across countries, and the objective of model 3 is to explore whether this variation or random slope (s2) has an influence on the variations of consensus across countries (s1). Actually, when introducing perception as a (random slope) predictor in model 3, we observe that the cross level interaction turns out to be significantly negative. To understand this effect it is necessary to consider first that the direct effect of income on the just gap is still positive, depicted in Graph 15 as that most of the country regression lines have a positive slope. When introducing perceptions of inequality in model 3, there is a negative variation of the slopes, i.e. they tend to be less steep (more parallel to the X axis), which is considered an influence in the direction of consensus. Therefore, the evidence points out that countries with higher income inequality show higher consensus relative to perception than less unequal countries.

The variability in inequality perceptions between countries constitutes one of the key aspects in explaining legitimacy of inequality in countries with high inequality, which can be represented as follows:

---

[74] Probably other context variables could be used to explain country differences in this regard, which is out of the scope of this research and remains open for future studies.

Figure 17: Perceived and just gap with cross national variation

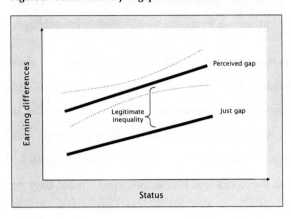

The graph is a schematic illustration of the relationship between status and both perceived and just gaps similar to the one presented in Chapter 5 (see Figure 12), but now adds dotted lines representing the variations of the perceived gap according to status (as a random slope across countries). According to the cross level interaction of model 2 in Table 32, the steepness of the slope can be explained based on the inequality level of the country, being steeper the higher the context level inequality, whereas in countries with lower inequality the slope tends to level off (parallel to the X axis). As a consequence, *the difference between the perceived and the just inequality appears to become smaller in low status groups in more unequal countries.* In the framework of the multidimensional model of legitimacy, this evidence is interpreted as a tendency to higher legitimacy of inequality both in the contextual and the consensual dimensions in countries with a high level of income inequality, which can be considered as an extension of the *consensus relative to perception* to the cross national level.

6.4 SUMMARY

This chapter dealt with the empirical study of the legitimacy of economic inequality in international comparison. The focus of the empirical analysis was the influence of the income inequality level on people's justifications of income inequality which, in the framework of the multidimensional model of legitimacy, corresponds to the *contextual dimension*. The analysis of the ISSP data showed evidence that in societies with high inequality people on average prefer larger income differences, in line with the contextual legitimacy hypothesis. As in the previous chapter, two concepts were considered to advance the explanation of legitimacy: perceptions of inequality and justice ideologies. Perceptions of inequality showed up to be status dependent and have a strong impact on the just earnings gap, replicating the results of the Chilean case now in an international setting. On the other hand, hypotheses regarding justice ideologies receive only partial support. Even though individualism depicts a positive influence on the preferences for larger inequalities at a country level, ideologies play a subordinate role in explaining legitimacy when compared to the perception of inequality. Therefore, existential standards as the income inequality level and perception of inequality play a predominant role in comparison to utopian standards in form of justice ideologies. Justice is first and foremost justice in context, and people in contexts with high inequality report a different conception of justice than those in societies with lower inequality. As a result, in the countries under study, economic inequality appears more legitimate in those societies with larger economic differences.

SUMMARY AND DISCUSSION

This research was aimed at the empirical study of the legitimacy of economic inequality with a focus on Chile as a case study, guided by the question: *How does a high level of economic inequality influence the legitimacy of inequality?* The central hypothesis adopted an alternative perspective to traditional views that typically predict a crisis in legitimacy in contexts of high inequality. Instead, this research was oriented by the proposal that individual perceptions and beliefs play a chief role in legitimacy processes while simultaneously being strongly influenced by context characteristics. *Context influences* refer to those individual normative preferences regarding economic inequality bounded to the current distribution of their social reality, which would lead those living in societies with a high level of inequality to comparatively prefer higher inequality.

The focus on the impact of a high level of inequality on legitimacy is the reason for the examination of the case of Chile, as it is one of the countries with the highest indexes of income inequality worldwide. After conducting empirical analysis, two conclusions can be drawn regarding the research question, based on the two legitimacy dimensions under study (consensual and contextual legitimacy). The first

216

one is that there is *partial* evidence of a consensus regarding distribution in a country with a high level of inequality such as Chile, related to the hypothesis of *consensual legitimacy*. The adjective *partial* means that although there is not absolute consensus regarding differences in earnings, there is evidence of consensus relative to the perception of economic inequality; that is, individuals agree on the differences between perceived earnings and just earnings. The second conclusion is that a preference for economic inequality is not particular to Chile, as it acquires a more general character when contemplated within an international comparative framework: countries with higher levels of economic inequality tend to exhibit a preference for larger occupational earning differences, associated to the hypothesis of *contextual legitimacy*.

The empirical approach for the research question required a conceptual framework for explaining the phenomenon of legitimacy. In accordance with Kurt Lewins' famous saying that *nothing is as practical as a good theory*, the first section of this study consisted of a theoretical discussion regarding the definition of a concept of legitimacy suitable for empirical research. The theoretical and empirical proposals of this study constituted the two areas around which this final summary and discussion is organized. I begin with the theoretical contributions, centered on the multidimensional concept of legitimacy and its link with social justice research. In a second point I highlight the issues regarding the empirical implementation and the repercussion of the research results, both for the Chilean case as well as in a cross-national scenario. In both the theoretical and empirical sections, I comment on several critical aspects and include proposals for future studies.

A. THEORETICAL LINKS: LEGITIMACY, INEQUALITY, AND SOCIAL JUSTICE

The starting point for the generation of an explanatory model of legitimacy was the diffuse character of this concept in the literature. After a first review of the different definitions, objects, and levels associated with the term *legitimacy* in the social sciences, I could well understand Beetham's remark about legitimacy literature: "I was very confused myself." Despite its diffuse character, the growing use of the concept of legitimacy in theoretical discussion and the empirical literature reflects that it accounts for a relevant social phenomenon that is not reduced to similar concepts such as support, obedience, or endorsement. There is something unique in the concept of legitimacy that accounts for situations that appear to contradict rational interests, including the suppression of the individual will on behalf of an external rule, as reflected in the Weberian expression of *voluntary submission*. It is certainly the reference to such a paradoxical situation the origin of the numerous theoretical debates and the confusion in several empirical attempts for the study of legitimacy, but at the same it is what keeps maintaining the attractive and unique character of the concept.

Beetham's multidimensional concept of legitimacy represents an important step for bridging the gap between theoretical and empirical perspectives. With the identification of different aspects or dimensions of legitimacy, the multidimensional concept not only offers guidelines for empirical research but also aids understanding the contribution of previous empirical approaches that have addressed several layers of a single phenomenon. In this framework, the confusion in the legitimacy literature can be attributed to the fact that several approaches restrict legitimacy to the study of some kind of belief (as Easton's *diffuse support*), which Beetham attributes to the original Weberian notion of *Legitimitätsglaube*. The proposal of the use of a multidimensional concept of legitimacy is precisely aimed at overcoming the restrictive consideration of legitimacy as solely a belief by including other aspects such as *consent* and *conformity*, which were redefined for empirical implementation in this study as subjective (belief/justification), consensual (consent), and contextual (conformity) dimensions.

Having identified the dimensions of legitimacy that must be taken into account in empirical research, the next task consisted of determining the means of measuring the legitimacy of inequality in a society, i.e. based on survey data. The first challenge was specifying the subjective dimension of legitimacy, which Beetham argued must refer to the capacity to justify a particular rule. The assessment of the individual justification of inequality represents the link between legitimacy and social justice

218

studies. Based on the accumulated knowledge of empirical social justice, I proposed an operationalization of the subjective dimension of legitimacy based on responses to survey questions assessing just occupational earnings. Regarding the measurement of the consensual dimension, support for earnings inequality despite status differences could be considered an indication of consensus. The contextual dimension can be empirically assessed by contrasting individual preferences for inequality with the level of the economic inequality of the society.

Two aspects of the empirical implementation of Beetham's concept require additional discussion: the definition of *consent* as *consensus* and the consideration of *income inequality level* as the only context predictor. Regarding the first aspect, the consensual dimension of legitimacy is related to the notion of consent proposed by Beetham. Nevertheless, by *consent* Beetham mostly means *actions* that denote endorsement of the rules, not precisely an *overall consensus* as it was conceived in this research. The proposal of consensus as consent is based on the one hand on methodological difficulties in assessing concrete actions reflecting endorsement in public opinion research. But on the other hand, although it would have been possible to consider variables as political participation or voting behavior as indicating consent, this would have meant changing the focus of the research to a different dependent variable. Therefore, I opted to concentrate on the justice of earnings as the main object of study, leaving open the consideration of consent as actions denoting endorsement for future research.

The second aspect refers to income inequality as a context predictor. The strong association between income inequality and individual beliefs regarding distribution provides support for the central research hypothesis, but at the same time opens a series of new questions. One of these questions concerns the direction of the causality, which the first chapter addressed by arguing that the determinants of income inequality are mostly related to the position of a country within the global economic order, and as such is not strongly impacted by individual preferences. Even though I subscribe to this argument, it might well be that individual preferences, primarily affected by context standards, play then a role in the maintenance of inequality. Such a proposal requires additional research for its empirical assessment, ideally based on time-series-cross-section or panel datasets including societies with high levels of inequality, a type of data that currently does not exist. A further question that emerges refers to the inclusion of context predictors other than income inequality, such as gross domestic product (GDP), the human development index (HDI), democracy indicators, among others. The specific focus only in income inequality as context predictor was intended for calling the attention into this indicator for legitimacy research, and on the other hand the inclusion of additional context variables run into methodological limitations due to the small number of countries in the dataset (ISSP), which also remains open to be overcome in further studies.

Overall, my view of the multidimensional concept is that it constitutes a general framework for empirical legitimacy studies that embraces areas beyond those examined in this study. As such, its application is not restricted to the area of economic inequality, but it could also be extended to the study of legitimacy of authorities and political systems. In the area of economic inequality, the conceptual model could also be expanded by considering additional explanatory concepts for consensus and/or alternative standards for contextual legitimacy as predictors. In this sense, the multidimensional model opens several possibilities for new research initiatives while simultaneously inspiring further theoretical–empirical exchange in the area of legitimacy.

B. THE EMPIRICAL APPROACH TO THE LEGITIMACY OF ECONOMIC INEQUALITY

Despite numerous theoretical discussions concerning the assumed threat that economic inequality represents to social integration and political stability, attempts to deal with this topic empirically at a large society scale it still an uncommon enterprise in social sciences. This has led to an unbalanced presence of theoretical approaches in comparison with the empirical ones, even though several authors recognize that legitimacy is first and foremost a matter of empirical research.

220

Therefore, for the assessment of legitimacy in the Chilean case, it was not only necessary to tackle the definition of the concept, but most of all to deal with its empirical implementation. In this regard, the main contributions of this research can be summarized around three main points: the link between legitimacy and empirical social justice research, the empirical assessment of the utopian-existential debate, and the study of legitimacy at a country level based on public opinion studies.

Concerning the first point, this research proposed integration between social justice and legitimacy. The multidimensional approach to legitimacy allows for differentiation between justice and legitimacy by establishing that individual beliefs about justice belong to only one of the dimensions to take into account (the subjective dimension) in studying legitimacy. Therefore, the inclusion of the term *legitimacy* only makes sense when considering beliefs regarding justice in relationship to the distributive rules that characterize a society (the contextual dimension) or the degree of consensus among the population regarding the distributive rule (the consensual dimension). After addressing this basic distinction, it is possible to begin to integrate into legitimacy research the vast number of theoretical and empirical developments in social justice. Concepts such as justice ideologies, the perception of inequality, and the justice of earnings shed significant light into individual beliefs regarding inequality and distribution and offer the advantage of being operationalizable based on public opinion data, opening the door for legitimacy research on the scale of large societies.

The just earnings gap constitutes the central proposal for assessing the subjective dimension of the legitimacy of inequality based on social justice literature. This proposal possesses three main advantages. Firstly, by considering the ratio of earnings considered just for high- and low-status occupations, it enables an indirect approach to individual normative justice conceptions, decreasing the impact of the social desirability that characterizes direct questions regarding distribution. Second, by obtaining responses in currency units, it permits the attainment of a continuous variable. Third, the ratio term generates a comparable measure across countries, avoiding the need to calculate differences in currencies or standardize values. The

221

advantages of using a term associated with two simple questions should encourage its consideration in not only further public opinion studies of legitimacy, but also in other areas in which the just earnings gap could act as predictor variable.

The second aspect of discussion corresponds to the empirical approach regarding the utopian-existential debate in social justice. The existential determination of justice constitutes the core aspect of the argument regarding the legitimacy of inequality in contexts of high inequality, such as Chile. In other words, context matters as a reference standard for normative judgments. That context matters is something taken for granted in current social research, but still the relevant question to this regard is whether the context or *what is* keeps determining beliefs about *what ought to be* even in situations where the current distribution can lead to challenge utopian justice principles. This means, even accepting that context matters, it could be expected that utopian standards of equality begin to play a stronger role than existential standards in extreme situations of inequality. This debate is expressed in empirical terms in the counterpoint between justice ideologies (utopian standards) and the perception of inequality (existential standards). From this empirical implementation of the utopian-existential debate, the answer from this study is that although utopian standards play a relevant role, even in contexts of high levels of inequality such as Chile, standards of justice regarding distribution are predominantly existential: *what is* remains a central referent for *what ought to be*.

The preference for larger differences in earnings in Chile is undoubtedly a provocative finding. It raises a series of questions regarding traditional approaches used in legitimacy studies that highlight ideological domination and false consciousness phenomena as main explanatory concepts. As a counterpoint to traditional approaches, legitimacy here is mostly explained by contextual standards and perceptual phenomena; when the status dependency of perception is considered (i.e., low status individuals perceive less inequality), different status groups have similar views regarding a just distribution. Therefore, according to the empirical evidence, individuals need not be indoctrinated into supporting a high level of inequality; they simply do not perceive much inequality. I am aware that such an explanation gives economic inequality a deterministic character, making it appear a self-reproducing and static process with no possibility of changing. However, the purpose of this emphasis was to highlight an alternative explanation of the phenomenon of legitimacy and to open the debate in this area. On the other hand, this static character has been influenced by the analysis of cross-sectional data that did not offer the opportunity to examine time variations in legitimacy. With the availability of the ISSP 2009 dataset, which will include replication on countries with high levels of inequality such as Brazil and Chile, an opportunity will be provided to advance in understanding the dynamics of legitimacy by implementing time-series-cross-sectional analysis.

The third and last point to discuss concerning empirical contributions refers to innovations in analysis techniques, survey design, and data acquisition. The use of structural equations and multilevel-model techniques has enabled the analysis of legitimacy in its multidimensional character by allowing inclusion of individual and country-level data, latent constructs, and direct and indirect associations. This type of methods certainly entails a degree of complexity, but this effort is widely compensated by enabling an explanatory approach to the data analysis. By explanatory I refer to the possibility of hypothesis testing based on theoretically driven explanatory models, which encourages a growing exchange between the theoretical and empirical perspectives.

Regarding survey design, the implementation of a factorial survey in Chile in this study was without precedent outside Western academic institutions. Even though it was of an exploratory character, it offered an innovative way of studying the legitimacy of current differences in earnings and led to such findings as that the basic just salary corresponds to the current minimum salary. Again, the complexity of a questionnaire design as the factorial survey is rewarded by the insight it permits into the black box of justice judgments and the legitimacy of differences in earnings.

Last but not least is the issue of data acquisition. This research was implemented due to the possibility to collect data for a country that typically does not conduct specialized public opinion studies. The economic gap between countries discussed in the first chapter is also expressed in an academic gap, which in some particular research areas has exhibited paradoxical consequences: so far, empirical studies regarding the legitimacy of inequality have not focused on societies with high levels of inequality. Such disregard is not due to a lack of awareness but rather the difficulties in obtaining research funding and establishing academic cooperation. Overcoming these challenges requires special effort, which in this case meant devoting two years to collecting and preparing the Chilean data for its analysis with the supervision and strong support of the ISJP German research team. Having been involved in this process, I can well understand the difficulties associated with bridging this particular research gap and the lack of presence of a large part of the world in comparative specialized public opinion studies. Nevertheless, attending to the results of this study I recognize the growing importance of considering data from societies with different economic and political backgrounds, which allows the contrast with previous evidence and to advance in the generalizability of empirical results about the legitimacy of economic inequality.

Aalberg, T. (2003). *Achieving justice: comparative public opinion on income distribution*. Leiden: Brill.

Abercrombie, N. (1990). Popular culture and ideological effects. In N. Abercrombie, S. Hill, & B. Turner (Eds.), *Dominant Ideologies*. Boston: Unwin Hyman.

Abercrombie, N., Hill, S., & Turner, B. (1980). *The dominant ideology thesis*. London: Allen & Unwin.

Adamopoulos, J. (2008). On the Entanglement of Culture and Individual Behavior. In F. Vijver, D. Hemert, & Y. Poortinga (Eds.), *Multilevel Analysis of Individuals and Cultures* (pp. 27-62). New York: Lawrence Erlbaum Associates.

Adams, J. (1963). Towards an Understanding of Inequity. *Journal of Abnormal Psychology*, *67*, 422-36.

Adloff, F. (2005). Die Reziprozität der Gesellschaft - Zum Paradigma der Gabe in der Moderne. In M. Corsten, H. Rosa, & R. Schrader (Eds.), *Die Gerechtigkeit der Gesellschaft* (pp. 25-51). Wiesbaden: VS Verlag.

Aghion, P., Caroli, E., & Garcia-Peñalosa, C. (1999). Inequality and Economic Growth: The Perspective of the New Growth Theories. *Journal of Economic Literature*, *37*(4), 1615-1660.

Ajzen, I., & Fishbein, M. (1975). *Belief, Attitude, Intention, and Behavior. An Introduction to Theory and Research*. Massachusetts: Addison-Wesley.

Alderson, A., & Nielsen, F. (1999). Income Inequality, Development, and Dependence: A Reconsideration. *American Sociological Review*, *64*(4), 606–631.

Alexander, C., & Becker, H. (1978). The Use of Vignettes in Survey Research. *The Public Opinion Quarterly*, *42*(1), 93-104.

Altimir, O. (1996). Economic Development and Social Equity: A Latin American Perspective. *Journal of Interamerican Studies and World Affairs*, *38*(2/3), 47-71.

Alves, W. (1982). Modeling distributive justice judgements. In P. Rossi & S. Nock (Eds.),

Measuring Social Judgments: The Factorial Survey Approach. Beverly Hills: Sage.

Alves, W., & Rossi, P. (1978). Who Should Get What? Fairness Judgments of the Distribution of Earnings. *The American Journal of Sociology, 84*(3), 541-564.

Alwin, D., Gornev, G., & Khakhulina, L. (1995). Comparative Referential Structures, System Legitimacy, and Justice Sentiments: An International Comparison. In J. Kluegel, D. Mason, & B. Wegener (Eds.), *Social Justice and Political Change. Public Opinion in Capitalist and Post-Communist States* (pp. 109-130). New York: Aldine de Gruyter.

Alwin, D., & Wegener, B. (1995). Methods of the International Social Justice Project. In J. Kluegel, D. Mason, & B. Wegener (Eds.), *Social Justice and Political Change. Public Opinion in Capitalist and Post-Communist States* (pp. 321-330). New York: Aldine de Gruyter.

Amiel, Y., & Bishop, J. (2003). *Inequality, Welfare and Poverty: Theory and Measurement*. Boston: JAI.

Anderson, C. (2008). The Sensitive Left and the Impervious Right: Multilevel Models and the Politics of Inequality, Ideology, and Legitimacy in Europe. *Comparative Political Studies, 41*, 564-599.

Andreassen, T., Lorentzen, B., & Olsson, U. (2006). The Impact of Non-Normality and Estimation Methods in SEM on Satisfaction Research in Marketing. *Quality and Quantity, 40*(1), 39-58.

Aristotle. (1999). *Nichomaquean Ethics*. Kitchener: Batoche Books.

Arts, W., & Gelissen, J. (2001). Welfare States, Solidarity and Justice Principles: Does the Type Really Matter? *Acta Sociologica, 44*, 283-299.

Arts, W., Hermkens, P., & Wijck, V. (1991). Income and the Idea of Justice: Principles, Justice and Their Framing. *Journal of Economic Psychology, 12*, 121-140.

Arts, W., & van der Veen, R. (1992). Sociological Approaches to Distributive and Procedural Justice. In K. Scherer (Ed.), *Justice: Interdisciplinary Perspectives* (pp. 141-176). Cambridge: Cambridge University Press.

Arts, W., & Vermunt, R. (1989). New Directions in Social Stratification and Income Distribution: Introduction. *Social Justice Resarch, 3*(34), 181-186.

Arts, W., & van Wijck, P. (1989). Share and Share Alike? Social Constraints on Income Equalization. *Social Justice Research*, *3*(3), 233-249.

Atria, R. (2006). Crecimiento Económico Y Estratificación Social: Observaciones Sobre El Caso Caso Chileno. *Revista Chilena de Sociologia*, *20*, 45-68.

Austen, S. (2002). An International Comparison of Attitudes to Inequality. *Economics*, *29*(3), 218-237.

Barker, R. S. (2001). *Legitimating Identities: The Self-Presentation of Rulers and Subjects*. Cambridge: Cambridge University Press.

Baron, R., & Kenny, D. (1986). The Moderator-Mediator Variable Distinction in Social Psychological Research: Conceptual, Strategic, and Statistical Considerations. *Journal of Personality and Social Psychology*, *51*(6), 1173-1182.

Barry, B. (1989). *Theories of Justice*. Berkeley: University of California Press.

Bay, A., & Pedersen, A. (2006). The Limits of Social Solidarity: Basic Income, Immigration and the Legitimacy of the Universal Welfare State. *Acta Sociologica*, *49*(4), 419-436.

Beetham, D. (1991a). *The Legitimation of Power*. Hampshire: Palgrave.

Beetham, D. (1991b). Max Weber and the Legitimacy of the Modern State. *Analyse & Kritik*, (13), 34-45.

Beetham, D. (1993). In Defence of Legitimacy. *Political Studies*, *41*(3), 488-491.

Beetham, D. (2004). Political Legitimacy. In K. Nash & A. Scott (Eds.), *The Blackwell Companion to Political Sociology* (pp. 107-116). Oxford: Blackwell.

Bell, D. (1960). *The End of Ideology: On the Exhaustion of Political Ideas in the Fifties*. Glencoe, Illinois: Free Press.

Bell, D. (1972). On Equality: I. Meritocracy and Equality. *The Public Interest*, *29*, 29-68.

Bellei, C. (2005). *The Private-Public School Controversy: The Case of Chile*. Paper presented at the "Conference on Mobilizing the Private Sector for Public Education" (October, 5-6). Boston: Harvard University.

Ben-Ari, R., Schwarzwald, J., & Horiner-Levi, E. (1994). The Effects of Prevalent Social Stereotypes on Intergroup Attribution. *Journal of Cross-Cultural Psychology*, *25*(4),

489-500.

Berger, J., Fisek, M., & Norman, R. (1989). The Evolution of Status Expectations: A Theoretical Extension. In J. Berger, M. Zelditch, & B. Anderson (Eds.), *Sociological Theories in Progress. New Formulations* (pp. 100-130). Newbury Park: Sage.

Berger, J., Ridgeway, C., Fisek, M., & Norman, R. (1998). The Legitimation and Delegitimation of Power and Prestige Orders. *American Sociological Review, 63*(3), 379-405.

Berger, J., & Zelditch, M. (1998). *Status, Power, and Legitimacy: Strategies & Theories.* New Brunswick: Transaction Publishers.

Berger, J., Zelditch, M., Anderson, B., & Cohen, B. P. (1972). Structural Aspects of Distributive Justice: A Status Value Formulation. In J. Berger, M. Zelditch, & B. Anderson (Eds.), *Sociological Theories in Progress* (Vol. 2, pp. 119-246). New York: Houghton Mifflin.

Berger, P., & Luckmann, T. (1967). *The Social Construction of Reality.* New York: Anchor.

Bergesen, A., & Bata, M. (2002). Global and National Inequality: Are They Connected? *Journal of World-Systems Research, 8*(1), 130–144.

Berkowitz, L., & Walster, E. (1976). *Equity Theory: Toward a General Theory of Social Interaction.* New York: Academic Press.

Berman, J., & Murphy-Berman, V. (1996). Cultural Differences in Perceptions of Allocators of Resources. *Journal of Cross-Cultural Psychology, 27*(4), 494-509.

Berry, A. (1997). The Income Distribution Threat in Latin America. *Latin American Research Review, 32*(2), 3-40.

Berry, J. (1999). Emics and Etics: A Symbiotic Conception. *Culture & Psychology, 5*(2), 165-171.

Beyer, H., & Le Foulon, C. (2002). Un Recorrido por las Desigualdades Salariales en Chile. *Estudios Públicos, 85*, 139-75.

Beyer, H., Rojas, P., & Vergara, R. (2000). Apertura Comercial y Desigualdad Salarial en Chile. *Estudios Públicos, 77*, 69-95.

Birchfield, V., & Dion, M. (2007). *Income Inequality and Popular Support for Redistribution:*

A Cross-Regional and Global Perspective. Paper prepared for presentation at the Annual Conference of the International Sociological Association (September 6-8). Florence, Italy: University of Florence.

Blackburn, R., & Prandy, K. (1997). The Reproduction of Social Inequality. *Sociology, 31*(3), 491-509.

Blau, P. (1963). Critical Remarks on Weber's Theory of Authority. *The American Political Science Review, 57*(2), 305-316.

Blau, P., & Duncan, O. (1967). *The American Occupational Structure*. New York: Free Press.

Blomberg, H., & Kroll, C. (1999). Do Structural Contexts Matter? Macro-sociological Factors and Popular Attitudes towards Public Welfare Services. *Acta Sociologica, 42*(4), 319-335.

Blomström, M., & Hettne, B. (1987). *Development Theory in Transition*. London: Zed Books.

Boix, C., & Stokes, S. C. (2003). Endogenous Democratization. *World Politics, 55*(4), 517-549.

Bollen, K. (1983). World System Position, Dependency, and Democracy: The Cross-National Evidence. *American Sociological Review, 48*(4), 468-79.

Bollen, K. (1989). *Structural Equation Models with Latent Variables*. New York: Wiley & Sons.

Borge, L., & Rattsø, J. (2004). Income Distribution and Tax Structure: Empirical Test of the Meltzer-Richard Hypothesis. *European Economic Review, 48*(4), 805-826.

Borghi, E. (2005). *Trade Openness and Wage Distribution in Chile*. (Working Paper N°173). Centro di Ricerca sui Processi di Innovazione e Internazionalizzazione. Milano: Università Commerciale "Luigi Bocconi".

Bornschier, V., & Trezzini, B. (1996). Jenseits von Dependencia-versus Modernisierungstheorie: Differenzierungsprozesse in der Weltgesellschaft und ihre Erklärung. In H. Müller (Ed.), *Weltsystem und kulturelles Erbe*. (pp. 53-79). Berlin: Reimer.

Borzutzky, S. (2005). From Chicago to Santiago: Neoliberalism and Social Security Privatization in Chile. *Governance, 18*(4), 655-674.

Borzutzky, S. (2009). Anti-Poverty Politics in Chile: A Preliminary Assessment of the Chile Solidario Program. *Poverty & Public Policy*, *1*(1), 1-16.

Bourdieu, P. (1983). *Die feinen Unterschiede: Kritik der ges. Urteilskraft* (2nd ed.). Frankfurt a. M: Suhrkamp.

Bourguignon, F., & Morrisson, C. (2002). Inequality among World Citizens: 1820-1992. *The American Economic Review*, *92*(4), 727-744.

Bourricaud, F. (1987). Legitimacy and Legitimization. *Current Sociology*, *35*(2), 57-67.

Bowles, S. (1998). Endogenous Preferences: The Cultural Consequences of Markets and other Economic Institutions. *Journal of Economic Literature*, *36*(1), 75-111.

Braun, M., & Uher, R. (2003). The ISSP and its Approach to Background Variables. *Advances in Cross-National Comparison. A European Working Book for Demographic and Socio-Economic Variables*, 33-47.

Brauns, H., Scherer, S., & Steinmann, S. (2003). The CASMIN Educational Clasification in International Comparative Research. In J. Hoffmeyer-Zlotnik & C. Wolf (Eds.), *Advances in Cross-national Comparison: A European Working Book for Demographic and Socio-economic Variables*. New York: Kluwer Academic/Plenum Publishers.

Breen, R. (1997). Inequality, Economic Growth and Social Mobility. *The British Journal of Sociology*, *48*(3), 429-449.

Briceno-Leon, R. (2002). Introduction: Latin America - A Challenge for Sociology. *Current Sociology*, *50*(1), 9-18.

Brown, T. (2006). *Confirmatory Factor Analysis for Applied Research*. New York: The Guilford Press.

Bryk, A., & Raudenbush, S. (1992a). *Hierarchical linear models: Applications and data analysis methods*. London: Sage.

Bryk, A., & Raudenbush, S. (1992b). *Hierarchical Linear Models: Applications and Data Analysis Methods*. Newbury Park: Sage.

Brynin, M. (2003). Using CASMIN: the Effect of Education on Wages in Britain and Germany. In J. Hoffmeyer-Zlotnik & C. Wolf (Eds.), *Advances in Cross-National*

Comparison: A European Working Book for Demographic and Socio-Economic Variables. New York: Kluwer Academic/Plenum Publishers.

Bullock, H. (1999). Attributions for Poverty: A Comparison of Middle-Class and Welfare Recipient Attitudes. *Journal of Applied Social Psychology, 29*(10), 2059-2082.

Burgoyne, C., Routh, D., & Sidorenko-Stephenson, S. (1999). Perceptions, Attributions and Policy in the Economic Domain: A Theoretical and Comparative Analysis. *International Journal of Comparative Sociology, 40*(1), 79-93.

Burton, M., & Grusky, D. (1992). A Quantitative History of Comparative Stratification Research. *Contemporary Sociology, 21*(5), 623-631.

Calder, B. (1977). Endogenous-Exogenous Versus Internal-External Attributions: Implications for the Development of Attribution Theory. *Personality Social Psychological Bulletin, 3*(3), 400-406.

Campbell, R. (1983). Status Attainment Research: End of the Beginning or Beginning of the End? *Sociology of Education, 56*(1), 47-62.

Cancian, F. (1976). Social Stratification. *Annual Review of Anthropology, 5*(1), 227-248.

Cardoso, F., & Faletto, E. (1979). *Dependency and Development in Latin America.* Berkeley: University of California Press.

Carnoy, M. (1998). National Voucher Plans in Chile and Sweden: Did Privatization Reforms Make for Better Education? *Comparative Education Review, 42*(3), 309-337.

Castillo, J. (2007). *Legitimation and Justice Ideologies in Contexts of Extreme Economic Inequalities.* (International Social Justice Project - Working Paper N°125). Paper presented at the 30th conference of the International Society of Political Psychology (Portland, 4-7 July). Berlin: Humboldt University.

Castillo, J. (2009). ¿Cuál es la Brecha Salarial Justa? Opinión Pública y Legitimación de la Desigualdad Económica en Chile. *Estudios Públicos,* (113), 237-266.

Castillo, J., Gerlitz, J., & Schrenker, M. (2008). *Perception and Legitimacy of Income Inequality in International Comparison.* Paper presented at the Annual Meeting of the American Political Science Association (Boston, 28-31 August).

CEPAL. (2006). *Social Panorama of Latin America.* Santiago: CEPAL.

Chapman, G., & Johnson, E. (1999). Anchoring, Activation, and the Construction of Values. *Organizational Behavior and Human Decision Processes, 79*(2), 115-153.

Chase-Dunn, C. (1975). The Effects of International Economic Dependence on Development and Inequality: A Cross-National Study. *American Sociological Review, 40*(6), 720-738.

Cheal, D. (1979). Hegemony, Ideology and Contradictory Consciousness. *The Sociological Quarterly, 20*(1), 109-117.

Cheung, M., Leung, K., & Au, K. (2006). Evaluating Multilevel Models in Cross-Cultural Research: An Illustration with Social Axioms. *Journal of Cross-Cultural Psychology, 37*(5), 522-541.

Chiapello, E. (2003). Reconciling the Two Principal Meanings of the Notion of Ideology: The Example of the Concept of the `Spirit of Capitalism'. *European Journal of Social Theory, 6*(2), 155-171.

Chirot, D., & Hall, T. (1982). World-System Theory. *Annual Review of Sociology, 8*(1), 81-106.

Christoph, B., Jardin, G., Lippl, B., Stark, G., & Wegener, B. (1998). *Documentation of the German International Social Justice Project. Replication 1996* (International Social Justice Project - Working Paper N°37). Berlin: Humboldt University.

Cipriani, R. (1987). The Sociology of Legitimation: An Introduction. *Current Sociology, 35*(2), 1-20.

Citrin, J. (1977). Political Alienation as a Social Indicator: Attitudes and Action. *Social Indicators Research, 4*(1), 381-419.

Claps, D. (2007). *Flexibilidad Laboral desde la Perspectiva de la Dispersión Salarial, el caso de Chile a partir del Año 1990*. Santiago de Chile: Instituto Nacional de Estadisticas.

Coburn, D. (2000). Income Inequality, Social Cohesion and the Health Status of Populations: The role of Neo-liberalism. *Social Science & Medicine, 51*(1), 135-146.

Cohen, J., Hazelrigg, L., & Pope, W. (1975). De-Parsonizing Weber: A Critique of Parsons' Interpretation of Weber's Sociology. *American Sociological Review, 40*(2), 229-241.

Cohen, R. (1987). Distributive justice: Theory and research. *Social Justice Research, 1*(1), 19-

40.

Cohen, R., & Kennedy, P. (2000). *Global sociology*. Macmillan Houndmills, Basingstoke, Hampshire.

Coleman, J. S. (1986). Social Theory, Social Research, and a Theory of Action. *The American Journal of Sociology, 91*(6), 1309-1335.

Collier, S., & Sater, W. (1996). *A History of Chile, 1808-1994*. Cambridge: Cambridge University Press.

Collins, R. (1980). Weber's Last Theory of Capitalism: A Systematization. *American Sociological Review, 45*(6), 925-942.

Colodro, M. (2002). Gobernar los Cambios: Chile, más allá de la Crisis Cultura y Cambio Político en Chile. La Caja Negra de los 90. Santiago: LOM.

Contreras, D., Cooper, R., Herman, J., & Neilson, C. (2004). *Dinámica de la Pobreza y Movilidad Social: Chile 1996-2001*. Santiago de Chile: Departamento de Economía, Universidad de Chile.

Contreras, D., & Gallegos, S. (2007). *Descomponiendo la Desigualdad Salarial en América Latina:¿ Una Década de Cambios?* (Serie Estudios Estadisticos y Prospectivos N°59). Santiago de Chile: CEPAL.

Converse, P. (2004). The Nature of Belief Systems in Mass Publics. In J. Jost & J. Sidanius (Eds.), *Political Psychology* (pp. 177-199). New York: Psychology Press.

Cook, K. (1975). Expectations, Evaluations and Equity. *American Sociological Review, 40*(3), 372-388.

Cook, K. (1987). Toward a More Interdisciplinary Research Agenda: The Potential Contributions of Sociology. *Social Justice Research, 1*(1), 5-18.

Cook, K., & Hegtvedt, K. (1983). Distributive Justice, Equity, and Equality. *Annual Review of Sociology*, (9), 217-241.

Crompton, R. (1998). *Class and Social Stratification*. Cambridge: Polity Press.

Crosby, F. (1979). Relative Deprivation Revisited: A Response to Miller, Bolce, and Halligan. *The American Political Science Review, 73*(1), 103-112.

Cullen, B. (1992). Philosophical Theories of Justice. In K. Scherer (Ed.), *Justice. Interdisciplinary Perspectives* (pp. 15-64). Cambridge: Cambridge University Press.

Cumsille, G., & Garretón, M. (2000). *Percepciones Culturales de la Desigualdad*. Santiago: Mideplan.

Curran, P. J. (2003). Have Multilevel Models Been Structural Equation Models All Along? *Multivariate Behavioral Research, 38*(4), 529-569.

Dahrendorf, R. (1959). *Class and Class Conflict in Industrial Society*. Stanford: Stanford University Press.

Dalton, R. (1999). Critical Citizens: Global Support for Democratic Government. In *Political Support in Advanced Industrial Democracies* (pp. 57-77). Oxford: Oxford University Press.

d'Anjou, L., Steijn, A., & Van Aarsen, D. (1995). Social Position, Ideology, and Distributive Justice. *Social Justice Research, 8*(4), 351-384.

Davey, L., Bobocel, D., Son Hing, L., & Zanna, M. (1999). Preference for the Merit Principle Scale: An Individual Difference Measure of Distributive Justice Preferences. *Social Justice Research, 12*(3), 223-240.

Davis, K., & Moore, W. (1945). Some Principles of Stratification. *American Sociological Review, 10*(2), 242-249.

Davis, N., & Robinson, R. (1991). Men's and Women's Consciousness of Gender Inequality: Austria, West Germany, Great Britain, and the United States. *American Sociological Review, 56*(1), 72-84.

De Ferranti, D., Perry, G., Ferreira, F., Walton, M., Coady, D., Cunningham, W., Gasparini, L., et al. (2003). *Inequality in Latin America and the Caribbean: Breaking with History?* Washington: The World Bank.

Deephouse, D. (1996). Does Isomorphism Legitimate. *Academy of Management Journal, 39*(4), 1024-1039.

Deininger, K., & Squire, L. (1996). A New Data Set Measuring Income Inequality. *World Bank Economic Review, 10*(3), 565-591.

Delhey, J. (1999). *Inequality and Attitudes: Post-Communism, Western Capitalism and*

Beyond. Forschungsschwerpunktes Sozialer Wandel, Institutionen und Vermittlungsprozesse. Berlin: Wissenschaftszentrum Berlin für Sozialforschung (WZB).

Della Fave, R. (1974). On the Structure of Egalitarianism. *Social Problems, 22*(2), 199-213.

Della Fave, R. (1980). The Meek Shall Not Inherit the Earth: Self Evaluation and the Legitimacy of Stratification. *American Sociological Review, 45*(6), 955-971.

Della Fave, R. (1986a). The Dialectics of Legitimation and Counternorms. *Sociological Perspectives, 29*(4), 435-460.

Della Fave, R. (1986b). Toward an Explication of the Legitimacion Process. *Social Forces, 65*(2), 476-500.

Deutsch, M. (1975). Equity, Equality, and Need: What Determines Which Value Will Be Used as a Basis of Distributive Justice? *Journal of Social Issues, 31*(3), 137-150.

Devroye, D., & Freeman, R. (2001). *Does Inequality in Skills Explain Inequality in Earnings Across Advanced Countries?* (Working Paper N°8140). Cambridge: National Bureau of Economic Research.

Dewey, M. (2008). *Procedimientos fallidos* (Doctoral Dissertation). Rostock University.

DiMaggio, P., & Powell, W. (1991). *The New Institutionalism in Organizational Analysis.* Chicago: University of Chicago Press.

Dimitrov, D. (2006). Comparing Groups on Latent Variables: A Structural Equation Modeling Approach. *Work,* (26), 429-436.

Djilas, M. (1957). *The New Class: An Analysis of the Communist System.* New York: Praeger.

Donald, R., & Montiel, C. (1999). Poverty in Developing Nations: A Cross-Cultural Attributional Analysis. *European Journal of Social Psychology, 29*(7), 943-959.

Dornbusch, S., & Scott, W. (1975). *Evaluation and the Exercise of Authority.* San Francisco: Jossey-Bass Publishers.

Dowling, J., & Pfeffer, J. (1975). Organizational Legitimacy: Social Values and Organizational Behavior. *Pacific Sociological Review, 18*(1), 122-136.

Durkheim, É. (1982). *The Rules of the Sociological Method.* New York: Free Press.

Durkheim, É. (1988). *Über soziale Arbeitsteilung: Studie über die Organisation höherer Gesellschaften* (2nd ed.). Frankfurt/M: Suhrkamp.

Dworkin, R. (1981). What is Equality? Part 2: Equality of Resources. *Philosophy and Public Affairs, 10*(4), 283-345.

Dworkin, R. (2000). *Sovereign Virtue: The Theory and Practice of Equality*. Cambridge: Harvard University Press.

Dyer, N. G., Hanges, P. J., & Hall, R. J. (2005). Applying Multilevel Confirmatory Factor Analysis Techniques to the Study of Leadership. *The Leadership Quarterly, 16*(1), 149-167.

Easton, D. (1965). *A Systems Analysis of Political Life*. New York: Wiley & Sons.

Easton, D. (1975). A Re-Assessment of the Concept of Political Support. *British Journal of Political Science, 5*(4), 435-457.

Easton, D. (1976). Theoretical Approaches to Political Support. *Canadian Journal of Political Science/Revue canadienne de science politique, 9*(3), 431-448.

Elizaga, R. (2006). Sociology and the South: The Latin American Experience. *Current Sociology, 54*(3), 413-425.

Elsbach, K. (2001). The Architecture of Legitimacy: Constructing Accounts of Organizational Controversies. In J. Jost & B. Major (Eds.), *The Psychology of Legitimacy*. Cambridge: Cambridge University Press.

Elsbach, K., & Sutton, R. (1992). Acquiring Organizational Legitimacy through Illegitimate Actions: A Marriage of Institutional and Impression Management Theories. *Academy of Management Journal, 35*(4), 699-738.

Elster, J. (1995). The Empirical Study of Justice. In D. Miller & M. Walzer (Eds.), *Pluralism, Justice and Equality* (pp. 81-99). Oxford: Oxford University Press.

Epp, A. (1998). *Divergierende Konzepte von "Verfahrensgerechtigkeit": Eine Kritik der procedural-justice-forschung* (Forschungsschwerpunkt Technik, Arbeit, Umwelt). Berlin: Wissenschaftszentrum Berlin für Sozialforschung (WZB).

Erikson, R., & Goldthorpe, J. (1992). *The Constant Flux: A Study of Class Mobility in Industrial Societies*. Oxford: Clarendon Press.

Erikson, R., Goldthorpe, J., & Portocarrero, L. (1979). Intergenerational Class Mobility in Three Western European Societies: England, France and Sweden. *The British Journal of Sociology, 30*(4), 415-441.

Escobar, P. (2003). The New Labor Market: The Effects of the Neoliberal Experiment in Chile. *Latin American Perspectives, 30*(5), 70-78.

Esping-Andersen, G. (1990). *The Three Worlds of Welfare Capitalism*. Cambridge: Polity Press.

Esping-Andersen, G. (2007). More Inequality and Fewer Opportunities? Structural Determinants and Human Agency in the Dinamics of Income Distribution. In D. Held & A. Kaya (Eds.), *Global Inequality: Patterns and Explanations* (pp. 216-251). Cambridge: Polity press.

Evans, M., & Kelley, J. (2004). Subjective Social Location: Data From 21 Nations. *International Journal of Public Opinion Research, 16*(1), 3-38.

Evans, M., & Kelley, J. (2006). *Economic Development and Inequality Attitudes: The Long Shadow of the Past*. Paper presented at the annual meeting of the American Sociological Association (Montreal, 10-14 August).

Feagin, J. (1972). When it Comes to Poverty, it's Still,God Helps Those Who Help Themselves.'. *Psychology Today, 6*, 101-129.

Featherstone, M. (1987). Lifestyle and Consumer Culture. *Theory Culture Society, 4*(1), 55-70.

Festinger, L. (1962). *A Theory of Cognitive Dissonance*. Stanford: Stanford University Press.

Filgueira, C. (2001). *La Actualidad de Viejas Temáticas: Sobre los Estudios de Clase, Estratificación y Movilidad Social en América Latina* (No. 51). Serie Politicas Sociales. Santiago de Chile: CEPAL.

Finch, J. (1987). The Vignette Technique in Survey Research. *Sociology, 21*(1), 105-114.

Firebaugh, G. (1999). Empirics of World Income Inequality. *American Journal of Sociology, 104*(6), 1597-1630.

Fleischacker, S. (2004). *A Short History of Distributive Justice*. Cambridge, MA: Harvard University Press.

Fletcher, J., & Howe, P. (2002). *A Structural Model of Specific and Diffuse Support for the Supreme Court of Canada*. Paper presented at the Annual Meeting of the American Political Science Association (August 31st). Boston.

Flora, D., & Curran, P. (2004). An Empirical Evaluation of Alternative Methods of Estimation for Confirmatory Factor Analysis with Ordinal Data. *Psychological Methods, 9*(4), 466-491.

Folger, R. (1984). Emerging Issues in the Social Psychology of Justice. In R. Folger (Ed.), *The Sense of Injustice: Social Psychological Perspectives*. New York: Plenum Press.

Foner, A. (1979). Ascribed and Achieved Bases of Stratification. *Annual Review of Sociology, 5*(1), 219-242.

Forster, M., Jesuit, D., & Smeeding, T. (2005). Regional Poverty and Income Inequality in Central and Eastern Europe: Evidence from the Luxembourg Income Study. In R. Kanbur & A. Venables (Eds.), *Spatial Inequality and Development*. Oxford: Oxford University Press.

Fox, T. G., & Miller, S. M. (1965). Economic, Political and Social Determinants of Mobility: An International Cross-Sectional Analysis. *Acta Sociologica, 9*(1), 76-93.

Frank, A. (1979). *Dependent Accumulation and Underdevelopment*. New York: Monthly Review Pr.

Frank, A. (2000). The Development of Underdevelopment. In S. Corbridge (Ed.), *Development: Critical Concepts in the Social Sciences*. New York: Routledge.

Fraser, J. (1974). Validating a Measure of National Political Legitimacy. *American Journal of Political Science, 18*(1), 117-134.

Frazier, P. A., Tix, A. P., & Barron, K. E. (2004). Testing Moderator and Mediator Effects in Counseling Psychology Research. *Journal of Counseling Psychology, 51*(1), 115-134.

Frohlich, N., Oppenheimer, J., & Eavey, C. (1987). Choices of Principles of Distributive Justice in Experimental Groups. *American Journal of Political Science, 31*(3), 606-637.

Ganzeboom, H., & Treiman, D. (1996). Internationally Comparable Measures of Occupational Status for the 1988 International Standard Classification of Occupations.

Social Science Research, 25(3), 201-239.

Ganzeboom, H., & Treiman, D. (2003). Three Internationally Standarized Measures for Comparative Research on Occupational Status. In J. Hoffmeyer-Zlotnik & C. Wolf (Eds.), *Advances in Cross-national Comparison: A European Working Book for Demographic and Socio-economic Variables* (pp. 150-193). New York: Kluwer Academic/Plenum Publishers.

Ganzeboom, H., Treiman, D., & Ultee, W. (1991). Comparative Intergenerational Stratification Research: Three Generations and Beyond. *Annual Review of Sociology, 17*, 277-302.

Gargarella, R. (1999). Las Teorías de la Justicia Después De Rawls: Un Breve Manual de Filosofía Política. Buenos Aires: Editorial Paidós.

Garretón, M., & Cumsille, G. (2002). Las Percepciones de la Desigualdad en Chile. *Revista Proposiciones, 34*, 1-9.

Gaviria, A. (2007). Social Mobility and Preferences for Redistribution in Latin America. *Economía, 8*(1), 55-96.

Gelman, A., & Hill, J. (2007). *Data Analysis Using Regression and Multilevel/Hierarchical Models*. Analytical methods for social research. Cambridge: Cambridge University Press.

Gibson, J., Caldeira, G., & Spence, L. (2005). Why Do People Accept Public Policies They Oppose? Testing Legitimacy Theory with a Survey-Based Experiment. *Political Research Quarterly, 58*(2), 187-201.

Giddens, A. (1979). *Central Problems in Social Theory. Action, Structure and Contradiction in Social Analysis.* Berkeley: University of California Press.

Gijsberts, M. (1999). *The Legitimation of Inequality in State-Socialist and Market Societies, 1987-1996*. Amsterdam: Thela Thesis.

Gilley, B. (2006a). The Meaning and Measure of State Legitimacy: Results for 72 Countries. *European Journal of Political Research, 45*(3), 499-525.

Gilley, B. (2006b). The Determinants of State Legitimacy: Results for 72 Countries. *International Political Science Review/ Revue internationale de science pol, 27*(1), 47-

71.

Glaser, J. (2005). Intergroup Bias and Inequity: Legitimizing Beliefs and Policy Attitudes. *Social Justice Research*, *18*(3), 257-282.

Goesling, B. (2001). Changing Income Inequalities within and between Nations: New Evidence. *American Sociological Review*, *66*(5), 745-761.

Goldthorpe, J. (2003). Progress in Sociology: The Case of Social Mobility Research. Oxford: Sociology Working Papers.

Góngora, M. (1975). Urban Social Stratification in Colonial Chile. *The Hispanic American Historical Review*, *55*(3), 421-448.

Gottschalk, P., & Joyce, M. (1998). Cross-National Differences in the Rise in Earnings Inequality: Market and Institutional Factors. *The Review of Economics and Statistics*, *80*(4), 489-502.

Gottschalk, P., & Smeeding, T. (1997). Cross-National Comparisons of Earnings and Income Inequality. *Journal of Economic Literature*, *35*(2), 633-687.

Grafstein, R. (1981). The Failure of Weber's Conception of Legitimacy: Its Causes and Implications. *The Journal of Politics*, *43*(2), 456-472.

Gramsci, A. (1971). *Selections from the Prison Notebooks*. London: Lawrence & Wishart.

Greenland, S. (2000). Principles of Multilevel Modelling. *International Journal of Epidemiology*, *29*(1), 158-167.

Greenwald, B., & Stiglitz, J. (1987). Keynesian, New Keynesian and New Classical Economics. *Oxford Economic Papers*, *39*(1), 119-133.

Greif, A. (1994). Cultural Beliefs and the Organization of Society: A Historical and Theoretical Reflection on Collectivist and Individualist Societies. *The Journal of Political Economy*, *102*(5), 912-950.

Griffith, B. (2006). *The Paradox of Neoliberalism: A Critique of the Washington Consensus in the Age of Globalization* (Doctoral Dissertation). Connecticut College.

Grimes, M. (2006). Organizing Consent: The Role of Procedural Fairness in Political Trust and Compliance. *European Journal of Political Research*, *45*(2), 285-315.

Grimes, M. (2008). Consent, Political Trust and Compliance: Rejoinder to Kaina's Remarks on 'Organizing Consent'. *European Journal of Political Research, 47*(4), 522-535.

Gronow, J. (1988). The Element of Irrationality: Max Weber's Diagnosis of Modern Culture. *Acta Sociologica, 31*(4), 319-331.

Groß, M. (2003). Educational Systems and Perceived Social Inequality. *European Societies, 5*(2), 193-225.

Grusky, D. (1994). *Social Stratification: Class, Race, and Gender in Sociological Perspective*. Boulder: Westview Press.

Grusky, D. (2001). The Past, Present, and Future of Social Inequality. In D. Grusky (Ed.), *Social Stratification: Class, Race, and Gender in Sociological Perspective*. Boulder: Westview Press.

Grusky, D. (2006). *Social Stratification*. Center for the Study of Inequality, Cornell University.

Grusky, D., & Kanbur, R. (2006). *Poverty and Inequality*. California: Stanford University Press.

Grusky, D., & Sorensen, J. (1998). Can Class Analysis Be Salvaged? *The American Journal of Sociology, 103*(5), 1187-1234.

Gurr, T. (1971). *Why Men Rebel*. Princeton: Princeton University Press.

Habermas, J. (1973). *Legitimationsprobleme im Spätkapitalismus* (1st ed.). Frankfurt a. M: Suhrkamp.

Hadler, M. (2004). Die Mehrebenen-Analyse. Ihre praktische Anwendung und theoretische Annahmen. *Osterreichische Zeitschrift für Soziologie, 29*(1), 53-74.

Hadler, M. (2005). Why Do People Accept Different Income Ratios? *Acta Sociologica, 48*(242), 131-154.

Hall, P., & Taylor, R. (1996). *Political Science and the Three New Institutionalisms* (MPIFG Discussion Paper 96/6). Köln: Max-Planck-Institut für Gesellschaftsforschung.

Haller, M. (1989). Die Klassenstruktur im sozialen Bewußtsein. Ergebnisse vergleichender Umfrageforschung zu Ungleichheitsvorstellungen. In M. Haller, H. Hoffman-Nowottny, & W. Zapf (Eds.), *Kultur und Gesellschaft* (pp. 447-469). Frankfurt:

Campus.

Haller, M., Mach, B., & Zwicky, H. (1995). Egalitarismus und Antiegalitarismus zwischen gesellschaftlichen Interessen und kulturellen Leitbildern. In H. Müller & B. Wegener (Eds.), *Soziale Ungleichheit und soziale Gerechtigkeit* (pp. 7-49). Opladen: Leske+ Budrich.

Hans, S. (2006). *Die Analyse gepoolter Daten mit Mehrebenenmodellen* (Arbeitsbericht N°6). Berliner Studien zur Soziologie Europas. Berlin: Freie Universität zu Berlin.

Harkness, J., Klein, S., & Scholz, E. (2003). *ISSP Study Monitoring 1999* (ZUMA Methodenbericht 2003/03). Manheim: ZUMA.

Hasse, K. (2002). Gerechtigkeit und Unparteilichkeit. Zum Verhältnis von normativen und empirischen Theorien der Gerechtigkeit. In S. Liebig & H. Lengfeld (Eds.), *Interdiziplinäre Gerechtigkeitsforschung. Zur Verknüpfung empirischer und normativer Perspektive* (pp. 219-242). Frankfurt: Campus.

Haug, M. (1977). Measurement in Social Stratification. *Annual Review of Sociology, 3*(1), 51-77.

Hauss, K., Mika, T., & Wegener, B. (2000). *Documentation of the German International Social Justice Project. Replication 2000* (International Social Justice Project - Technical Report 75). Berlin: Humboldt University.

von Hayek, F. (1976). *Law, Legislation and Liberty*. London: Routledge & Kegan Paul.

Headey, B. (1991). Distributive Justice and Occupational Incomes: Perceptions of Justice Determine Perceptions of Fact. *The British Journal of Sociology, 42*(4), 581-596.

Heck, R., & Thomas, S. (1999). *An Introduction to Multilevel Modeling Techniques*. Mahwah, NJ: Lawrence Erlbaum.

Heck, R., & Thomas, S. (2009). *An Introduction to Multilevel Modeling Techniques* (2nd ed.). New York: Routledge.

Hegtvedt, K. (1992). When is a Distribution Rule Just? *Rationality and Society, 4*(3), 308-331.

Hegtvedt, K. (2006). Justice Frameworks. In P. J. Burke (Ed.), *Contemporary Social Psychological Theories* (pp. 46-69). Stanford: Stanford Social Sciences.

Hegtvedt, K., Clay-Warner, J., & Johnson, C. (2003). The Social Context of Responses to Injustice: Considering the Indirect and Direct Effects of Group-Level Factors. *Social Justice Research, 16*(4), 343-366.

Hegtvedt, K., & Johnson, C. (2000). Justice beyond the Individual: A Future with Legitimation. *Social Psychology Quarterly, 63*(4), 298-311.

Held, D., & Kaya, A. (2007). *Global Inequality: Patterns and Explanations.* Cambridge: Polity Press.

Helfrich, H. (1999). Beyond the Dilemma of Cross-Cultural Psychology: Resolving the Tension between Etic and Emic Approaches. *Culture & Psychology, 5*(2), 131-153.

Herbert, S. (2003). Review of Trust in the Law: Encouraging Public Cooperation with the Police and Courts. *Social Forces, 82*(2), 840-841.

Hermkes, P., & Boerman, F. (1989). Consensus with Respect to the Fairness of Income: Differences Between Social Groups. *Social Justice Resarch, 3*(35), 201-215.

Hochschild, J. (1981). *What's Fair?: American Beliefs about Distributive Justice.* Cambridge: Harvard University Press.

Hoffman, E. (2003). International Statistical Comparison of Occupational and Social Structures. In J. Hoffmeyer-Zlotnik & C. Wolf (Eds.), *Advances in Cross-national Comparison: A European Working Book for Demographic and Socio-economic Variables.* New York: Kluwer Academic/Plenum Publishers.

Hoffman, K., & Centeno, M. (2003). The Lopsided Continent: Inequality in Latin America. *Annual Review of Sociology, 29*(1), 363-390.

Hoffmeyer-Zlotnik, J. (2003). The Classification of Education as a Sociological Background Characteristic. In J. Hoffmeyer-Zlotnik & C. Wolf (Eds.), *Advances in Cross-national Comparison: A European Working Book for Demographic and Socio-economic Variables.* New York: Kluwer Academic/Plenum Publishers.

Hofstede, G. (2001). *Culture's Consequences: Comparing Values, Behaviors, Institutions, and Organizations Across Nations* (2nd ed.). Thousand Oaks: Sage.

Hojman, D. (1996). Poverty and Inequality in Chile: Are Democratic Politics and Neoliberal Economics Good for You? *Journal of Interamerican Studies and World Affairs, 38*(2),

73-96.

Hollander, J. A., & Howard, J. A. (2000). Social Psychological Theories on Social Inequalities. *Social Psychology Quarterly, 63*(4), 338-351.

Holmes, S. (1982). Two Concepts of Legitimacy: France after the Revolution. *Political Theory, 10*(2), 165-183.

Homans, G. (1961). *Social Behavior: Its Elementary Forms*. New York: Harcourt, Brace & World.

Homans, G. (1976). Commentary. In L. Berkowitz & E. Walster (Eds.), *Equity Theory: Toward a General Theory of Social Interaction* (pp. 231-244). New York: Academic Press.

Hornsey, M., Spears, R., Cremers, I., & Hogg, M. (2003). Relations Between High and Low Power Groups: The Importance of Legitimacy. *Personality and Social Psychology Bulletin, 29*(2), 216-227.

Horton, J. (1966). Order and Conflict Theories of Social Problems as Competing Ideologies. *The American Journal of Sociology, 71*(6), 701-713.

Howard, J. A. (1994). A Social Cognitive Conception of Social Structure. *Social Psychology Quarterly, 57*(3), 210-227.

Howe, C. (1992). *Political Ideology and Class Formation: A Study of the Middle Class*. Westport: Praeger.

Hu, L., & Bentler, P. (1998). Fit Indices in Covariance Structure Modeling: Sensitivity to Underparameterized Model Misspecification. *Psychological methods, 3*(4), 424-453.

Hu, L., & Bentler, P. (1999). Cutoff Criteria for Fit Indexes in Covariance Structure Analysis: Conventional Criteria Versus new Alternatives. *Structural Equation Modeling, 6*(1), 1-55.

Huber, J., & Form, W. (1973). *Income and Ideology: An Analysis of the American Political Formula*. New York: Free Press.

Huber, J., Form, W., & Pease, J. (1970). Income and Stratification Ideology: Beliefs About the American Opportunity Structure. *The American Journal of Sociology, 75*(4), 703-716.

Iglesias, E. (2006). El Papel del Estado y los Paradigmas Economicos en America Latina. *Revista de la Cepal, 90,* 7-15.

ILO. (2008a). *Income Inequalities in the Age of Financial Globalization.* World of Work Report. Geneva: International Labor Organization.

ILO. (2008b). *Minimum Wages and Collective Bargaining: Towards Policy Coherence* (Global Wage Report 2008/09). Geneva: International Labour Office.

INE. (2007). *Ingresos de Personas y Hogares Chile 2007.* Santiago de Chile: Instituto Nacional de Estadisticas.

Inglehart, R., & Baker, W. (2000). Modernization, Cultural Change, and the Persistence of Traditional Values. *American Sociological Review, 65*(1), 19-51.

Inglehart, R., & Welzel, C. (2005). *Modernization, cultural change, and democracy: The human development sequence.* Cambridge Univ Pr.

Izzo, A. (1987). Legitimation and Society: A Critical Review. *Current Sociology, 35*(2), 41-56.

Jackman, M., & Muha, M. (1984). Education and Intergroup Attitudes: Moral Enlightenment, Superficial Democratic Commitment, or Ideological Refinement?. *American Sociological Review, 49*(6), 751-69.

Jackson, B. (2005). The Conceptual History of Social Justice. *Political Studies Review, 3*(3), 356-373.

Jacowitz, K., & Kahneman, D. (1995). Measures of Anchoring in Estimation Tasks. *Personality and Social Psychology Bulletin, 21*(1), 1161-1166.

Jasso, G. (1978). On the Justice of Earnings: A New Specification of the Justice Evaluation Function. *American Journal of Sociology, 83*(6), 1398-1419.

Jasso, G. (1980). A New Theory of Distributive Justice. *American Sociological Review, 45*(1), 3-32.

Jasso, G. (1981). Further Notes on the Theory of Distributive Justice. *American Sociological Review, 46*(3), 352-360.

Jasso, G. (1989). The Theory of the Distributive-Justice Force in Human Affairs: Analyzing the Three Central Questions. In J. Berger, M. Zelditch, & B. Anderson (Eds.),

Sociological Theories in Progress (pp. 354-387). Newbury Park: Sage.

Jasso, G. (1999). How Much Injustice Is There in the World? Two New Justice Indexes. *American Sociological Review, 64*(1), 133-168.

Jasso, G. (2000). Trends in the Experience of Injustice: Justice Indexes About Earnings in Six Societies, 1991-1996. *Social Justice Research, 13*(2), 101-121.

Jasso, G. (2006a). Factorial Survey Methods for Studying Beliefs and Judgments. *Sociological Methods & Research, 34*(3), 334.

Jasso, G. (2006b). *Theoretical Unification in Justice and Beyond.* Presentation at the 11th International Social Justice Conference in Berlin 2.-5. August, .

Jasso, G. (2007). *Studying Justice: Measurement, Estimation, and Analysis of the Actual Reward and the Just Reward* (IZA Discussion Paper Series N°2592). Bonn: Institute for the Study of Labor.

Jasso, G., & Rossi, P. (1977). Distributive Justice and Earned Income. *American Sociological Review, 42*(4), 639-651.

Jasso, G., & Wegener, B. (1997). Methods for Empirical Justice Analysis: Part 1. Framework, Models, and Quantities. *Social Justice Research, 10*(4), 393-430.

Johnson, C., Dowd, T., & Ridgeway, C. (2006). Legitimacy as a Social Process. *Annual Review of Sociology, 32*, 53-78.

Johnson, D. (1981). Economism and Determinism in Dependency Theory. *Latin American Perspectives, 8*(3), 30-31.

Jöreskog, K., & Sorbom, D. (1986). *LISREL VI; Analysis of Linear Structural Relationships by Maximum Likelihood, Instrumental Variables, and Least Squares.* Uppsala: University of Uppsala.

Jöreskog, K. G. (1970). A General Method for Analysis of Covariance Structures. *Biometrika, 57*(2), 239-251.

Jost, J. (2002). *System Justification Theory as Compliment, Complement, and Corrective to Theories of Social Identification and Social Dominance* (Research Paper N°1672). Stanford: Stanford University.

Jost, J., Blount, S., Pfeffer, J., & Hunyady, G. (2003). Fair Market Ideology: Its Cognitive-

Motivational Underpinnings. *Research in Organizational Behavior, 25*, 53-91.

Jost, J., & Hunyady, O. (2003). The Psychology of System Justification and the Palliative Function of Ideology. *European Review of Social Psychology, 13*, 111-153.

Jost, J., & Major, B. (2001a). *The Psychology of Legitimacy*. Cambridge: Cambridge University Press.

Jost, J., & Major, B. (2001b). Emerging Perspectives on the Psychology of Legitimacy. In J. Jost & B. Major (Eds.), *The Psychology of Legitimacy*. Cambridge: Cambridge University Press.

Jost, J., Pelham, B., Sheldon, O., & Ni Sullivan, B. (2003). Social Inequality and the Reduction of Ideological Dissonance on Behalf of the System: Evidence of Enhanced System Justification Among the Disadvantaged. *European Journal of Social Psychology, 33*, 13-36.

Kaina, V. (2008). Legitimacy, Trust and Procedural Fairness: Remarks on Marcia Grimes' Study. *European Journal of Political Research, 47*(4), 510-521.

Kaminsky, G., & Pereira, A. (1996). The Debt Crisis: Lessons of the 1980s for the 1990s. *Journal of Development Economics, 50*(1), 1-24.

Kay, C. (1979). Review: Chile Since 1920. *Latin American Research Review, 14*(3), 264-279.

Kay, C. (1993). For a Renewal of Development Studies: Latin American Theories and Neoliberalism in the Era of Structural Adjustment. *Third World Quarterly, 14*(4), 691-702.

Keith, R. (1971). Encomienda, Hacienda and Corregimiento in Spanish America: A Structural Analysis. *The Hispanic American Historical Review, 51*(3), 431-446.

Kelley, J., & Evans, M. (1993). The Legitimation of Inequality: Occupational Earnings in Nine Nations. *The American Journal of Sociology, 99*(1), 75-125.

Kelley, J., & Zagorski, K. (2004). Economic Change and the Legitimation of Inequality: The Transition from Socialism to Free Market in Central-East Europe. *Research in Social Stratification and Mobility, 22*, 319-364.

Kenworthy, L. (1999). Do Social-Welfare Policies Reduce Poverty? A Cross-National Assessment. *Social Forces, 77*(3), 1119-1139.

Kenworthy, L. (2007). Inequality and Sociology. *American Behavioral Scientist, 50*(5), 584-602.

Kerbo, H. (1991). *Social Stratification and Inequality: Class Conflict in Historical and Comparative Perspective.* New York: McGraw-Hill.

Kerckhoff, A. (1995). Social Stratification and Mobility Processes. In K. S. Cook, G. A. Fine, & J. S. House (Eds.), *Sociological Perspectives on Social Psychology* (pp. 476-496). Boston: Allyn and Bacon.

Kiecolt, K. (1988). Recent Developments in Attitudes and Social Structure. *Annual Review of Sociology, 14*(167), 381-403.

Kluegel, J. (1989). *Perceptions of Justice in the Us: Split Consciousness Among the American Public.* Paper presented at the Conference on Perception of Social Justice in East and West. Dubrovnik.

Kluegel, J., Csepeli, G., Kolosi, T., Orkeny, A., & Nemenyi, M. (1995). Accounting for the Rich and the Poor: Existencial Justice in Comparative Perspective. In J. Kluegel, D. Mason, & B. Wegener (Eds.), *Social Justice and Political Change: Public Opinion in Capitalist and Post-Communist States* (pp. 179-207). New York: Aldine de Gruyter.

Kluegel, J., Mason, D., & Wegener, B. (1995). *Social Justice and Political Change: Public Opinion in Capitalist and Post-Communist States.* New York: Aldine de Gruyter.

Kluegel, J., Mason, D., & Wegener, B. (1999). The Legitimation of Capitalism in the Postcommunist Transition: Public Opinion about Market Justice, 1991-1996. *European Sociological Review, 15*(3), 251-283.

Kluegel, J., & Smith, E. (1981). Beliefs About Stratification. *Annual Review of Sociology, 7,* 29-56.

Kluegel, J., & Smith, E. (1986). *Beliefs About Inequality: Americans' Views of What Is and What Ought to Be.* New York: Aldine de Gruyter.

Kopp, M., & Müller, H. P. (1980). *Herrschaft und Legitimität in modernen Industriegesellschaften: Eine Untersuchung der Ansätze von Max Weber, Niklas Luhmann, Claus Offe, Jürgen Habermas.* München: Tuduv-Verlagsgesellschaft.

Korpi, W., & Palme, J. (1998). The Paradox of Redistribution and Strategies of Equality:

Welfare State Institutions, Inequality, and Poverty in the Western Countries. *American Sociological Review, 63*(5), 661-687.

Korzeniewicz, R., & Moran, T. (1997). World-Economic Trends in the Distribution of Income, 1965-1992. *The American Journal of Sociology, 102*(4), 1000-1039.

Korzeniewicz, R., & Smith, W. (2000). Poverty, Inequality, and Growth in Latin America: Searching for the High Road to Globalization. *Latin American Research Review, 35*(3), 7-54.

Kraatz, M., & Zajuac, E. (1996). Exploring the Limits of the New Institutionalism: The Causes and Consequences of Illegitimate Organizational Change. *American sociological review, 61*(5), 812-836.

Krebs, A. (2000). *Gleichheit oder Gerechtigkeit*. Frankfurt/Main: Suhrkamp.

Kreft, I., & de Leeuw, J. (1998). *Introducing Multilevel Modeling*. London: Sage.

Kreidl, M. (2000a). *What Make Inequalities Legitimate? an International Comparison*. Sociological Papers. Prag: Academy of Sciences of the Czech Republic.

Kreidl, M. (2000b). Perceptions of Poverty and Wealth in Western and Post-Communist Countries. *Social Justice Research, 13*(2), 151-176.

Kremermann, M. (2004). *Distribución de Ingreso en Chile: Una Bomba de Tiempo*. Santiago de Chile: Fundacion Terram.

Kuhn, A. (2005). *Subjective Evaluations of Wage Inequality and Preferences for Redistribution*. Zurich: Institute for Empirical Research in Economics.

Kuznets, S. (1955). Economic Growth and Income Inequality. *The American Economic Review, 45*(1), 1-28.

Lagos, M. (2005). *Informe Latinobarómetro 1995-2005*. Santiago de Chile: Corporacion Latinobarómetro.

Lane, R. (1959). The Fear of Equality. *American Political Science Review, 53*(1), 35-51.

Lane, R. (1962). *Political Ideology: Why the American Common Man Believes what He Does*. New York: Free Press.

Lane, R. (1986). Market Justice, Political Justice. *The American Political Science Review,*

80(2), 383-402.

Larraín, J. (1983). *The Concept of Ideology*. Vermont: Gregg Revivals.

Laurell, A. (2000). Structural Adjustment and the Globalization of Social Policy in Latin America. *International Sociology, 15*(2), 306-325.

Lechner, N. (1999). Los Desafios de la Gobernabilidad en una Sociedad Gobal. Mexico: Flacso.

Legewie, J., Gerlitz, J., Mühleck, K., Scheller, P., & Schrenker, M. (2006). *Documentation of the German International Social Justice Project. Replication 2006* (International Social Justice Project - Working Paper N°118). Berlin: Humboldt University.

Lehmann, C., & Hinzpeter, X. (2000). *Los Pobres No Pueden Esperar, La Desigualdad Si*. Puntos de Referencia. Santiago de Chile: Centro de Estudios Públicos.

Lehmann, C., & Hinzpeter, X. (2001). *Los Pobres No Pueden Esperar, La Desigualdad Si (parte II)*. Puntos de Referencia. Santiago de Chile: Centro de Estudios Públicos.

Lenski, G. (1966). *Power and Privilege: A Theory of Social Stratification*. New York: McGraw-HIll.

Lerner, M. (1980). *The Belief in a Just World. A Fundamental Delusion*. New York: Plenum Press.

Leventhal, G. (1976). *What Should Be Done with Equity Theory? New Approaches to the Study of Fairness in Social Relationships*. Michigan: Wayne State University.

Lichbach, M. (1989). An Evaluation of "Does Economic Inequality Breed Political Conflict?" Studies. *World Politics, 41*(4), 431-470.

Liebig, S., & Lengfeld, H. (2002). *Interdisziplinäre Gerechtigkeitsforschung: Zur Verknüpfung empirischer und normativer Perspektiven*. Frankfurt/Main: Campus.

Liebig, S., Lengfeld, H., & Mau, S. (2001). *Interdisciplinary Social Justice Research*. ISJR-Newsletter. International Society for Justice Research.

Lind, E., & Tyler, T. (1988). *The Social Psychology of Procedural Justice*. New York: Plenum Press.

Linz, J. (1988). Legitimacy of Democracy and the Socioeconomic System. In M. Dogan

(Ed.), *Comparing Pluralist Democracies: Strains on Legitimacy* (pp. 65-113). London: Westview Press.

Linz, J., & Stepan, A. (1978). *The Breakdown of Democratic Regimes: Latin America*. Baltimore: Johns Hopkins Univ. Press.

Lippl, B. (1999). *Justice Evaluation and the Welfare State in Europe*. Paper presented to the 4th European Conference of Sociology. Amsterdam.

Lippl, B. (2003). *Sozialer Wandel, wohlfahrtsstaatliche Arrangements und Gerechtigkeitsäußerungen im internationalen Vergleich-Analysen in postkommunistischen und westlich-kapitalistischen Ländern* (Doctoral Dissertation). Berlin: Institut of Social Sciences, Humboldt University.

Lipset, S. (1959). Some Social Requisites of Democracy: Economic Development and Political Legitimacy. *The American Political Science Review, 53*(1), 69-105.

Lipset, S. (1968). Social Class. In D. Sills (Ed.), *Encyclopedia of the Social Sciences*. New York: Macmillan.

Lipset, S. (1981). Political Man. Baltimore: Johns Hopkins University Press.

Lipset, S., & Bendix, R. (1967). *Social mobility in industrial society* (1st ed.). Berkeley: University of California Press.

Lipset, S., & Solari, A. (1967). *Elites in Latin America*. New York: Oxford University Press.

Longford, N., & Muthén, B. (1992). Factor Analysis for Clustered Observations. *Psychometrika, 57*(4), 581-597.

Lübker, M. (2007). Inequality and the Demand for Redistribution: Are the Assumptions of the New Growth Theory Valid? *Socioeconomic Review, 5*(1), 117-148.

Luckmann, T. (1987). Comments on Legitimation. *Current Sociology, 35*(2), 109-117.

Luhmann, N. (1969). *Legitimation durch Verfahren*. Neuwied: Luchterhand.

Luhmann, N. (1989). *Legitimation durch Verfahren* (2nd ed.). Frankfurt/M: Suhrkamp.

MacCallum, R., & Austin, J. (2000). Applications of Structural Equation Modeling in Psychological Research. *Annual Review of Psychology, 51*(1), 201-226.

Machiavelli, N. (1908). *The Prince* (Translated by W.K. Marriot.). Retrieved from www.constitution.org.

Maffettone, S. (2001). John Rawls: An Interpretation. *Croatian Journal of Philosophy, 1*(3), 189-216.

Major, B., & Schmader, T. (2001). Legitimacy and the Construal of Social Disadvantage. In J. Jost & B. Major (Eds.), *The Psychology of Legitimacy*. Cambridge: Cambridge University Press.

Mann, M. (1970). The Social Cohesion of Liberal Democracies. *American Sociological Review, 35*(3), 423-439.

Manzano, L. (2006). Estratos y Clases Sociales en Chile 1973-1990. *Revista Chilena de Sociologia, 20*, 97-130.

Marcel, M., & Solimano, A. (1993). *Developmentalism, Socialism and Free Market Reform: Three Decades of Income Distribution in Chile*. Policy Research Working Papers. Washington: World Bank.

March, J., & Olsen, J. (1984). The New Institutionalism: Organizational Factors in Political Life. *The American Political Science Review, 78*(3), 734-749.

Märker, A. (2000). *Über die politische Relevanz von Gerechtigkeitsvorstellungen und Ungerechtigkeitserfahrungen* - (ISJP-Arbeitsbericht N°20). Berlin: Humboldt University.

Markovsky, B. (1985). Toward a Multilevel Distributive Justice Theory. *American Sociological Review, 50*(6), 822-839.

Markovsky, B. (1988). Anchoring Justice. *Social Psychology Quarterly, 51*(3), 213-224.

Markovsky, B., & Younts, C. (2001). Prospects for Distributive Justice Theory. *Social Justice Research, 14*(1), 45-59.

Marshall, G., & Swift, A. (1993). Social Class and Social Justice. *The British Journal of Sociology, 44*(2), 187-211.

Martin, J., Kleindorfer, G., & Brashers, W. (1987). The Theory of Bounded Rationality and The Problem of Legitimation. *Journal for the Theory of Social Behaviour, 17*(1), 63-82.

Martínez, J., & Díaz, A. H. (1996). *Chile, the Great Transformation*. Washington, D.C:

Brookings Institution.

Marx, K., & Engels, F. (1932). *Das Kommunistische Manifest*. Wien: Internationaler Arbeiter-Verlag.

Marx, K., & Engels, F. (1953). *Die deutsche Ideologie*. Berlin: Dietz.

Mason, D., & Kluegel, J. (2000). *Marketing Democracy: Changing Opinion about Inequality and Politics in East Central Europe*. Lanham: Rowman & Littlefield Publishers.

Massey, J. (2001). Managing Organizational Legitimacy: Communication Strategies for Organizations in Crisis. *Journal of Business Communication, 38*(2), 153-182.

Matheson, C. (1987). Weber and the Classification of Forms of Legitimacy. *The British Journal of Sociology, 38*(2), 199-215.

Mau, S. (1997). *Ungleichheits-und Gerechtigkeitsorientierungen in modernen Wohlfahrtsstaaten*. Forschungsschwerpunktes Sozialer Wandel, Institutionen und Vermittlungsprozesse. Berlin: Wissenschaftszentrum Berlin für Sozialforschung (WZB).

Mau, S., & Veghte, B. (2007). *Social Justice, Legitimacy and the Welfare State*. Hampshire: Ashgate Publishing.

McBride, W. (1975). The Concept of Justice in Marx. *Ethics, 85*(3), 204-218.

McClelland, D. (1961). *The Achieving Society*. Princeton, NJ: Nostrand.

McClosky, H. (1964). Consensus and Ideology in American Politics. *American Political Science Review, 58*(2), 361-82.

McCranie, E., & Kimberly, J. (1973). Rank Inconsistency, Conflicting Expectations and Injustice. *Sociometry, 36*(2), 152-176.

Mehta, P., & Neale, M. (2005). People Are Variables Too: Multilevel Structural Equations Modelling. *Psychological Methods, 10*(3), 259-28426.

Melchior, A., Telle, K., & Wiig, H. (2000). *Globalisation and Inequality: World Income Distribution and Living Standards, 1960–1998* (Studies on Foreign Policy Issues Report 6b). Oslo: Norwegian Institute of International Affairs.

Meltzer, A., & Richard, S. (1981). A Rational Theory of the Size of Government. *The Journal of Political Economy, 89*(5), 914.

Merkel, W. (1998). The Consolidation of Post-Autocratic Democracies: A Multi-Level Model. *Democratization, 5*(3), 33 - 67.

Merkel, W. (2001). Soziale Gerechtigkeit und die Drei Welten des Wohlfahrtskapitalismus. *Berliner Journal für Soziologie, 11*, 135–157.

Merkel, W. (2007). Soziale Gerechtigkeit im OECD-Vergleich. In S. Empter & R. Vehrkamp (Eds.), *Soziale Gerechtigkeit - eine Bestandaufnahme*. Gütersloh: Verlag Bertelsmann Stiftung.

Merkel, W., & Kruck, M. (2004). Social Justice and Democracy: Investigating the Link. *Internationale Politik und Gesellschaft*, 134-158.

Merton, R. (1988). The Matthew Effect in Science, II: Cumulative Advantage and the Symbolism of Intellectual Property. *Isis, 79*(4), 606-623.

Meyer, J., & Rowan, B. (1977). Institutionalized Organizations: Formal Structure as Myth and Ceremony. *American Journal of Sociology, 83*(2), 340-363.

MIDEPLAN. (2006). *Distribución del Ingreso e Impacto Distributivo del Gasto Social CASEN 2006*. Serie analisis CASEN. Santiago de Chile: Ministerio de Planificacion y Cooperacion.

Mideplan. (2006). Resumen resultados nacionales CASEN 2006.

Milanovic, B. (2000). The Median-Voter Hypothesis, Income Inequality, and Income Redistribution: An Empirical Test with the Required Data. *European Journal of Political Economy, 16*(3), 367-410.

Milanovic, B. (2007). Globalization and Inequality. In D. Held & A. Kaya (Eds.), *Global Inequality: Patterns and Explanations*. Cambridge: Polity press.

Mill, J. S. (1863). *Utilitarianism*. London: Parker, Son, and Bourn. Retrieved from http://www.utilitarianism.com

Miller, A. (1974). Political Issues and Trust in Government: 1964-1970. *American Political Science Review, 68*(3), 951-72.

Miller, D. (1992). Distributive Justice: What the People Think. *Ethics, 102*(3), 555-593.

Miller, D. (2003). A response. In D. Bell & A. De-Shalit (Eds.), *Forms of Justice: Critical Perspectives on David Miller's Political Philosophy*. Oxford: Rowman & Littlefield Publishers.

Mizala, A., & Romaguera, P. (2005). Teachers'salary Structure and Incentives in Chile. In E. Vegas (Ed.), *Incentives to Improve Teaching* (pp. 103-150). Washington: World Bank.

Mizala, A., Romaguera, P., & Ostoic, C. (2004). *A Hierarchical Model for Studying Equity and Achievement in the Chilean School Choice System*. Center for Applied Economics, Department of Industrial Engineering: Universidad de Chile.

Montada, L., & Lerner, M. (1996). *Current Societal Concerns about Justice*. New York: Plenum Press.

Moran, T. (2003). On the Theoretical and Methodological Context of Cross-National Inequality Data. *International Sociology, 18*(2), 351-378.

Morley, S. (2001). *The Income Distribution Problen in Latin America and the Caribbean*. Santiago de Chile: CEPAL.

Morris, M., & Western, B. (1999). Inequality in Earnings at the Close of the Twentieth Century. *Annual Review of Sociology, 25*(1), 623-657.

Mosca, G. (2001). The Ruling Class. In D. Grusky (Ed.), *Social Stratification: Class, Race and Gender in Sociological Perspective*. Boulder: Westview Press.

Mueller, C., & Landsman, M. (2004). Legitimacy and Justice Perceptions. *Social Psychology Quarterly, 67*(2), 189-202.

Mühleck, K., & Wegener, B. (2002). *Social Stratification, Attitudes and Justice Evaluation* (International Social Justice Project - Arbeitsbericht N°83). Berlin: Humboldt University.

Mulhall, S., & Swift, A. (1996). *Liberals and communitarians*. Oxford: Blackwell.

Muller, E., & Jukam, T. (1977). On the Meaning of Political Support. *The American Political Science Review, 71*(4), 1561-1595.

Muller, E., Jukam, T., & Seligson, M. (1982). Diffuse Political Support and Antisystem Political Behavior: A Comparative Analysis. *American Journal of Political Science, 26*(2), 240-264.

Müller, H., & Wegener, B. (1995). Die Soziologie vor der Gerechtigkeit. Konturen einer soziologischen Gerechtigkeitsforschung. In H. Müller & B. Wegener (Eds.), *Soziale Ungleichheit und soziale Gerechtigkeit* (pp. 7-49). Opladen: Leske+ Budrich.

Müller, H. (2007). *Max Weber: eine Einführung in sein Werk*. Köln: Böhlau.

Müller, W., Lüttinger, P., König, W., & Karle, W. (1989). Class and Education in Industrial Nations. *International Journal of Sociology, 19*, 3-39.

Müller-Planterberg, U. (2001). Rawls global. *Revista de la Universidad Bolivariana, 1*(2), 1-15.

Mummendey, A., Kessler, T., Klink, A., & Mielke, R. (1999). Strategies to Cope with Negative Social Identity: Predictions by Social Identity Theory and Relative Deprivation Theory. *Journal of Personality and Social Psychology, 76*(2), 229-245.

Muthén, B. (1994). Multilevel Covariance Structure Analysis. *Sociological Methods & Research, 22*(3), 376.

Muthén, B. (2002). Beyond Sem: General Latent Variable Modeling. *Behaviormetrika, 29*(1), 81-117.

Muthén, B. (2004). Latent variable analysis. In D. Kaplan (Ed.), *The Sage Handbook of Quantitative Methodology for the Social Sciences.* (pp. 345–68). Thousand Oaks: Sage Publications.

Muthén, B., & Muthén, L. (2007). *Mplus User's Guide* (4th ed.). Los Angeles: Muthén & Muthén.

Nakao, K. (1992). Occupations and Stratification: Issues of Measurement. *Contemporary Sociology, 21*(5), 658-662.

Neckerman, K., & Torche, F. (2007). Inequality: Causes and Consequences. *Annual Review of Sociology, 33*, 335-357.

Nee, V. (1989). A Theory of Market Transition: From Redistribution to Markets in State Socialism. *American Sociological Review, 54*(5), 663-681.

Noel, A., & Therien, J. (2002). Public Opinion and Global Justice. *Comparative Political Studies, 35*(6), 631-656.

Nohlen, D. (1999). Das Zentrum-Pheripherie Modell der internationalen

Wirtschaftsbeziehungen. *Entwicklung und Zusammenarbeit*, *11*, 316-319.

Nozick, R. (1974). *Anarchy, State, and Utopia*. Oxford: Blackwell.

Núñez, J., & Gutiérrez, R. (2004a). Classism, Discrimination and Meritocracy in the Labor Market: The Case of Chile. Working Paper - Departamento de Economía, Universidad de Chile.

Núñez, J., & Gutiérrez, R. (2004b). Class Discrimination and Meritocracy in the Labor Market: Evidence from Chile. *Estudios de Economía*, *31*(2), 113-132.

Núñez, J., & Tartakowsky, A. (2007). Inequality of Outcomes Vs. Inequality of Opportunities in a Developing Country: An Exploratory Analysis for Chile. *Estudios de economía*, *34*, 185-202.

O'Donnell, G. (1996). Illusions about Consolidation. *Journal of Democracy*, *7*(2), 34-51.

O'Kane, R. (1993). Against Legitimacy. *Political Studies*, *41*(3), 471-487.

Osberg, L., & Smeeding, T. (2006). "Fair" Inequality? Attitudes toward Pay Differentials: the United States in Comparative Perspective. *American Sociological Review*, 450-473.

Palma, A. (2008). *Explaining Earnings and Income Inequality in Chile* (Doctoral Dissertation). Göteborg University, Department of Economics.

Palma, G. (1978). Dependency: A Formal Theory of Underdevelopment or a Methodology for the Analysis of Concrete Situations of Underdevelopment? *World Development*, *6*(7), 881-924.

Parkin, F. (1967). Working Class Conservatives. *British Journal of Sociology*, *18*, 278-290.

Parkin, F. (1971). *Class Inequality and Political Order: Social Stratification in Capitalist and Communist Societies*. New York: Praeger.

Parsons, T. (1940). An Analytical Approach to the Theory of Social Stratification. *The American Journal of Sociology*, *45*(6), 841-862.

Parsons, T. (1951). *The Social System*. Glencoe, Illinois: Free Press.

Parsons, T. (1970). Equality and Inequality in Modern Society, or Social Stratification Revisited. *Sociological Inquiry*, *40*(2), 13-72.

Paynter, R. (1989). The Archaeology of Equality and Inequality. *Annual Review of*

Anthropology, 18, 369-399.

Pike, F. (1963). Aspects of Class Relations in Chile, 1850-1960. *The Hispanic American Historical Review, 43*(1), 14-33.

Pogge, T. (2007). Why inequality matters. In D. Held & A. Kaya (Eds.), *Global Inequality: Patterns and Explanations*. Cambridge: Polity press.

Polanyi, K. (1990). *The Great Transformation. Politische und ökonomische Ursprünge von Gesellschaften und Wirtschaftssystemen*. Frankfurt: Suhrkamp.

Pope, W., Cohen, J., & Hazelrigg, L. (1975). On the Divergence of Weber and Durkheim: A Critique of Parsons' Convergence Thesis. *American Sociological Review, 40*(4513), 417-427.

Portes, A. (1976). On the Sociology of National Development: Theories and Issues. *The American Journal of Sociology, 82*(1), 55-85.

Portes, A., & Canak, W. (1981). Latin America: Social Structures and Sociology. *Annual Review of Sociology, 7*(1), 225-248.

Prebisch, R. (1972). *International Economics and Development*. New York: Academic Press.

Prebisch, R. (1950). *The Economic Development of Latin America and its Principal Problems*. New York: U.N. Dep. of Economic Affairs.

Przeworski, A., & Limongi Neto, F. P. (1997). Modernization: Theories and Facts. *World Politics, 49*(2), 155-183. doi:10.1353/wp.1997.0004

Rainwater, L. (1974). *What Money Buys: Inequality and the Social Meanings of Income*. New York: Basic Books.

Raven, B., & French, J. (1958). Group Support, Legitimate Power, and Social Influence. *Journal of Personality, 26*(3), 400.

Rawls, J. (1971). *A Theory of Justice*. Cambridge: Harvard University Press.

Rawls, J., & Hinsch, W. (1992). *Die Idee des politischen Liberalismus*. Frankfurt: Suhrkamp.

Raykov, T., & Marcoulides, G. A. (2006). *A First Course in Structural Equation Modeling* (2nd ed.). Mahwah, NJ: Lawrence Erlbaum Associates.

Richter, M. (1982). Toward a Concept of Political Illegitimacy: Bonapartist Dictatorship and

Democratic Legitimacy. *Political Theory*, *10*(2), 185-214.

Ridgeway, C. (1991). The Social Construction of Status Value: Gender and Other Nominal Characteristics. *Social Forces*, *70*(2), 367-386.

Ridgeway, C. (2006). Status construction theory. In P. J. Burke (Ed.), *Contemporary Social Psychological Theories* (p. 382). Stanford: Stanford Social Sciences.

Ridgeway, C., & Walker, H. (1995). Status Structures. In K. S. Cook, G. A. Fine, & J. S. House (Eds.), *Sociological Perspectives on Social Psychology*. Boston: Allyn and Bacon.

Riedemann, B. (1984). *Die Aussenwirtschaftsbeziehungen und die wirtschaftliche Entwicklung Chiles, 1974-1980*. Frankfurt am Main: P. Lang.

Robertson, R., & Lechner, F. (1985). Modernization, Globalization and the Problem of Culture in World-Systems Theory. *Theory Culture Society*, *2*(3), 103-117.

Robinson, R., & Bell, W. (1978). Equality, Success, and Social Justice in England and the United States. *American Sociological Review*, *43*(2), 125-143.

Roemer, J. (1982). New Directions in the Marxian Theory of Exploitation and Class. *Politics Society*, *11*(3), 253-287.

Rossem, R. (1996). The World System Paradigm as General Theory of Development: A Cross-National Test. *American Sociological Review*, *61*(3), 508-527.

Rossi, P., & Nock, S. (1982). *Measuring Social Judgments: The Factorial Survey Approach*. Beverly Hills: Sage.

Rostow, W. (1959). The Stages of Economic Growth. *The Economic History Review*, *12*(1), 1-16.

Rudra, N. (2002). Globalization and the Decline of the Welfare State in Less-Developed Countries. *International Organization*, *56*(2), 411-445.

Ruiz, M. (2000). *Introducción a los Modelos de Ecuaciones Estructurales*. Madrid: Universidad Nacional de Educación a Distancia.

Ruiz-Tagle V, J. (2007). Forecasting Wage Inequality. *Estudios de economía*, *34*, 141-162.

Ruiz-Tagle, J. (1999). *Chile: 40 Años de Desigualdad de Ingresos*. Santiago de Chile:

Departamento de Economía, Universidad de Chile.

Runciman, W. (1966). *Relative Deprivation and Social Justice. A Study of Attitudes to Social Inequality in Twentieth Century England*. London: Routledge & Kegan Paul.

Sabbagh, C. (2001). A Taxonomy of Normative and Empirically Oriented Theories of Distributive Justice. *Social Justice Research, 14*(3), 237-263.

Sabbagh, C., & Golden, D. (2007). Reflecting Upon Etic and Emic Perspectives on Distributive Justice. *Social Justice Resarch, 20*(3).

Sandel, M. (1998). *Liberalism and the Limits of Justice*. Cambridge: Cambridge University Press.

Santos, T. (1998). La Teoría de la Dependencia: Un Balance Histórico y Teórico. In F. Lopez (Ed.), *Los Retos De La Globalización. Ensayo En Homenaje a Theotonio Dos Santos*. Caracas: Unesco.

Savage, M. (2005). Class and Stratification: Current Problems and Revival Prospects. In C. Calhoun, C. Rojek, & B. Turner (Eds.), *The Sage Handbook of Sociology* (pp. 236–253). London: Sage Publications.

Scharpf, F. (2007). *Reflections on Multilevel Legitimacy* (- Working paper 07/3). Köln: Max-Planck Institut für Gesellschaftsforschung.

Schluchter, W. (1985). *The Rise of Western Rationalism Max Weber's Developmental History*. Berkeley: Univ. of California Press.

Schmidt-Hebbel, K. (2006). Chile's Economic Growth. *Cuadernos de Economia, 43*(127), 5-48.

Schrenker, M. (2007). *Was ist eine gerechte Rente? Ergebnisse einer Vignettenstudie*. (ISJP-Arbeitsbericht N°126). Berlin: Humboldt University.

Scott, J. (1996). *Stratification and Power: Structures of Class, Status and Command*. Cambridge: Polity Press.

Scott, J., Matland, R., Michelbach, P., & Bornstein, B. (2001). Just Deserts: An Experimental Study of Distributive Justice Norms. *American Journal of Political Science, 45*(4), 749-767.

Selig, J., Card, N., & Little, T. (2008). Latent Variable Structural Equation Modeling in Cross

Cultural Research: Multigroup and Multilevel Approaches. In F. Vijver, D. Hemert, & Y. Poortinga (Eds.), *Multilevel Analysis of Individuals and Cultures*. New York: Lawrence Erlbaum Associates.

Seligson, M. (1983). On the Measurement of Diffuse Support: Some Evidence from Mexico. *Social Indicators Research*, *12*(1), 1-24.

Sen, A. (1992). *Inequality Reexamined*. New York: Russell Sage Foundation.

Sennett, R., & Cobb, J. (1972). *The Hidden Injuries of Class*. Cambridge: Cambridge Universitiy Press.

Shepelak, N. (1987). The Role of Self-Explanations and Self-Evaluations in Legitimating Inequality. *American Sociological Review*, *52*(4), 495-503.

Shepelak, N. (1989). Ideological Stratification: American Beliefs About Economic Justice. *Social Justice Resarch*, *3*(3), 217-231.

Shepelak, N., & Alwin, D. (1986). Beliefs about Inequality and Perceptions of Distributive Justice. *American Sociological Review*, *51*(1), 30-46.

Sidanius, J., Levin, S., Federico, C., & Pratto, F. (2001). Legitimizing Ideologies: The Social Dominance Approach. In J. Jost & B. Major (Eds.), *The Psychology of Legitimacy*. Cambridge: Cambridge University Press.

Sidanius, J., Levin, S., & Pratto, F. (1996). Consensual Social Dominance Orientation and its Correlates within the Hierarchical Structure of American Society. *International Journal of Intercultural Relations*, *30*(3), 385-408.

Sidanius, J., Liu, J., Shaw, J., & Pratto, F. (1994). Social Dominance Orientation, Hierarchy Attenuators and Hierarchy Enhancers: Social Dominance Theory and the Criminal Justice System. *Journal of Applied Social Psychology*, *24*(4), 338-366.

Sidanius, J., & Pratto, F. (1999). *Social Dominance: An Intergroup Theory of Social Hierarchy and Oppression*. Cambridge, UK: Cambridge University Press.

Simonsen, E., Padilla, I., & Vargas, S. (2008). El 50% de los Gerentes de Grandes Empresas Egresó de Cinco Colegios. *Sección Educacion, Diario La Tercera*.

Skrondal, A., & Rabe-Hesketh, S. (2004). *Generalized Latent Variable Modeling: Multilevel, Longitudinal, and Structural Equation Models*. Boca Raton: Chapman & Hall.

Skrondal, A., & Rabe-Hesketh, S. (2005). *Multilevel and Longitudinal Modeling Using Stata*. College Station, Texas: Stata Press.

Smith, T. (2008). *The International Social Survey Program Research*. Summary of ISSP Participant Countries' Publications. International Social Survey Program.

Solomon, S. (1978). Measuring Dispositional and Situational Attributions. *Personality Social Psychological Bulletin, 4*(4), 589-594.

Soltan, K. (1982). Empirical Studies of Distributive Justice. *Ethics, 92*(4), 673-691.

Sorensen, A. (1996). The Structural Basis of Social Inequality. *The American Journal of Sociology, 101*(5), 1333-1365.

Spencer, M. (1970). Weber on Legitimate Norms and Authority. *The British Journal of Sociology, 21*(2), 123-134.

Steiner, P., & Atzmüller, C. (2006). Experimentelle Vignettendesigns in Faktoriellen Surveys. *Kölner Zeitschrift für Soziologie und Sozialpsychologie, 58*(1), 117-146.

Stephenson, S. (2000). Public Beliefs in the Causes of Wealth and Poverty and Legitimization of Inequalities in Russia and Estonia. *Social Justice Research, 13*(2), 83-100.

Stollte, J. (1983). The Legitimation of Structural Inequality: Reformulation and Test of the Self-Evaluation Argument. *American Sociological Review, 48*(3), 331-342.

Stouffer, S., Suchman, E., Devinney, L., Star, S., & Williams, R. (1949). *The American Soldier*. Princeton: Princeton University Press.

Suchman, M. (1995). Managing Legitimacy: Strategic and Institutional Approaches. *The Academy of Management Review, 20*(3), 571-610.

Sunshine, J., & Tyler, T. (2003). The Role of Procedural Justice and Legitimacy in Shaping Public Support for Policing. *Law & society, 37*(3), 513-548.

Swift, A. (1999). Public Opinion and Political Philosophy: The Relation between Social-Scientific and Philosophical Analyses of Distributive Justice. *Ethical Theory and Moral Practice, 2*(4), 337-363.

Swift, A., Marshall, G., Burgoyne, C., & Routh, D. (1995). Distributive justice: Does it matter what the people think. In J. Kluegel, D. Mason, & B. Wegener (Eds.), *Social Justice and Political Change: Public Opinion in Capitalist and Post-Communist States* (pp.

15–47). New York: Aldine de Gruyter.

Szelenyi, I. (1978). Social Inequalities in State Socialist Redistributive Economies: Dilemmas for Social Policy in Contemporary Socialist Societies of Eastern Europe. *International Journal of Comparative Sociology, 19*(1), 63-87.

Szirmai, A. (1988). *Inequality Observed: A Study of Attitudes Towards Income Inequality.* Aldershot: Avebury.

Tajfel, H. (1982). Social Psychology of Intergroup Relations. *Annual Review of Psychology, 33*, 1-39.

Taylor-Sutphin, S., & Simpson, B. (2009). The Role of Self-Evaluations in Legitimizing Social Inequality. *Social Science Research, 38*(3). Retrieved from http://www.sciencedirect.com/science/article/B6WX8-4VHSDC6-1/2/d7cb7e5502af48016c6f7c24817f8b4d

Thibaut, J., & Walker, L. (1975). *Procedural Justice: A Psychological Analysis.* Hillsdale, NJ: Erlbaum.

Thome, H. (1981). *Legitimitätstheorien und die Dynamik kollektiver Einstellungen: Probleme der Verknüpfung von Theorie und Empirie.* Opladen: Westdt. Verl.

Thucydides. (1954). *History ofthe Peloponnesian War.* Harmondsworth: Penguin Books.

Tilly, C. (1998). *Durable Inequality.* Berkeley: University of California Press.

Torche, F. (2005a). *Desigual pero Fluido: El Patrón Chileno de Movilidad en Perspectiva Comparada.* En Foco N°57. Santiago de Chile: Expansiva.

Torche, F. (2005b). Privatization Reform and Inequality of Educational Opportunity: The Case of Chile. *Sociology of Education, 78*(4), 28.

Torche, F. (2006). Una Clasificación De Clases Para La Sociedad Chilena. *Revista Chilena de Sociologia, *(20), 15-44.

Torche, F., & Wormald, G. (2004). *Estratificación y Movilidad Social en Chile: Entre la Adscripción y el Logro.* (Politicas Sociales N°98). Santiago de Chile: CEPAL.

Triandis, H. C. (1995). *Individualism and Collectivism.* New Directions in Social Psychology. Boulder: Westvien Press.

Trottier, Y. (1997). *The End of Ideology in Chile?*. (Master Thesis). Queen's University.

Tversky, A., & Kahneman, D. (1974). Judgment under Uncertainty: Heuristics and Biases. *Science, 185*(4), 1124-1131.

Tyler, T. (1988). What is Procedural Justice? Criteria Used by Citizens to Assess the Fairness of Legal Procedures. *Law & Society Review, 22*(1), 103-135.

Tyler, T. (1990). *Why People Obey the Law*. New Haven: Yale University Press.

Tyler, T. (1997). *Social Justice in a Diverse Society*. Boulder: Westview Press.

Tyler, T. (2005). Introduction: Legitimating Ideologies. *Social Justice Research, 18*(3), 211-215.

Tyler, T. (2006). Psychological Perspectives on Legitimacy and Legitimation. *Annual Review of Psychology, 5*, 375-400.

Tyler, T., & Huo, Y. (2002). *Trust in the Law. Encouraging Public Cooperation with the Police and the Courts*. New York: Russell Sage Foundation.

Ullrich, C. (2000). Die soziale Akzeptanz des Wohlfahrtsstaates: Ergebnisse, Kritik und Perspektiven einer Forschungsrichtung. *Soziale Welt, 51*(2225).

UNDP. (1998). *Desarrollo Humano en Chile: Las Paradojas de la Modernización*. Santiago: Programa de Naciones Unidas para el Desarrollo.

UNDP. (2004). *Desarrollo humano en Chile: El poder, ¿Para qué y para quién?* Santiago: Programa de Naciones Unidas para el Desarrollo.

UNDP. (2007). Human Development Report: 2007/2008. New York: United Nations Development Programme.

Valda, D. (2007). *Comparación de las Distribuciones de Ingreso de Chile con las de Otros Países, antes y después del Gasto e Impuestos*. Consejo Asesor Presidencial Trabajo y Equidad. Santiago de Chile.

Valenzuela, J., & Valenzuela, A. (1978). Modernization and Dependency: Alternative Perspectives in the Study of Latin American Underdevelopment. *Comparative Politics, 10*(4), 535-557.

Valenzuela, M. (2007). *Desafíos para la Equidad en el Trabajo: Chile* (OIT Notas). Trabajo

Decente y Equidad de Género en America Latina. Santiago: Oficina Internacional del Trabajo.

Van der Sar, N., & Van Praag, B. (1989). Social Stratification: Individual Importance and Social Welfare. *Social Justice Research, 3*(3), 187-200.

Verwiebe, R., & Wegener, B. (2000). Social Inequality and the Perceived Income Justice Gap. *Social Justice Research, 13*(2), 123-149.

Vijver, F., Hemert, D., & Poortinga, Y. (Eds.). (2008). *Multilevel Analysis of Individuals and Cultures*. New York: Lawrence Erlbaum Associates.

Wade, R. (2004). Is Globalization Reducing Poverty and Inequality? *World Development, 32*(4), 567-589.

Waisman, C. (1992). Capitalism, the Market, and Democracy. *American Behavioral Scientist, 35*(4), 500-516.

Waissbluth, M. (2006). *La Reforma del Estado en Chile 1990-2005: De la Confrontación al Consenso*. Santiago de Chile: Departamento de Ingeniería Industrial, Universidad de Chile.

Walder, A. (1996). Markets and Inequality in Transitional Economies: Toward Testable Theories. *The American Journal of Sociology, 101*(4), 1060-1073.

Wallander, L. (2009). 25 Years of Factorial Surveys in Sociology: A Review. *Social Science Research, 38*(3), 505-520.

Wallerstein, I. (1974). The Rise and Future Demise of the World Capitalist System: Concepts for Comparative Analysis. *Comparative Studies in Society and History, 16*(4), 387-415.

Wallerstein, I. (2004). *World Systems Analysis: An Introduction*. Durham: Duke University Press.

Walster, E., & Walster, G. (1975). Equity and Social Justice. *Journal of Social Issues, 31*(3).

Walzer, M. (1983). *Spheres of Justice: A Defense of Pluralism and Equality*. New York Oxford: Basic Books.

Warner, U., & Hoffmeyer-Zlotnik, J. (2003). How to Measure Income. In J. Hoffmeyer-Zlotnik & C. Wolf (Eds.), *Advances in Cross-national Comparison: A European*

Working Book for Demographic and Socio-economic Variables. New York: Kluwer Academic/Plenum Publishers.

Wassermann, F. (1947). The Melian Dialogue. *Transactions and Proceedings of the American Philological Association, 78*, 18-36.

Waxman, C. (1968). *The End of Ideology Debate*. New York: Simon and Schuster.

Weakliem, D. L. (2002). The Effects of Education on Political Opinions: An International Study. *International Journal of Public Opinion Research, 14*(2), 141-157.

Weatherford, M. (1987). How Does Government Performance Influence Political Support? *Political Behavior, 9*(1), 5-28.

Weatherford, M. (1992). Measuring Political Legitimacy. *The American Political Science Review, 86*(1), 149-166.

Weber, M. (1947). *The Theory of Social and Economic Organization*. New York: Free Press.

Weber, M. (2003). *General Economic History*. Mineola: Dover.

Wegener, B. (1987). The Illusion of Distributive Justice. *European Sociological Review, 3*(1), 1-13.

Wegener, B. (1990). Equity, Relative Deprivation, and the Value Consensus Paradox. *Social Justice Research, 4*(1), 65-86.

Wegener, B. (1991). Relative Deprivation and Social Mobility: Structural Constraints on Distributive Justice Judgments. *European Sociological Review, 7*(1), 3-18.

Wegener, B. (1992). Gerechtigkeitsforschung und Legitimationsnormen. *Zeitschrift für Soziologie, 21*(4), 269-283.

Wegener, B. (1995). Gerechtigkeitstheorie und empirische Gerechtigkeitsforschung. In H. Müller & B. Wegener (Eds.), *Soziale Ungleichheit und soziale Gerechtigkeit* (pp. 195-220). Opladen: Leske+Budrich.

Wegener, B. (1998). *Belohnungs- und Prinzipiengerechtigkeit. Die zwei Welten der empirischen Gerechtigkeitsforschung.* (ISJP-Arbeitsbericht Nr. 56). Berlin: Humboldt University.

Wegener, B. (1999). Belohnungs- und Prinzipiengerechtigkeit. Die zwei Welten der empirischen Gerechtigkeitsforschung. In U. Druwe & V. Kunz (Eds.), *Politische Gerechtigkeit* (pp. 167-214). Opladen: Leske + Budrich.

Wegener, B. (2000). Political Culture and Post-Communist Transition—A Social Justice Approach: Introduction. *Social Justice Research, 13*(2), 75-82.

Wegener, B. (2001). Ist soziale Gerechtigkeit das, was die Leute dafür halten? Zum Verhältnis von normativer und empirischer Gerechtigkeitsforschung. In P. Koller (Ed.), *Gerechtigkeit. Ihre Bedeutung im politischen Diskurs der Gegenwart* (pp. 123-164). Wien: Passagen Verlag.

Wegener, B. (2003). Solidarity, Justice, and Social Change: Germany's Ten Years of Unification. In D. Pollack, J. Jacobs, O. Müller, & G. Pickel (Eds.), *Political Culture in Post-Communist Europe: Attitudes in New Democracies* (pp. 207-233). Aldershot: Ashgate.

Wegener, B., & Liebig, S. (1993). Eine Grid-Group-Analyse Sozialer Gerechtigkeit. Die neuen und alten Bundesländer im Vergleich. *Kölner Zeitschrift für Soziologie und Sozialpsychologie, 45*(4), 668-690.

Wegener, B., & Liebig, S. (1995a). Hierarchical and Social Closure Conceptions of Distributive Social Justice: A Comparison of East and West Germany. In J. Kluegel, D. Mason, & B. Wegener (Eds.), *Social Justice and Political Change. Public Opinion in Capitalist and Post-communist States.* (pp. 263-284). New York: Aldine de Gruyter.

Wegener, B., & Liebig, S. (1995b). Dominant Ideologies and the Variation of Distributive Justice Norms: A Comparison of East and West Germany, and the United States. In J. Kluegel, D. Mason, & B. Wegener (Eds.), *Social Justice and Political Change. Public Opinion in Capitalist and Post-Communist States* (pp. 239-259). New York: Aldine.

Wegener, B., & Liebig, S. (2000). Is the "Inner Wall" Here To Stay? Justice Ideologies in Unified Germany. *Social Justice Research, 13*(2), 177-197.

Wegener, B., Lippl, B., & Christoph, B. (2000). Justice Ideologies, Perceptions of Reward Justice, and Transformation: East and West Germany in Comparison. In D. Mason & J. Kluegel (Eds.), *Marketing Democracy: Changing Opinion about Inequality and Politics in East Central Europe* (pp. 122-160). Lanham: Rowman & Littlefield Publishers.

Wegener, B., & Steinmann, S. (1995). Justice Psychophysics in the Real World. In J. Kluegel, D. Mason, & B. Wegener (Eds.), *Social Justice and Political Change. Public Opinion in Capitalist and Post-Communist States* (pp. 239-259). New York: Aldine de Gruyter.

Westle, B. (1989). *Politische Legitimität: Theorien, Konzepte, empirische Befunde*. Baden-Baden: Nomos.

Wiley, N. (1988). The Micro-Macro Problem in Social Theory. *Sociological Theory, 6*(2), 254-261.

Wood, A. (1972). The Marxian Critique of Justice. *Philosophy and Public Affairs, 1*(3), 244-282.

Young, M. (1962). *The Rise of the Meritocracy*. Baltimore: Penguin Books.

Younts, C., & Mueller, C. (2001). Justice Processes: Specifying the Mediating Role of Perceptions of Distributive Justice. *American Sociological Review, 66*(1), 125-145.

Yu, C. Y. (2002). *Evaluating Cutoff Criteria of Model Fit Indices for Latent Variable Models with Binary and Continuous Outcomes* (Doctoral Dissertation). UCLA.

Yzerbyt, V., & Rogier, A. (2001). Blame it on the Group: Entitativity, Subjective Essentialism, and Social Attribution. In J. Jost & B. Major (Eds.), *The Psychology of Legitimacy* (pp. 103-134). Cambridge: Cambridge University Press.

Zelditch, M. (2001). Theories of Legitimacy. In J. Jost & B. Major (Eds.), *The Psychology of Legitimacy* (pp. 33-53). Cambridge: Cambridge University Press.

Zelditch, M., & Walker, H. (1998). Legitimacy and the Stability of Authority. In J. Berger & M. Zelditch (Eds.), *Status, Power, and Legitimacy: Strategies & Theories* (pp. 315-338). New Brunswick: Transaction Publishers.

Zuckerman, A. (1977). The Concept "Political Elite": Lessons from Mosca and Pareto. *The Journal of Politics, 39*(2), 324-344.

Lightning Source UK Ltd.
Milton Keynes UK

176503UK00004B/15/P